DIAMONDS
Are Forever

D0458074

DIAM

Are F

DIAMONDS
Are Forever

The Business of
BASEBALL

Paul M. Sommers, Editor

The Brookings Institution
Washington, D.C.

About Brookings

The Brookings Institution is a private nonprofit organization devoted to research, education, and publication on important issues of domestic and foreign policy. Its principal purpose is to bring knowledge to bear on the current and emerging policy problems facing the American people.

A board of trustees is responsible for general supervision of the Institution and safeguarding of its independence. The president is the chief administrative officer and bears final responsibility for the decision to publish a manuscript as a Brookings book. Publication of a work signifies that it is deemed a competent treatment worthy of public consideration but does not imply endorsement of conclusions or recommendations. The Institution itself does not take positions on policy issues.

Copyright © 1992
THE BROOKINGS INSTITUTION
1775 Massachusetts Avenue, N.W., Washington, D.C. 20036
All rights reserved

Library of Congress Cataloging-in-Publication Data:

Diamonds are forever : the business of baseball /
  Paul M. Sommers, editor.
      p.   cm.
  Includes bibliographical references and index.
  ISBN 0-8157-8042-7 (alk. paper)
  1. Baseball—Economic aspects—United States.
  2. Baseball players—Salaries, etc.—United States.
  3. Collective bargaining—Baseball—United States.
  I. Sommers, Paul M.
  GV880.D53   1992
  338.4'3796357'640973—dc20   91-47699
                                                          CIP

9 8 7 6 5 4 3 2 1

The paper used in this publication meets the minimum
requirements of the American National Standard for
Information Sciences—Permanence of paper for Printed
Library Materials, ANSI Z39.48-1984

Preface

THERE admittedly is no shortage of books about baseball—the more memorable players, the unforgettable summers, and the sterile statistical arcana of accomplishment. The publication of another tome on baseball reminds one of Yogi Berra, who, looking with incredulity on some recurring phenomenon, said, "It's déjà vu all over again." However, the studies in this book take a fresh look at the vital issues that have affected the game since the publication of an earlier Brookings book, *Government and the Sports Business*, edited by Roger G. Noll. That book was published in 1974, the same year that final-offer salary arbitration was negotiated into baseball's Basic Agreement, but two years before the demise of the sport's restrictive reserve system. Clearly a lot of changes have taken place since then; indeed, one could say it's a whole new ball game.

George F. Will properly notes that "every spring baseball brings American boys to places they otherwise would never visit, or even hear of." In the spring of 1991, the subject of baseball brought together a team of scholars in a small college town nestled in the backwoods of Vermont for the annual Middlebury College Conference on Economic Issues. The starting players in the two-day series of presentations came from across the nation and from universities, independent research organizations, and government. (No major leaguers attended the conference, although invitations were extended to Mickey Mantle, Joe DiMaggio, and Ted Williams.)

In addition to the contributors to this volume, others who provided stimulation and added to the discussion of the issues were Gerald W. Scully, Rudolf K. Haerle, Jr., Brian W. Huff, Karl L. Lindholm, Brett C. Millier, Kevin P. Ryan, William Sharp, and the students in my undergraduate senior seminar on the business of baseball.

I want to thank the conferees for their contributions and their willingness to revise promptly. I also gratefully acknowledge the secretarial and managerial skills of Sheila Cassin. I also appreciate the editing by Nancy D. Davidson and Cathy Kreyche. Roshna M. Kapadia and Laura A. Kelly verified the factual content of the manuscript, and Max Franke prepared the index. Finally, I extend my appreciation to Jones International, whose generosity gives Middlebury College the wherewithal to run an annual conference on economic issues.

The views expressed in this book are those of the authors and should not be ascribed to Jones International, to Middlebury College, to any agency that funded research reported here, or to the trustees, officers, or staff members of the Brookings Institution.

PAUL M. SOMMERS

March 1992
Middlebury, Vermont

Contents

Tables

Figures

The Top of the First

Paul M. Sommers

THE LAST fifteen years have been good for baseball. They have been good for fans, attested to by the growth in attendance, the spread of cable television, and the burgeoning interest in cards and other baseball memorabilia. They have been good for players, as evidenced by the emergence of a powerful players' union and average salaries almost twenty times their pre-1976 levels. One could also argue that they have on the whole been good for club owners, as seen by the appreciation of franchise values.

Yet at this moment of prosperity major economic issues trouble baseball: the threat of franchise relocation, the continual flash points in collective bargaining, the growing commercialization of the game, the club owners' collusive response to free agency, lingering concerns about racial discrimination, and the arguably tenuous link between player pay and performance. This volume is about such issues and their probable impact on the business of baseball.

Historical Background

Soon after the institutionalization of the game of baseball, owners recognized the need to curtail ballplayers' freedom. Until that time, professional ballplayers were free to move from team to team and sign with the highest bidder, without any compensation to their original team. The players enjoyed this freedom, but the owners became weary of escalating salaries and the lack of continuity that this revolving system brought to baseball. In 1879, the team owners agreed to a "reserve rule," now com-

This introduction draws on portions of Durland and Sommers (1991). This material is used with the permission of the University of South Alabama.

monly referred to as the reserve clause. The reserve clause stated that once a player signed a contract he lost his free agent status and thus became tied to the team that signed him, indefinitely. In other words, the reserve clause made each major league baseball team a monopsony, because a player could not sell his future services to any team other than the one with which he first signed a contract. The owners were allowed to have forty players in this reserve category.[1] Minor as well as major league players were (and still are) covered by this reserve clause.

The reserve clause controversy intensified in the late 1960s. In 1969, Curt Flood's contract was sold by the St. Louis Cardinals. Flood refused to report to his new team, the Philadelphia Phillies, claiming that he should have the right to decide where he played. Flood, who believed the reserve clause violated U.S. antitrust laws, sued the then commissioner of baseball, Bowie Kuhn.[2] Flood lost his case when the U.S. Supreme Court ruled that antitrust laws do not apply to baseball. Although Flood eventually became a free agent in 1971, he had sat out the 1970 season and the inactivity cost him a year's salary. The Washington Senators signed him for the 1971 season, but sacrificing one year's pay was not how other players hoped to gain mobility in baseball.

Less than two years later, shortly after the players staged a thirteen-day strike, the players and owners reached an agreement. The owners' main concession in the 1973 Basic Agreement gave players the option of filing for final-offer salary arbitration following the 1974 season. Under this agreement any player who had between two and six years of major league experience could file for arbitration. If the player had less than two years of experience, he was not eligible. If he had more than six years of experience, his club had to agree to a hearing.[3] Under final-offer arbitration, both the player and the club submit offers to an independent arbitrator, who must select one of the two offers as binding.

In December 1975, Dave McNally and Andy Messersmith were declared free agents by arbitrator Peter M. Seitz. At issue was paragraph 10A of a player's contract, which states that an owner may renew the contract unilaterally "for a period of one year on the same terms" for the following year. This renewal is known as the option year on a contract.

1. This number started out at five but has risen to forty.
2. *Flood* v. *Kuhn*, 407 U.S. 258.
3. After the 1986 season, the minimum number of years of playing experience needed to file for arbitration was raised from two to three. More recently, this number has fluctuated between two and three years of major league service.

The disagreement between management and the players stemmed from the interpretation of this clause. The owners believed that the "same terms" meant that they could continually renew a player's contract, whereas the players regarded the renewal clause as good for one year and one year only. Seitz agreed with the players, specifically McNally and Messersmith.

Under the 1976 Basic Agreement, players with at least six years of playing experience who signed after July 12 could become free agents. The agreement nonetheless limited the number of teams a player could negotiate with, as well as the number of free agents a team could attempt to sign. Players with six or more years of experience who signed before the agreement would have to play out the option year on their contracts before being able to declare themselves free agents. Players would play out the option year only if their team exercised the option year in their contracts.

In November 1976, when twenty-five players entered Major League Baseball's first reentry draft, the effects of Peter Seitz's decision were immediate. The average salary rose from $51,501 in 1976 to $76,349 in 1977, and the number of multiyear contracts grew dramatically in 1977. There were two reasons for the increase in multiyear contracts. First, long-term contracts were a way to lure free agents to sign. Second, those contracts served as a form of security to ensure owners that players would remain with the team.

Many fans of the game regard 1976 as a watershed in player-owner relations. In the years immediately following the 1976 revision of the reserve clause in Major League Baseball, the market for baseball players no longer exhibited monopsonistic characteristics to the same degree it did before that year.

In 1981 the owners tried unsuccessfully to raise the compensation for players lost through free agency to a level that might discourage fierce bidding for free agents. After a decade in which there was an active market for free agents, the market curiously disappeared beginning in 1985. Owners (such as George Steinbrenner) who had previously spent lavishly on mediocre free agents did not pursue even the topnotch players (like Jack Morris) they needed, who appeared available at comparatively low salaries.

In September 1987 arbitrator Thomas T. Roberts decided in favor of Major League Baseball's 1985 free agents, ruling that team owners had colluded and had thus violated their labor agreement with the players. Several executives had made statements that verged on acknowledgment of an agreement not to pursue other teams' players. In particular, Roberts's decision was based on statements emerging from a series of management meetings in late 1985. At the general managers' meeting in November of that year, Commissioner Peter Ueberroth told the owners that "it is not smart to sign long-term contracts." The following month, at the annual major league meeting, the owners agreed to abstain from bidding for agents until the free agents were released by their former clubs. As far as Roberts was concerned, this action constituted a violation of article XVIII(H) of the Basic Agreement. In 1988 arbitrator George Nicolau decided in favor of the 1986 free agents, arguing that the owners had again conspired against the players to hold down salaries. Nicolau, also the arbitrator for the 1987 free agents, found for the players in the third collusion case in July 1990.[4]

An intriguing development is the resurgence of free agent activity. In 1989 a record ninety players filed for free agency. Several players then signed contracts for annual salaries of $3 million or more. The 1988 contracts of Orel Hershiser and Frank Viola were indicators that collusion might be over. But not until 1989, when so many free agents signed such large contracts, did it become apparent that the owners were no longer colluding. The renewed willingness of owners to dig deep into their pockets explains how in 1991, for the first time this century, two teams could in the span of a single season go from worst in their divisions to first in their respective leagues.

Issues of the Game

About twenty years ago, a conference of experts on the economics of sports was held at the Brookings Institution. The resulting volume of papers, *Government and the Sports Business*, edited by Roger G. Noll, is an oft-cited seminal work on the role government policy has played in shaping the sports business.[5] But the business of baseball has changed dramatically in the last two decades. The years since the 1971 Brookings conference have been eventful and therefore interesting to those of us involved in the study of professional team sports, especially baseball. This volume seeks to address some of the vital issues of the game in the tumultuous era since 1971.

Major League Baseball, like any professional sport, is a collection of

4. Durland and Sommers (1991).
5. Noll (1974).

teams, each of which exercises control over an inventory of player re-sources. If a league seeks to possess a monopoly with respect to its sport, then it must be able to discourage defections of players (notably, star players) to potential rival leagues. In 1913, for example, the National and American League clubs threatened ballplayers who jumped to the rival Federal League with banishment for life. Within a league, the primary concern is competitive balance and hence the distribution of playing strengths across teams. After all, competitive league balance leads to exciting pennant races, which in turn drive fan interest. The lead-off chapter in Part I by George G. Daly is concerned with the effect of the contracting structure of professional sports leagues on competitive balance and "contest legitimacy." Until now, the conventional wisdom has been that in the absence of restrictions, such as the reserve clause, "rich" teams from large markets would acquire a disproportionate share of the best players, thereby skewing the distribution of playing talent. Daly contends that the reserve clause affects the distribution of playing talent across teams in a more benign way than does free agency. Further, if competitive balance is promoted by restricting player movement, then allowing players to be freely sold may undercut the league's attempt to foster competition.

The next two chapters in the volume deal with the salary arbitration process in Major League Baseball. David M. Frederick, William H. Kaempfer, and Richard L. Wobbekind ask: Does prior experience with the arbitration process enhance players' salaries? Do ballplayers who win rather than lose their first arbitration case behave differently when they go through arbitration for a second time? What might be the effects of collusion on the arbitration process? To date, no one has investigated in any context, let alone in the context of organized baseball, the effect of repeating final-offer salary arbitration. Their findings suggest that players going through Major League Baseball's salary arbitration procedure for a second time do behave differently than first-time entrants. In particular, players who reenter arbitration are likely to lower significantly the spread between their final salary offer and the final offer of their team. This spread lowering in turn suggests that more repeated use of arbitration will lead to player salaries that more closely reflect market values.

The chapter by Paul L. Burgess and Daniel R. Marburger is representative of numerous economic studies of Major League Baseball currently being done to attach a numerical value to an activity or a player characteristic. Here the two authors seek to estimate the value of the pure bargaining-power effect of arbitration eligibility. By comparing the salaries of arbitration-eligible players with those of ineligible players, they conclude that hitters, starting pitchers, and relief pitchers obtain increases of 86 percent, 89 percent, and 58 percent, respectively, upon gaining final-offer arbitration eligibility.

Part II examines the role of the baseball fan as a contributor to team winning, as ticket purchaser, and as card-collecting hobbyist. Philip K. Porter contends that "fan fickleness" helps allocate players to markets where the demand for high quality is greatest. These same markets may not necessarily be the ones with the largest populations or the largest media markets. In short, teams are rewarded for bidding hardest for the players the fans want to see most. Competitive viability therefore depends on the fans' demand for quality.

David J. Salant (who enjoys the enviable distinction of holding season tickets to Boston Red Sox games) next considers the role of the fan as ticket holder. He argues that teams behave as if they have an implicit contract with their fans. In return for loyalty in bad years, season ticket holders enjoy priority in seat selection, the opportunity to renew season tickets, and an option for playoff and World Series tickets. Part of this implicit contract is that these options can be exercised at a price below what the market will bear.

Many of us could have made big money in baseball, if only we (or our mothers) had saved our gum cards as kids. If we knew then what we know now, we might not have flipped baseball cards or placed them in the spokes of our bikes to make the Schwinn sound more like a Harley. At a Sotheby auction held in March 1991, a near-perfect Honus Wagner baseball card sold for $451,000. Bidding for a mint 1952 Topps Mickey Mantle card stopped just short of $50,000. Baseball and bubble gum have become big business. John A. Vernon's sleuthing in archival material reveals the fascinating particulars of a restraint-of-trade action filed before the Federal Trade Commission by one bubble gum card manufacturer against another in 1962. This chapter, more a case study than a traditional economic analysis, provides an interesting look at what the picture card industry was like during its infancy.

Part III is concerned with the link between player pay and performance. In baseball, there is no such thing as a free agent. To a fan and to an economist alike, "free agent" has become something of an oxymoron. Most major leaguers are now pulling down princely sums. But are salaries earned? The headlines in 1930 shouted that Babe Ruth earned more than the president of the United States. When reminded that Herbert Hoover's $75,000 salary was $5,000 under his, Ruth replied: "I had a better year than he did." A 1982 study of the first family of free agents found that in 1977 Reggie Jackson was worth $1.13 million,[6] or at then prevailing prices ($350 per ounce) his weight in gold. Yet some of the potential anger of the fan today is deflected by the belief that marquee players make more for their owners than the owners pay in salaries.

Novelist Maxim Gorki wrote a story of a man who walks through a Russian village showing off some remarkable machine. It does all sorts of things: peels potatoes, fixes shoes, distills spirits. Finally, one old peasant silently watches the gadget perform and asks: "Yes, but will it whistle?" Of course, this is the big question about the pay and performance models developed in the chapters by Andrew Zimbalist and Rodney Fort. Do their models whistle? Do they tell us what we want to know? Are players' salaries earned? Zimbalist and Fort offer their views of players' worth in Major League Baseball and what the authors perceive to be the impact of free agency on the salary determination process. First, the chapter by Zimbalist comments and expands on the seminal empirical work of Gerald W. Scully on pay and performance of baseball players.[7] Zimbalist employs more robust measures of performance and presents a novel way of calculating a ballplayer's marginal revenue product. Fort's analysis spans twenty-five years and isolates those salary determinants that have been more important in the free agency period than in the reserve clause period. If it is usually presumed that unions reduce salary inequality (and the players' union is thought of as a traditional union), then Fort's finding of increasing salary inequality over time, especially in the free agency period, is surprising. Moreover, if increased salary inequality implies that player talent across teams has become less equally distributed over time, then Fort's chapter raises the following question: Does free agency hurt competitive balance? In theory, Daly would say yes. If pay and performance are related and if high-revenue teams buy all of the talent, Fort would also possibly say yes.

Part IV deals with the delicate subject of racial discrimination in baseball. In 1987, a team executive remarked on national television that blacks lacked "some of the necessities to be a field manager or perhaps a general manager." Although the executive resigned within forty-eight hours of making the statement, the image of the game had suffered. The incident served to fuel the public's perception of unequal treatment accorded professional black athletes. There are still lingering concerns that racial

6. Sommers (1989); Sommers and Quinton (1982).
7. Scully (1974).

discrimination continues to pervade baseball and other professional team sports. Lawrence M. Kahn's survey of discrimination finds little evidence of salary or hiring discrimination in Major League Baseball. Additionally, he finds no evidence that customer discrimination has affected team revenues since free agency, although customer preferences may affect baseball player salaries without causing a racial salary differential. Yet there are unexplained racial differences in career length and persistent, though slowly changing, vestiges of positional segregation. Noteworthy is the low incidence of black pitchers and blacks in managerial and executive positions. Although Kahn's survey says race does not affect salary, Bruce K. Johnson suggests that a player's salary might depend on the racial composition of his team. That is, having more black players on a team raises salaries of white players and reduces salaries of black players. Johnson's findings are consistent with the coworker discrimination model cited in Kahn's chapter, which predicts that white players require a premium to work with members of minority groups.

The broad coverage of these chapters provides enough baseball to keep a fan engaged, enough theory to keep a theorist engaged, and enough numbers to keep an econometrician engaged. Homer Hankies and the Tomahawk Chop might have been the rage in 1991, but diamonds are forever.

References

Durland, Dan W., Jr., and Paul M. Sommers. 1991. "Collusion in Major League Baseball: An Empirical Test." *Journal of Sport Behavior* 14:19–29.

Noll, Roger G., ed. 1974. *Government and the Sports Business*. Brookings.

Scully, Gerald W. 1974. "Pay and Performance in Major League Baseball." *American Economic Review* 64:915–30.

Sommers, Paul M. 1989. "The Golden Boys of Summer, 1987." *Journal of Recreational Mathematics* 21:161–65.

Sommers, Paul M., and Noel Quinton. 1982. "Pay and Performance in Major League Baseball: The Case of the First Family of Free Agents." *Journal of Human Resources* 17:426–36.

Part I

The Baseball Player's Labor Market

CHAPTER ONE

The Baseball Player's Labor Market Revisited

George G. Daly

A PRACTICE universal among the world's major professional sports leagues is the use of labor-contracting methods that limit the mobility of players among teams. In North America, this practice is embodied principally in player reservation, in drafting methods that assign to individual teams the exclusive and marketable rights to negotiate with particular players, and in league conventions or rules that limit the sale of players for cash.[1]

Why these policies exist and, indeed, persist is an issue of considerable practical as well as theoretical interest. Many American economists who have studied this issue have concluded that, although often justified on other grounds, the sole cause and consequence of these practices is to enhance the bargaining power of teams in their negotiations with players, thereby transferring to the teams rents associated with the display of the unique skills of the players.

This chapter reexamines this issue from a different analytical perspective, one that focuses on the benefits and costs of alternative contracting methods. I argue that previous investigators have omitted from their analyses two matters of great importance to understanding this issue: the existence of contracting costs, and contest legitimacy as an important

In addition to his full-time academic responsibilities, the author serves as a consultant to the National Football League. The views expressed herein are his own and do not necessarily reflect the views of the University of Iowa, the National Football League, or any of the NFL's member clubs. He has received helpful comments from Armen Alchian of UCLA, his Iowa colleagues Gary Fethke, John Kennan, George Neumann, and Robert Tamura, and the participants in the Industrial Organization/Game Theory/Managerial Economics Workshop at the Iowa Business School.

1. Also included within the generic term *player reservation* are mandatory compensatory payments from teams that sign players from another team's rosters and limitations on total salary expenditures made by a single team.

factor influencing such costs. Consideration of these factors suggests conclusions different from those of the previous analyses. The most general and important of these conclusions is that, whatever their distributive effects, the traditional labor-contracting practices of sports leagues have an efficiency rationale that arises from their ability to secure and thereby encourage organization-specific investments in both leagues and their constituent teams.

The Contracting Structure of Professional Sports Leagues

A professional sports league is a distinctive organizational arrangement characterized by several unusual contracting practices. These include the fact that the league itself is a composite structure made up of a number of independently owned and managed teams. Individual teams are granted franchises, which consist of a variety of rights and related restrictions governing many aspects of their operations. The teams collectively own the league, making it, in effect, a franchisee-owned franchiser.

Sports leagues also have unusual policies governing transactions between teams and between teams and players. The most general aspect of these policies is a strong reliance on a set of predetermined, written rules, including a constitution to govern league affairs. This rule structure plays an important role in the allocation of league resources and, among other things, requires a central authority, usually in the form of a commissioner, to oversee its application.

Teams within a sports league generally share revenues, a practice that redistributes funds from the more prosperous to the less prosperous league members. In addition, player transactions between teams are dominated by barter, in which the rights to one player's professional services are exchanged for those to others rather than for money. Indeed, in one major American sports league, the National Football League, player sales are banned, and in others they are severely restricted by custom and convention.[2]

By far the most celebrated and controversial of sports leagues' contracting practices, however, are the restrictions placed on individual play-

---

2. Interteam sales of players were more common in the early years of baseball and remain common in English football. However, they have played a negligible role during baseball's last fifty years, rarely involving first-line players. Indeed, this factor was cited by Commissioner Bowie Kuhn in voiding a number of such transactions precipitated by the revision of the reserve clause in 1976. See Kuhn (1987, chap. 14).

ers' rights to negotiate with other teams. Of special significance is the reserve clause of Major League Baseball, which "reserves" to a single team the exclusive right to employ a particular player. A closely related feature, the rookie draft, is used to assign the rights to new players among individual teams, usually in inverse order of the team's position in league standings at the conclusion of the previous season.

These rules, especially the reserve clause, have been a source of controversy over virtually the entire history of Major League Baseball, a controversy that continues today.[3] Professional athletes and others acting in their behalf (especially player agents and associations) frequently allege that these restrictive practices are nothing more than monopsonistic methods of reducing players' incomes to benefit those owning the teams. The inevitable result, they argue, is exploitation, which reduces the players' share of the wealth created by the display of their playing skills.

The traditional response to these arguments by team owners and those sympathetic to them is that these rules are necessary if the league is to produce an attractive, commercially viable product. In particular, they contend that in the absence of restrictions such as the reserve clause and rookie draft, "rich" teams from large markets would acquire a disproportionate share of the best players, thus producing unbalanced and, ultimately, uninteresting competitions.

The Invariance Proposition

In a provocative and seminal paper written over thirty-five years ago, Simon Rottenberg produced an ingenious and seemingly devastating counterargument to the sports world's conventional wisdom regarding the apparent effects of the reserve clause.[4] If player contracts can be freely exchanged, he argued, their allocation should be uninfluenced by their ownership. Because both team owners and players presumably wish to maximize their personal wealth, they should behave identically with re-

---

3. The reserve clause came into being in 1879, only a few years after the beginning of professional baseball. Among the problems it was designed to alleviate were highly uneven league competitions; the practice of "revolving," whereby teams signed each other's players in mid-season, thus harming the apparent integrity of contests; and escalating player salaries, which threatened the solvency of a number of teams. Shortly thereafter, a virtually identical clause, the retain and transfer rule, was developed in the newly emerging sport of professional football (soccer) in England and for virtually identical reasons. See Seymour (1960, chaps. 7–12); Levine (1985); and Tischler (1981).

4. Rottenberg (1956).

gard to the allocation of the identical asset, in this case the rights to a player's professional services. If, in the absence of the reserve clause, a player would rationally sell these services to a large-city (-market) team because it made him the largest offer, then, under the reserve clause, a rationally managed team owning his contract would do the same. Restrictions on players' mobility influence the ownership of an asset and thus the distribution of income arising from it, but not its allocation.

Rottenberg's invariance proposition proved compelling to many economists, some of whom viewed its logic to be so unassailable as to constitute proof of its empirical validity. Its grip on economists' thinking persists to this day.[5] The now substantial literature on economic aspects of professional sports is in many ways an outgrowth of Rottenberg's ideas and a testimony to their influence. A significant subset of this literature is concerned with policy issues, and much of it is critical of sports leagues' restrictive contracting practices in general and the reserve clause in particular.[6] If, it is argued, these rules do not alter actual contests but only the distribution of wealth arising from them, they are without an efficiency rationale. Instead, they are simply anticompetitive methods of supporting collusion among firms, and justifications offered for them are merely a "cover" for owners' wealth-maximizing behavior.

Contracting Costs in Professional Sports Leagues

Underlying the invariance result is the behavioral assumption of wealth maximization. Restrictive labor contracts are seen as serving this end by minimizing the price paid for an input class. Whatever the validity of such a claim, the potential implications of wealth maximization for contractual choice extend far beyond input prices; any contracting alternative that will reduce the costs of league operation or improve the demand for its product will also serve this end. Further, to the extent that the contractual choices affect real variables—resource supplies or output characteristics, for example—they have implications for efficiency as well.

The analytical methods used to derive the invariance result preclude this possibility by assuming that transactions are costless, a circumstance under which contractual choice is, by definition, unrelated to economic

5. See, for example, Noll (1988); Scully (1989, chap. 4).
6. Demmert (1973); El-Hodiri and Quirk (1971); Holahan (1978); Noll (1988); Scully (1989).

efficiency. Rottenberg's invariance proposition is a particular application of the Coase theorem: the proposition that in the absence of transaction costs and wealth effects, the efficient allocation of resources is independent of their ownership.[7] Yet the literal application of this theorem to sports leagues (or any other real world activity) ignores Coase's subsequent dictum: In the absence of transaction costs, all contracting methods are equally efficient, and the optimal form of contracting is indeterminate.[8] Under such conditions, the invariance proposition, like the Coase theorem itself, is a truism devoid of policy implications or empirical content. Only by including such costs can a meaningful analysis of sports league contracting be undertaken.

Contracting Costs, Resource Interdependencies, and Contractual Choice

The implications of contracting costs for the structure of economic institutions are the primary focus of a substantial economic literature.[9] A principal theme of this literature is that when the productivities of separately owned resources are interdependent, individual resource owners may have incentives to engage in unproductive forms of behavior to enlarge their share of jointly created wealth. Where this is so, contracting practices that limit such behavior and, more specifically, economize on the resources used in engaging in or preventing it, may enhance economic efficiency and thus fundamentally influence the form of institutions.

The concept of team production processes plays an important role in this context. A characteristic of such processes is that cooperation between separate productive agents is an important source of total productivity. The returns to this cooperation are inherently collective and thus cannot be attributed to particular productive agents nor, for that reason, transferred by them to other uses.[10] Two potential sources of inefficiency of

7. Cymrot and Dunlevy (1987); Daly and Moore (1981); Lehn (1982).

8. "While consideration of what would happen in a world of zero transaction costs can give us valuable insights, these insights are, in my view, without value except as steps on the way to the analysis of the real world of positive transaction costs." Coase (1981, p. 187).

9. The general area of contractual choice has been approached from a variety of perspectives or "schools" described by terms such as property rights economics, agency theory, transaction cost economics, and the "new" industrial organization. The work of Coase (1937), Williamson (1983, 1987), Alchian (Alchian and Demsetz [1972], Alchian and Woodward [1988], and Klein, Crawford, and Alchian [1978]), and Jensen and Meckling (1976) has been especially influential.

10. Alchian and Demsetz (1972).

particular importance to the contracting practices of sports leagues can arise under these circumstances. In one, what have been termed "small-number bargaining problems" are created when nonredeployable investments are required for economic efficiency and, once made, are subject to appropriation by strategic (that is, opportunistic) behavior. The second, often associated with the term *moral hazard* and closely related to the first, arises when such investments create indivisible benefits from which others cannot be costlessly excluded, creating incentives for free-riding behavior.

The examination of contracting in such contexts has yielded a number of insights about the efficiency properties of arrangements that, absent such considerations, may appear to be simply redistributive and thus "unfair" because of the restrictions they place on some parties to them.[11] What such arrangements have in common is a set of prior and frequently exclusive agreements that limit the potential for counterproductive behavior by one or more classes of resource owners. Among the contracting practices that have been usefully analyzed from this perspective are vertical integration, various tying arrangements, exclusive franchising, agreements assigning one party unilateral rights of termination, and a variety of means by which a potentially opportunistic party makes a "credible commitment" for the purpose of securing the consent of otherwise vulnerable parties.[12] More generally, such insights have greatly expanded the understanding of hierarchical contracting methods in which individual resource owners join organizations to whose rules they precommit because the coordination thereby achieved will result in greater productivity and individual rewards.

Sports leagues and teams are organizations in which value arises as a result of continued and complex associations among productive resources. Further, the fact that economic rents account for a large proportion of such organizations' expenditures suggests an environment conducive to strategic behavior and that transaction costs related to such conduct may constitute a relatively large proportion of the real costs involved.[13] For these reasons, it seems plausible that the efficiency of sports leagues and thus the long-term interests of the resource owners involved in them might be served by contracting methods that recognize such interdepen-

11. Klein (1980).
12. Williamson (1983).
13. In North American sports leagues, players' salaries generally constitute between 40 and 60 percent of total team expenditures. Obviously, a vast proportion of these payments represent compensation above the players' reservation prices.

dencies and serve to protect investments from actions capable of appropriating or dissipating them. If this is the case, contractual choice can influence the supply of resources, the manner in which they are combined, and the characteristics of the product that results, thereby contradicting the invariance result.

For example, the predictions of the invariance proposition arise from the belief that the highly specialized skills owned by professional athletes do not have alternative uses (earn economic rents) and, hence, that restrictions placed on their negotiating rights (or the removal of same) will not alter their supply and will therefore be without real (efficiency) effects. Such a conclusion rests on the tacit assumption that the supply decisions of other resource owners are similarly unaffected by these restrictions. If, instead, the supply of nonathletic resources varies according to the contractual protection afforded them and if sports league labor-contracting methods afford such protection, the invariance result no longer follows.

Contest Legitimacy and Contracting Costs in Sports Leagues

A second factor, omitted from earlier analyses but of considerable importance to sports leagues' contracting practices, is the concept of contest legitimacy. Sports leagues are unusual institutions in that the product they produce—a series of athletic contests—is a consequence of the joint efforts of separate entities, namely, the opposing teams.[14] This organizationally joint production involves both cooperative (economic) and noncooperative (athletic) elements. Specifically, teams must cooperate on economic matters (for example, playing sites must be determined and revenues divided), yet this cooperation must ultimately produce an athletic contest whose financial success depends, in part, on the perception that it involves strictly opposed behavior by two intense rivals. Contest legitimacy refers to the degree to which a league's fans perceive that the contests are fair and beyond manipulation and that the teams and players involved are doing their best to achieve athletic victory.

Because athletic contests are live performances whose production and consumption occur simultaneously, managerial actions that alter a team's composition or performance are immediately evident to informed spectators. As a result, contest legitimacy can be affected by managerial as well as athletic conduct. When this is so, the demand for a league's contests

14. Markham and Teplitz (1981); Neale (1964).

is sensitive to the nature of the economic transactions that take place within and among its constituent teams. Such effects can constitute an important opportunity cost associated with contractual choice and thus have decisive effects on it.

Such decisive effects appear to be present in major sports leagues. For example, contest legitimacy alone rationalizes limitations on any trans-actions other than those between a player and his own team in which individual athletic services are exchanged for monetary payments. The reason for this is simple: such exchanges can harm legitimacy by creating questions about the motivations of the selling party and thus can threaten the economic viability of the league and the wealth earned by its resources. If a player sells his services to a gambler or an owner sells his best players to a competing team, the league's legitimacy, and thus its economic wel-fare, is threatened. Thus it is hardly surprising that professional sports leagues adopt contracting procedures that restrict such transactions and go to considerable expense to ensure their enforcement.

A second implication of legitimacy concerns the manner in which leagues and their constituent teams are owned and organized. A league's legitimacy is enhanced by the independent ownership and management of individual teams and, conversely, is damaged by ownership integration and the potential conflicts of interests such arrangements might involve.[15] In turn, such separate ownership means transactions that in virtually any other industry would occur within a single organization instead take place between separate organizations (teams).

Although it is difficult to "prove" that the independent ownership of teams and the dominance of barter in major American sports leagues owe their existence to contest legitimacy, it is even more difficult to understand why a league would adopt these contracting rules in the absence of such a factor.[16] The existing, essentially neoclassical, analysis of a sports league views the contracting structure of a league and the demand for its output as exogenous and independent. Such methods cannot explain why these

15. In fact, in baseball's early days a number of individuals owned several teams, a practice known as "syndicalism." Immortals such as Wee Willie Keeler and Cy Young, for example, were shifted between teams by the decision of a single owner. Seymour writes of this period: "Declaring for honest competition, they [club owners] rejected syndicate ball by confirming separate ownership of clubs, and in time specifically prohibited anyone from holding stock in more than one club in a league." Seymour (1971, p. 39).

16. In leagues in which player sales or "transfers" are common, such as the English football league, legitimacy is established by other means, including promotion and relegation among league divisions, a strong tradition of nonfinancial objectives among ownership, and limitations on wealth extraction by owners of residual income claims.

institutions rationally choose to deny themselves the obvious efficiencies of unified ownership or impose on themselves the exchange inefficiencies of barter in players.[17]

Because legitimacy is a desirable characteristic of contests, the efficiency of a particular configuration of resources within a sports league is not independent of the contracting methods by which it has been achieved. This implies a dynamic inconsistency or path dependence because the contracting processes required to achieve efficiency over time will not necessarily result in resource allocations required for efficiency at an isolated moment. Thus some of the static optimality conditions associated with the invariance proposition—that each player be assigned to the team where his marginal returns are greatest and that, in the aggregate, the marginal returns to talent be equal across teams—no longer necessarily hold.[18]

Contracting Costs and Economic Efficiency in Sports Leagues

In a world of transaction costs and variable resource supplies, rather than under the static optimality conditions discussed above, efficiency requires the creation of a set of contracting rules that will lead rational, interdependent agents (players, fans, managers, owners) to behave in a manner that maximizes the wealth created by their joint activities. Such an outcome is characterized by the production of optimal output (contest) characteristics at the minimum social cost.

The traditional literature has emphasized two principal characteristics of a sports league's output that are important to spectator demand and thus to the wealth created by such an endeavor: (1) the absolute quality of athletic performances, and (2) league balance or relative parity of teams' athletic quality. To these characteristics must be added (3) contest legitimacy, for the reasons described above. The pertinent question concerns whether and how these characteristics are influenced by sports leagues' labor-contracting practices.

17. The advantages of unitary league ownership for residual claimants include the reduction of variance in returns to ownership (diversification across teams), ease of achieving product characteristics (for example, competitive balance), and the enhancement of bargaining power.

18. This is because the transaction costs, in terms of damage to league legitimacy, exceed the allocative gains associated with achieving the static neoclassical optimality conditions.

The contractually relevant interdependencies among the resources employed by sports leagues occur at two organizational levels. First, a variety of productive resources—athletic skills, managerial expertise, risk-taking abilities—must be combined into teams. These teams are then used as intermediate products or inputs into the production of a final product, the contests produced by the league.

Discussion of the contractual implications of these interdependencies is simplified by adapting some of the terminology used in the transaction cost economics literature to sports leagues.[19] Transaction-specific resource commitments are nonredeployable investments that, once made, are vulnerable to appropriation by strategic behavior. Such investments can be further subdivided by the source of this opportunistic behavior: Resource commitments that are vulnerable to actions by a resource of the same team are termed team specific; those vulnerable to resources employed by another team, league specific.[20]

Securing Team-Specific Investments

The creation of a professional sports team of the highest athletic quality requires team-specific investments by a variety of resource owners that cannot be costlessly shifted to other uses. The value of these investments is sensitive to the subsequent behavior of other team-specific resources. Moreover, the nature of the process through which teams and contests are produced greatly amplifies the consequences of this team specificity. The skills possessed by some athletes are unique or of "star" quality, capable of influencing team design and thus the nature of other athletic resources employed; in the vernacular, teams are sometimes "built around" such players. Economically meaningful measures of these skills are difficult to specify contractually. Many of the necessary investments, particularly those by owners of nonathletic resources, must be made before and thus, once made, are particularly vulnerable to actions that threaten the contests from which virtually all of the teams' revenues are derived.

The traditional bargaining settings between players and teams have often been described as monopsonistic or, in the case of star players, as bilateral monopolies. Such terms, however, fail to capture all of the rel-

19. Williamson (1987).
20. Although in general all investments in a league are specific in both senses (that is, they can be threatened by actions of resource owners from its own as well as other teams), distinguishing between them has important pedagogical advantages for the subsequent analysis.

evant economic considerations involved because an element of "double moral hazard" is present in that each party may be capable of inflicting economic harm on the other. If this is so, efficient (incentive-compatible) contracts must limit both parties from benefiting from strategic behavior.[21] That is, each party must make what Williamson has termed a "credible commitment" to the other as an implicit bond formed to prevent counterproductive, inefficient behavior.[22]

Team owners' incentives to devote resources to such behavior are limited by their ownership of residual claims as well as the rights of control. By virtue of their ownership of the team's residual income, and thus its most specific resource, franchise owners make such a commitment because they will incur the consequences of any inefficiency within the organization.[23] What is needed is an equivalent prior commitment from the owners of athletic skills whose subsequent behavior determines the value of these investments.

Alchian and Woodward have made a general observation about the relationship between bargaining environments and efficient contracting that is directly relevant to the circumstances confronting a team and its key players:

An owner of a unique resource will be more tempted to exploit the situation as the composite quasi-rent [cooperative return] grows large and as the unique resource's flow of services becomes more controlled (for example, by failing to pay the rent, or to show up for work). The more likely and foreseeable is this temptation, the greater is the likelihood that precautionary terms will be sought.[24]

It has been suggested that explicit, long-term contracting can efficiently deal with reliant investments in sports leagues.[25] Such a conclusion over-

21. Demski and Sappington (1991).

22. Williamson (1983).

23. In fact, Demski and Sappington (1991) show that an agreement to accept the ownership of residual claims of a firm on the unilateral decision of their current owner can serve as such a credible commitment for a resource owner negotiating with the firm when double moral hazard is present.

24. Alchian and Woodward (1988, p. 68). It would appear that the practical implications of this reality have not escaped those who have played a role in shaping the contracting rules of sports leagues, as a quotation from former Major League Player Association official Marvin Miller indicates: "I never before have seen a group of people [major league players] who are so irreplaceable in relation to their work." Quoted in Jennings (1990, p. 24).

25. Noll (1988).

looks several serious problems in this context. Some forms of long-term contracting have been shown to significantly affect player performance.[26] Indeed, writing efficient forms of such contracts may be impossible given the complex interdependent nature of player and team performances and the fact that many dimensions of this performance are under managerial control. The inalienability of human capital seriously impedes employers' ability to enforce these contracts, as indicated by the frequency with which they are renegotiated while in force under threats by players to take actions capable of degrading team performance (for example, "holding out").

Given these factors, efficient contracting between teams and players is likely to be described by hierarchical methods in which substantial rights over the conduct of players are assigned to the owner of residual claims. To protect and thereby encourage reliant investments required for efficient team operation, the rights so transferred or modified must include those whose subsequent exercise could be important sources of costly strategic behavior to the team. Chief among these is the right to be employed by another team in the league, the major comparable alternative source of income to the player and therefore a principal source of credible strategic behavior. The transfer of these rights via exclusive employment contracts thus constitutes a credible commitment from potentially opportunistic resource owners to the team's residual income claimant and thus, indirectly, to all owners of team-specific resources. If the player's income is an economic rent, whereas that of some or all of the other team-specific resources is not, restrictions on the former that protect the latter can enhance the supply of resources to the league and, accordingly, economic efficiency.

Although overlooked by the invariance proposition literature, such prior contractual commitments are common in organizational contexts that require unusual or unique human skills whose subsequent withdrawal could diminish the value of other investments.[27] Indeed, these commitments not only take the form of illiquid claims on residual income and other forms of compensation designed to avoid "agency" problems, but also include "noncompete" clauses, common in many executive and professional contracts, which restrict the employment options of human resources around which otherwise appropriable investments are made.[28]

26. Lehn (1982).
27. Alchian and Woodward (1988); Klein (1980).
28. Rubin and Shedd (1981).

Finally, among the relevant factors shaping contractual choice in a professional sports league is the concomitant need to protect the league-wide resources of competitive balance and contest legitimacy. As discussed below, these considerations reinforce the conclusion that prior contractual agreements that restrict the interteam mobility of players can enhance economic efficiency.

Securing League-Specific Investments

A league involves organizationally joint production through which successively matched pairs of teams produce a series of contests. As a consequence, the value of investments made in an individual team depends not only on its own activities but also on those of the other teams. The existing literature has tended to subsume all such interdependencies within a single variable described as "league balance." This results in oversimplification; many aspects of a single team are capable of influencing the returns earned by resources invested in other league members, including stadiums, market areas, management skills and behavior patterns, and ownership structures.

Such interdependence is not unique to professional sports leagues and is common in other activities that involve the distribution of a product with shared characteristics (in this case, identification with the league) in separate locations. Consider, for example, the case of a nationally distributed but locally produced product such as fast food. Here, a low-quality product delivered at a single location will, through reputation effects, damage the wealth of resources involved at other locations. Efficient production, however, is served by local ownership and control. How can the potential harm from these externalities be minimized? The contracting practice that has come to dominate the supply of such services is franchise arrangements that permit a central organization (the franchiser) to regulate the quality of service at individual locations. The methods commonly used in doing so include a variety of restrictions on the uses made of productive resources.[29]

Similar organizational arrangements are used in sports leagues. In this context, the relevant question becomes, What types of resource allocation decisions by individual franchises might, owing to the resource interdependencies involved, be capable of imposing significant costs on other franchises and, therefore, be appropriate candidates for such restrictions?

29. Mathewson and Winter (1985).

The answer is, Any of those shared output characteristics subject to managerial discretion of an individual franchise. Of these, however, the characteristics of league balance and legitimacy, because they are indivisible across teams, are of particular concern because of the moral hazard problems to which they are subject and the free-riding behavior, with its attendant inefficiencies, that can result.

Transactions that can result in the movement of players among teams are particularly strong candidates for such contractual restraints because of the dominant role played by the interteam distribution of talent in influencing both league balance and legitimacy. Among such transactions, those that result in the exchange of players for monetary payments (that is, player sales) are especially significant. Such transfers necessarily alter league balance (because, by definition, these transactions result in one team's playing strength growing while another's diminishes) and because a separate leaguewide asset—the legitimacy of its contests—can be diminished by such actions. The possibility that some franchise owners might be motivated by a desire for athletic success or other nonfinancial objective underscores this conclusion because such behavior is likely to be directed at altering the interteam distribution of talent and to use player purchases as a primary vehicle for achieving this end.

Thus, whatever their other effects, prior agreements restricting player mobility in major sports leagues can protect the leaguewide assets of balance and legitimacy. The combined effect of the barter constraint, player reservation, and inverse-order drafting procedures is to assign players among teams in an equalizing manner and subsequently to prohibit types of transactions (such as the exchange of player services for cash, whether between teams or between teams and individual players) that are capable of systematically harming league balance or legitimacy.[30]

Summary and Conclusions

This chapter has advanced the argument that prior contractual agreements limiting players' negotiating options within professional sports leagues can serve the cause of economic efficiency by protecting, and thereby encouraging, transaction-specific investments. Such investments have real

30. As noted by El-Hodiri and Quirk (1971) and others, given rational behavior, a team will not trade a good player for a poor one so that the a priori effect of such transactions on league balance is nil.

effects that can include a larger level of league output, higher-quality athletic performances by teams and players, and an enhancement of the legitimacy and competitive balance of contests.

The analysis does not deal with the "fairness" or other noneconomic effects of sports league contracting. Nor does it deny that the "bargaining power" rationale central to previous analyses may play a role in explaining the contracting practices of sports leagues. It does, however, argue that such distributive explanations cannot sensibly claim exclusivity as consequences or causes of these practices and, further, that policies based on such presumptions are likely to lead to unforeseen consequences, including a reduction in economic efficiency.

Relatively little attention has been devoted to empirical tests of the consequences of contracting alternatives in sports leagues. One reason for this is that restrictive labor-contracting practices are common to virtually all major revenue-generating sports leagues and have varied little across time, making comparisons difficult. The principal "evidence" offered in support of the invariance proposition has been its internal logic or consistency with existing concepts of neoclassical economics.[31] However, given its tautological nature, the proposition's logical consistency is neither surprising nor a relevant test of its validity.

The best available evidence with which to judge this issue comes from the use of and changes in contracting practices of sports leagues. In this regard, the following observations are justified.

1. In efforts to test directly the propositions of interest in this chapter, several authors have examined free agent movement and athletic performance in the years immediately following the 1976 revision of the reserve clause in Major League Baseball.[32] They each concluded that systematic changes in real outcomes had occurred following this contractual change.

2. The invariance proposition implies that drafting procedures employed by sports leagues have no effect, being offset by subsequent player sales between teams. Since interteam sales of first-line players are virtually nonexistent in major North American sports leagues (and, indeed, are prohibited in several leagues), transactions that the invariance proposition contends are critical to its validity do not occur.[33]

---

31. For example, two of the most influential papers in articulating the invariance proposition, by Rottenberg (1956) and El-Hodiri and Quirk (1971), are nonempirical.

32. Cymrot (1983); Cymrot and Dunlevy (1987); Daly and Moore (1981); Lehn (1982).

33. The criticality of cash sales to the validity of the invariance proposition has been noted by several authors, including El-Hodiri and Quirk (1971), Daly and Moore (1981), and Scully (1989).

3. The invariance proposition's hypothesis of ineffectuality of the player draft is not borne out by historical experience. Drafting procedures were instituted in both Japanese and American major league baseball during the 1960s. In both leagues, one of the major motivations for the change was the dominance of large-market teams. In both cases this dominance declined significantly in the decade following the adoption of the draft. Likewise, professional football, which employs a draft, produces contests that are significantly closer, on average, than those produced by major college football, which does not.

4. All major sports leagues in all countries (including revenue-generating amateur leagues in which residual claims are diffuse and the monopsonistic rationale is accordingly weakened) impose restrictions on the movement of players. In the absence of laws or regulations compelling their use, it is difficult to understand the widespread and persistent dominance of such institutional forms if they do not possess efficiency properties. If such properties do not exist, the implied "exploitation" of a unique resource critical to a league's existence would make it vulnerable to competition from leagues employing less restrictive methods.[34] Yet new leagues that have arisen to challenge existing ones have adopted similar player-contracting practices.

In sum, it is plausible to suppose that professional sports leagues, like most other economic organizations, operate more efficiently by using alternatives to market contracting for certain purposes, particularly for transactions involving economic agents whose subsequent behavior is capable of imposing significant costs on their operations. To label such practices as "unfair" or "anticompetitive" misses this point. Such assertions, as well as policy prescriptions based on them, should be reexamined.

References

Alchian, Armen A., and Harold Demsetz. 1972. "Production, Information Costs, and Economic Organization." *American Economic Review* 62:777–95.
Alchian, Armen A., and Susan Woodward. 1988. "The Firm is Dead; Long Live

34. As Fama and Jensen (1983, p. 327) note, "Most goods and services can be produced by any form of organization, and there is competition among organizational forms for survival in any activity. Absent fiat, the form of organization that survives in an activity is the one that delivers the product demanded by customers at the lowest price while covering costs. This is the telling dimension on which the economic environment chooses among organizational forms."

the Firm: A Review of Oliver E. Williamson's *The Economic Institutions of Capitalism.*" *Journal of Economic Literature* 26:65–79.

Coase, Ronald H. 1937. "The Nature of the Firm." *Economica* N.S. 4:386–405.

———. 1981. "The Coase Theorem and the Empty Core: Comment." *Journal of Law and Economics* 24:183–87.

Cymrot, Donald J. 1983. "Migration Trends and Earnings of Free Agents in Major League Baseball, 1976–1979." *Economic Inquiry* 21:545–56.

Cymrot, Donald J., and James A. Dunlevy. 1987. "Are Free Agents Perspicacious Peregrinators?" *Review of Economics and Statistics* 69:50–58.

Daly, George, and William J. Moore. 1981. "Externalities, Property Rights and the Allocation of Resources in Major League Baseball." *Economic Inquiry* 19:77–95.

Demmert, Henry G. 1973. *The Economics of Professional Team Sports.* Lexington-Heath.

Demski, Joel S., and David E. M. Sappington. 1991. "Resolving Double Moral Hazard Problems with Buyout Agreements." *Rand Journal of Economics* 22:232–40.

El-Hodiri, Mohammed, and James Quirk. 1971. "An Economic Model of a Professional Sports League." *Journal of Political Economy* 79:1302–19.

Fama, Eugene F., and Michael C. Jensen. 1983. "Agency Problems and Residual Claims." *Journal of Law and Economics* 26:327–49.

Holahan, William L. 1978. "The Long-Run Effects of Abolishing the Baseball Player Reserve System." *Journal of Legal Studies* 7:129–37.

Jennings, Kenneth M. 1990. *Balls and Strikes: The Money Game in Professional Baseball.* Praeger.

Jensen, Michael C., and William H. Meckling. 1976. "Theory of the Firm: Managerial Behavior, Agency Costs and Ownership Structure." *Journal of Financial Economics* 3:305–60.

Klein, Benjamin. 1980. "Transaction Cost Determinants of 'Unfair' Contractual Arrangements." *American Economic Association Papers and Proceedings* 70:356–62.

Klein, Benjamin, Robert G. Crawford, and Armen A. Alchian. 1978. "Vertical Integration, Appropriable Rents and the Competitive Contracting Process." *Journal of Law and Economics* 21:297–326.

Kuhn, Bowie. 1987. *Hardball: The Education of a Baseball Commissioner.* Times Books.

Lehn, Kenneth. 1982. "Property Rights, Risk Sharing, and Player Disability in Major League Baseball." *Journal of Law and Economics* 25:343–66.

Levine, Peter. 1985. *A. G. Spalding and the Rise of Baseball: The Promise of American Sport.* Oxford University Press.

Markham, Jesse W., and Paul V. Teplitz. 1981. *Baseball Economics and Public Policy.* Lexington Books.

Mathewson, G. Frank, and Ralph A. Winter. 1985. "The Economics of Franchise Contracts." *Journal of Law and Economics* 28:503–26.

Neale, Walter C. 1964. "The Peculiar Economics of Professional Sports." *Quarterly Journal of Economics* 78:1–14.

Noll, Roger G., ed. 1974. *Government and the Sports Business.* Brookings.

——— . 1988. "The Economics of Sports Leagues." In *Law of Professional and Amateur Sports,* edited by Gary A. Uberstine. New York: C. Boardman.

Rottenberg, Simon. 1956. "The Baseball Players' Labor Market." *Journal of Political Economy* 64:242–58.

Rubin, Paul H., and Peter Shedd. 1981. "Human Capital and Covenants Not to Compete." *Journal of Legal Studies* 10:93–110.

Scully, Gerald W. 1989. *The Business of Major League Baseball.* University of Chicago Press.

Seymour, Harold. 1960. *Baseball: The Early Years.* Oxford University Press.

——— . 1971. *Baseball: The Golden Age.* Oxford University Press.

Tischler, Steven. 1981. *Footballers and Businessmen: The Origins of Professional Soccer in England.* New York: Holmes and Meier.

Williamson, Oliver E. 1983. "Credible Commitments: Using Hostages to Support Exchange." *American Economic Review* 73:519–40.

——— . 1987. *The Economic Institutions of Capitalism: Firms, Markets, Relational Contracting.* Free Press.

CHAPTER TWO

Salary Arbitration as a Market Substitute

David M. Frederick, William H. Kaempfer, and Richard L. Wobbekind

T HE MARKET for Major League Baseball players could conceivably approximate a competitive market in that there are twenty-six potential bidders (the franchises) for any given player and an even larger, although qualitatively differentiated, potential group of players at every position. A competitive market generates prices that provide the best available predictor of the future value of any item of exchange. Consequently, market-determined player salaries should predict in an unbiased and reasonably accurate manner the expected value of players to their employers for the period under contract. However, the general agreement between the Players Association and Major League Baseball assigns to the franchises certain exclusive property rights over players at certain stages of their careers. In particular, teams hold exclusive rights to a player in the first portion of that player's career. This monopsony right on the part of the team forces the player's salary below the fair market value of that player's talent.

At one time clubs enjoyed the benefits of a reserve rule that granted these monopsony rights for the entire career of a player. During the 1970s, however, collective labor activity on the part of the Players Association and a set of favorable arbitration decisions broke the hold of clubs over players. Free agency in baseball has caused player salaries to increase dramatically toward their presumed market value during the last fifteen years. Another institution that should also approximate the market process and move salaries toward their true market values is final-offer salary arbitration.

Research on the effects of baseball's final-offer salary arbitration pro-

We are grateful to Tom Goodwin, Donnie Lichtenstein, and William Sharp for their helpful comments and to Rachel Hayes and Joe Kreikemeier for their able assistance.

cedure has expanded in recent years. Recent analyses suggest that, although the threat of arbitration has encouraged good faith bargaining and negotiated settlements, arbitration has not influenced bargaining efforts and consequently has not produced market convergence among the parties going to arbitration.[1] These studies imply that in arbitration owners' offers and players' demands have spread farther apart over time. Instead of narrowing the differences between players and owners, the arbitration process has widened them and has proved divisive and acrimonious.

Little is known, however, about the role experience plays for those players and owners repeating this process. Previously published studies aggregate the positions of all those in arbitration each year, including the parties experiencing the procedure for the first time. As a result, the richness of the arbitration process is not being fully captured. Thus this chapter has two objectives: to better understand the effect of baseball's final-offer salary arbitration procedure on bargaining and to investigate whether prior experience with the arbitration process enhances or inhibits approximation of the market solution.

This chapter predicts that, over time, baseball owners and players will submit reasonable final offers and final demands for salary arbitration. This view contrasts with evidence from previous studies that find the parties submit diverging final positions. The practical significance of this hypothesized finding lies in its implications for strategies utilized by Major League Baseball to determine player salaries. For example, repeated exposure to salary arbitration may be beneficial in obtaining the true market value of all players eligible for the process, both those who are and those who are not eligible for free agency.

This chapter first discusses some issues pertaining to the theory of behavior under final-offer arbitration and reviews previous analyses of baseball's salary arbitration procedure. We use these analyses to develop arguments that are the basis for our research issues and the testable implications of arbitration theory as applied to baseball. We then provide a description of the data and detail the research design and the empirical results.

Arbitration Theory

Arbitration is a dispute resolution procedure employed by joint agreement between two conflicting parties to avoid more costly resolutions such as

1. Dworkin (1981, 1986); Scully (1989); Jennings (1990).

lengthy court proceedings, the cessation of any transactions (that is, a strike), or outright hostilities (in the event of a dispute between nations). Under an arbitration agreement a neutral third party decides among the points of conflict of the disputing parties. Arbitration can be either binding, in which both parties commit in advance to the arbitrator's final judgment, or nonbinding, in which either party can reject the judgment. Nonbinding arbitration is typically a less successful dispute resolution technique.[2]

Conventional Binding Arbitration

Under conventional binding arbitration, the parties to the dispute present the arbitrator with arguments on their behalf, and the arbitrator decides the appropriate judgment. Typically this conventional arbitration judgment is a compromise between the positions of the disputants. The compromising nature of conventional binding arbitration offers the advantage that both parties receive a portion of their claim and are, as a result, at least partially satisfied.[3]

The disadvantage of conventional arbitration is that good faith negotiations before the arbitration are not rewarded and thus not encouraged. In fact, if the arbitrator does seek out an average between the initial offers of the disputing parties, then the participants have a strong incentive to exaggerate their offers as much as possible.

Final-Offer Arbitration

Stevens introduced the concept of final-offer arbitration as an alternative to conventional binding arbitration to avoid the destructive incentives inherent in conventional arbitration.[4] Under final-offer arbitration, rather than having discretion over the level of the judgment, the neutral judge is presented with the final offer of each of the disputants and then chooses one of the offers. A number of studies have developed a theoretical model of the final-offer arbitration process by which both parties should have strong disincentives to exaggerate their offers.[5]

2. Ashenfelter and Bloom (1984) provide an extensive analysis of both types of arbitration from the point of view of the neutral party's behavior.
3. From a different perspective, of course, both parties are left unfulfilled by the resolution as well.
4. Stevens (1966).
5. For example, Ashenfelter and Bloom (1983, 1984); Farber (1980).

These theoretical treatments of final-offer arbitration start from the presupposition that the behavior of the three parties—the arbitrator and the two disputants—will be shaped by their own objective functions and self-interest. For the arbitrator, this implies a preference to continue to receive the remuneration associated with hearing arbitration cases, which requires the appearance of impartiality to the disputants. Each of the disputants attempts to maximize net return, which depends on the level of their offer and the probability of its being selected. Central to the traditional theory of final-offer arbitration is the belief that, based on the arbitrator's behavior, the more exaggerated a disputant's offer, the lower the probability that it will be selected. However, this theoretical link between the level of an offer and its probability of selection has not always been put forth in analyses of final-offer arbitration in Major League Baseball.

Final-Offer Salary Arbitration in Baseball

The final-offer salary arbitration process in Major League Baseball is conducted entirely during the off-season. Players with between three and six years of major league service and teams can unilaterally choose to file for arbitration.[6] Offers by the disputants are submitted in January to a jointly selected arbitrator. A hearing is held in late February, and a ruling is issued soon thereafter. All the while, however, further negotiations between the parties can be pursued, and frequently players filing for arbitration sign contracts before their hearings.[7] Table 2-1 shows, however, that a sizable proportion (21.2 percent) of players who have filed for arbitration have gone through with the process.

In general, researchers of final-offer arbitration in baseball have assumed that arbitrators act out of self-interest and a desire to keep their positions.[8] Thus the arbitrator probably wishes to appear as fair as possible to the two disputants to maximize chances for retention. Researchers

6. Since salary arbitration was negotiated into the baseball labor agreement, the lower bound on player eligibility has fluctuated between two and three years of major league service. The current Basic Agreement "mandates that players with at least two years in the majors, and no more than three, can qualify for arbitration if they had a minimum of 86 days of major-league service [in 1990] and their total major-league service ranks in the top 17% of the eligible players in that group." Hal Bodley, "Arbitration Offers Might Set Marks," *USA Today*, January 18, 1991, p. 12C.

7. Both Dworkin (1981) and Jennings (1990) offer nuanced explanations of the arbitration process in Major League Baseball.

8. Dworkin (1981).

Table 2-1. *Arbitration Cases Filed and Heard, 1974–91*

Year	Number of arbitration cases filed	Number of cases heard
1974	53	29
1975	38	15
1978[a]	16	9
1979	40	14
1980	65	26
1981	96	21
1982	103	22
1983	88	30
1984	80	10
1985	98	13
1986	159	35
1987	109	26
1988	111	18
1989	136	12
1990	162	24
1991	157	17
Total	1,511	321

Sources: Hal Bodley, "Arbitration Offers Might Set Marks," *USA Today*, January 18, 1991, p. 12C; and "Club Owners 11-for-14 in Arbitration," *USA Today*, February 25, 1991, p. 7C.

a. There was no arbitration in 1976–77 because of players' negotiations concerning the reserve system.

have suggested three different types of decision behavior as ways for the arbitrators to project their fairness: offsetting behavior, conservative behavior, and parity behavior.

Scully and Dworkin both develop the notion that arbitrators engage in offsetting behavior.[9] According to this concept, the arbitrator tries to act as a compromiser, even under the constraints of final-offer arbitration. The arbitrator attempts to even out the number of decisions, offsetting a judgment favorable to a player with one favorable to a team. The greatest chance for an arbitrator to engage in offsetting decisions is when a player comes to arbitration against the same team in successive years. Then the arbitrator can directly offset the prior judgment.[10]

Jennings suggests arbitrators in baseball exhibit conservative behavior.[11] According to this proposition, the arbitrator will be more likely to side with the team as the degree of divergence between the player's final demand and the club's final offer grows. That is to say, the player is responsible for the large divergence and should not be rewarded. This

9. Scully (1989); Dworkin (1981).

10. Even if the arbitrator had changed from the previous year, the motivation for the new arbitrator to offset the prior judgment is still present.

11. Jennings (1990, pp. 203–04).

follows from Gibbons's more general point that arbitrators learn about the status of the market from the offers of the disputants.[12] Of course, a wide spread could be due to a "lowball" offer by a team, but the team is typically constrained more than the player because salaries must be above the league minimum and the player's salary during the previous year serves as an important point of reference.[13]

Finally, Dworkin discusses at length the notion of parity decisions.[14] Unlike the other two procedures, under the parity concept the arbitrator begins with an examination of the evidence at hand relating to the true market value of the player and makes a judgment of the player's worth for the upcoming season. This parity value is then compared with the player's final demand and the club's final offer. Whichever position is closer to the arbitrator's parity is selected.[15]

Research Issues

Of the three views of the salary arbitration process, a neutral third party may find the parity, or fair market value, concept most compelling. What matters, however, is how the participants in the arbitration process view the behavior of arbitrators and how that view changes the generation of final demands and final offers. Thus this study concentrates on all three types of arbitration decision behavior.

Each conceptualization is explored through a variety of research questions focused on arbitration outcomes and on the spreads between the final demands and final offers submitted to arbitration. We first use exclusively those players who repeat arbitration with the same team to investigate the predictions of the three conceptualizations with regard to arbitration outcomes. It should be noted that even though both sides have the right to invoke arbitration, the players have filed a vast majority

12. Gibbons (1988).

13. Although Jennings (1990) brings up the conservative point, he does not seem to endorse it and even presents evidence to dispute its occurrence when considering all cases that have gone to arbitration. However, the effects of this concept, if any, on the research issues addressed in the present study must still be determined.

14. Dworkin (1981, pp. 166–73, 187–95).

15. Erekson, Moser, and Schwartz (1989) estimate the parity values for players in arbitration during 1974–82 and find a bias on the part of the arbitrator in 30 percent of the rulings, most in favor of the players. This bias may only reflect the start of the general upward trend of player salaries at the time. The theoretical basis of parity decisions stems from the models of Ashenfelter and Bloom (1983, 1984) and Farber (1980).

(close to 90 percent) of the cases.[16] As a result, this study focuses extensively on player behavior in arbitration. Second, to examine the nature
of baseball's salary arbitration procedure on the spread between final
demands and final offers, we use a simple model of the arbitration process,
including in the model the following information: players who repeat
arbitration, years of service, small-market teams, and collusion. In this
manner, we use a multiple methodological approach and statistical tests
employing multiple measurement methods to examine the three conceptualizations of the arbitration process.

THE DECISION TO REPEAT ARBITRATION. Given the three models of
arbitrator behavior, under what conditions would a player previously
involved in an arbitration decision be expected to repeat the process in
another year? The offsetting concept implies that the arbitration process
assigns outcomes to maintain the impression that it is equitable. In es-
sence, this concept suggests that arbitrators seek to maintain their positions out of self-interest and consequently attempt to be perceived as fair
and neutral judges by equally dividing outcomes between players and
teams. This implies that, of those players who repeat arbitration with the
same team, a substantial number will be expected to obtain the opposite
ruling the second time.[17]

On receiving an arbitration decision, neither the owner nor the player
definitively knows what criteria were considered by the arbitrator or the
differential weights assigned to the specific criteria used to reach the
decision. The only feedback provided to the parties is the outcome or
ruling itself. Therefore, players who elect to repeat arbitration in a subsequent year have only one type of data on which to base their chances
of winning. Although this feedback is inadequate to understand the arbitration procedure, it is still useful to those experiencing the process
again.[18] If players accept the point of view that arbitrators make offsetting
judgments, then those players who won in arbitration their first time
through the process would be loath to repeat it, fearing that the odds
would be against them. First-time losers would be eager to repeat to have
their prior loss offset.

More recently, Hogarth and Einhorn have put forth a descriptive
model of belief revision that is relevant for player behavior under both
the parity and conservative conceptualizations of the arbitration process.[19]

16. Dworkin (1981, pp. 157–58).
17. Scully (1989).
18. See, for example, Harrell (1977); Hammond, Summers, and Deane (1973).
19. Hogarth and Einhorn (in press).

This model posits that belief revision is a sequential process and is influenced by the order in which evidence is received. Here, players obtain evidence in the form of an arbitrator's selection of a salary position. Thus a player who wins an earlier arbitration ruling takes that victory as an indication that he correctly approximated the criteria and weights perceived by the arbitrator in reaching the decision. Hogarth and Einhorn predict that this player subsequently perceives his probability of formulating a winning offer the second time through the arbitration process as having increased, or at least as having remained unchanged.

Consequently, when players believe parity judgments are reached, that the salary position awarded is the one closest to the arbitrator's judgment of true market value, those repeating the arbitration process will perceive their probability of formulating a winning offer the second time through as increasing if they won the first ruling. Thus players will be more likely to repeat the process if they won the first arbitration ruling, in contrast to behavior under the offsetting view.

This argument similarly holds when players believe arbitrators are conservative by nature, that they tend to award more outcomes in favor of the teams as the spreads increase between the players' salary requests and clubs' offers. Players who win the first time in arbitration will believe that the spread between the final demand and final offer was either appropriate or too narrow, whereas players who lost the first time will believe that the spread was too wide. This belief should lead those players who win the first ruling to choose to repeat the arbitration process, also in contrast to the behavior under the offsetting view.

In summary, the concept of offsetting arbitration outcomes predicts that the subsequent behavior of those players who win the first time in arbitration is to not repeat the arbitration process. Both the conservative view and the parity view predict just the opposite behavior, that players who won the first time in arbitration will be likely to go through the process again. Thus evidence will accumulate against the offsetting view if players who win the first arbitration decision repeat the process. If these players do not repeat the process, evidence will accumulate against both the conservative and parity concepts. At the same time, if it is found that the second arbitration decision is not the opposite of (dependent on) the first arbitration outcome, the offsetting view will not be substantiated.

PLAYERS' SALARY DEMANDS IN REPEATED ARBITRATION. The theory of arbitration suggests that if arbitration influences bargaining effort, the relative spread between the positions of disputants should converge over

Table 2-2. *Relative Spread at Arbitration, 1974–91*

Year	Relative spread[a]
1974[b]	1.20
1975[b]	1.21
1976[c]	. . .
1977[c]	. . .
1978[b]	. . .
1979	1.39
1980	1.44
1981	1.48
1982	1.53
1983	1.48
1984	1.45
1985	1.43
1986	1.44
1987	1.29
1988	1.28
1989	1.35
1990	1.47
1991	1.51

Sources: Dworkin (1981, pp. 191–95); *New York Times*, various issues 1982–84; *USA Today*, various issues 1985–91.
a. Player demand divided by team offer.
b. Incomplete data available.
c. No arbitration in 1976–77.

subsequent years of arbitration. Evidence from prior studies of final-offer arbitration for salaries in Major League Baseball, however, suggests the process is not causing the parties to submit reasonable final demands and final offers.[20] Table 2-2, which depicts the average relative spreads between the final salary positions since the inception of baseball's salary arbitration procedure, offers mixed evidence. Only during the years when there has either been no free agency (1974–75) or no free play in the market because of collusion (1987–89) has the average spread varied from a range of 1.40 to 1.53.

These conclusions are, perhaps, misleading because the prior research treats all participants in final-offer salary arbitration for any given year equally. If experience with the arbitration process influences behavior, then a player who has gone through arbitration in a previous year can be expected to behave differently than nonrepeating players.

For the parity view of arbitration, the importance of human capital experience begins with the view that arbitrators do attempt to assess fair

20. Dworkin (1986).

market value in their judgments but that the participants in the procedure need experience with the process to understand this behavior.[21] As a player gains this experience, he tries to improve the probability of an arbitration success by making a final salary demand that is closer to the true market value than is the club's final offer. Consequently, players (and teams) under the parity concept should make arbitration demands (and offers) that tend to converge toward market value as they repeat the arbitration process with each other.

The conservative view of the arbitration procedure hypothesizes that arbitrators side with the team when the divergence between the final salary demand and final salary offer is too great. Players with arbitration experience will consequently behave differently depending on whether they were first-time winners or losers. First-time losers will believe they lost previously because they asked for too much relative to the team's offer in their first arbitration case. As a result, they will lower their final demands in subsequent arbitration. First-time winners, however, will not have this pressure on the level of their final salary demand and may even feel that they can push the spread level upward.

In summary, players repeating the arbitration process and accepting the parity model of arbitrator behavior will try to improve their chance of winning by making a salary demand close to the parity judgment they expect the arbitrator to make. This should lead to a narrowing of final-demand spreads for players repeating arbitration whether they won or lost in their first attempt. In contrast, players repeating arbitration who believe in the conservative view should narrow the final spreads only if they lost the first ruling.

Although we have focused on player behavior for arbitration repeaters, teams can be viewed as having symmetric behavior. If teams believe arbitrators offset judgments, then there is incentive for teams to go into the process with lowball offers in repeat cases because the team would believe high offers do not improve the probability of winning. If teams believe arbitrators are motivated by conservative behavior, then the clubs will always want to make low offers to make the final spread between a player's demand and the team's offer appear too large. If the clubs hold the parity view, however, then in repeat cases they will seek to narrow the final-offer spreads to increase their probability of winning. However,

---

21. For reviews of the expertise literature, see Chi, Glaser, and Farr (1988) and Alba and Hutchinson (1987).

because teams file for arbitration in fewer than 10 percent of all cases, this study has focused on player behavior.

It should also be noted that average relative spreads are being used to differentiate between the parity and conservative concepts. This type of testing will be appropriate if no support is found for the offsetting concept during the tests of arbitration outcomes. However, if the tests of arbitration outcomes do not support the parity and conservative concepts, then this test of average spreads will not hold. If players are found to behave in accordance with the offsetting view, there should be upward pressure on the average spreads, as only those players who lost the first arbitration decision would repeat the process, expecting to win the second time.

Data Description and Research Design

The population for our study is all players who have participated in final-offer salary arbitration since its inception in 1974.[22] Each player has information associated with him regarding the arbitration decision. This information includes the year of arbitration, the offer from management, the amount requested by the player, whether he had participated in arbitration in a prior year, number of years of major league service, and baseball team.

Data Limitations

We were unable to secure data for the 1978 arbitration participants. We are aware that the clubs won seven of nine cases, but we do not know the players involved in those cases. Owing to similar data problems, the 1974, 1975, and 1979 numbers are incomplete. (Thus there are five additional player omissions from the data set.) This lack of a complete data set forces us to truncate our analysis to a time frame in which we are reasonably certain that our data are complete and accurate. Because one of our major explanatory variables is repeating the arbitration process, we need to be assured that we have correctly identified all second-time participants in the process. We are missing all of the participants in 1978

22. Our data were collected from various sources, including the *Baseball Encyclopedia*, *New York Times*, *Sporting News*, and *USA Today*.

and two from 1979 and therefore cannot determine if those players repeated in 1979, 1980, or 1981. It seems reasonable to assume that by 1982
the 1978 and 1979 participants would have been elevated to free agent
status. Therefore we analyzed the period 1982–91.

The Model

This equation relates the relative salary spread at arbitration to several
case-specific variables.

$$(1) \quad SPREAD = \alpha_1 + \beta_1\ REPEAT1 + \beta_2\ REPEAT2 + \beta_3\ YEARS$$
$$+ \beta_4\ MKTSIZE + \beta_5\ COLLUSION + \varepsilon$$

SPREAD is defined as the natural log of the amount requested by the
player divided by the offer from the team. The nonlog version of the
SPREAD variable is theoretically bounded by 0 and infinity. This nonlog
version can be viewed as a percentage difference between the player's
demand and the team's offer (for example, a SPREAD of 1.5 indicates a
player's demand that is 50 percent higher than the team's offer). In practical terms, however, its lower bound is a number greater than 1 with an
upper bound over 2. Given this limited range of outcomes, the natural
log was taken.

REPEAT1 and REPEAT2 are binary variables equal to 1 if the player
is repeating the arbitration process with the same team. The difference
between these two variables is that REPEAT1 encompasses those repeaters who won the first time and REPEAT2 comprises those who lost
their first decision. The parity view of arbitration would predict that the
coefficients on these variables will be negative; the conservative viewpoint
would predict the coefficient would be negative only for those who lost
their first decision. Table 2-3 lists the players who have repeated arbitration with the same team since the inception of baseball's salary arbitration, subject to the data limitations discussed above. Included in the
table are the relative spreads between the players and their clubs each
year and the arbitration outcomes.

YEARS is the recoded number of years of service of the player. This
variable ranges from 2 to 6, with any value greater than 6 recorded as 6.
The logic of this recoding lies in the belief that any player with six or
more years of service who is in arbitration is one year away from free
agency. A priori the coefficient of this variable is unknown.

Table 2-3. *Players Experiencing Arbitration Twice with Same Team, 1974–91*

Player	Club	Years	Spread[a]		Outcome[b]	
			1st	*2nd*	*1st*	*2nd*
S. Bando	Oak	74–75	1.333	1.250	P	C
S. Braun	Min	75–75	1.240	1.139	P	C
R. Fingers	Oak	74–75	1.182	1.187	P	P
K. Holtzman	Oak	74–75	1.163	1.204	P	C
R. Jackson	Oak	74–75	1.350	1.204	P	C
T. Kubiak	Oak	74–75	1.149	1.131	C	P
J. Essian	Oak	79–80	1.324	1.250	P	C
R. Langford	Oak	79–80	1.489	1.394	P	P
J. Newman	Oak	79–80	1.289	1.765	C	P
R. Scott	Mon	79–80	1.510	1.480	P	C
D. Collins	Cin	80–81	1.323	1.346	C	C
J. Cruz[c]	Sea	80–81	1.368	1.509	P	C
R. Jackson	Min	80–81	1.304	1.532	P	P
S. Kemp	Det	80–81	1.400	1.667	C	P
D. Aase	Cal	80–82	1.290	1.395	C	C
G. Minton	SF	81–82	1.472	1.443	C	C
J. Cruz[c]	Sea	82–83	1.875	1.177	P	C
M. Soto	Cin	82–83	1.475	1.389	P	P
R. Henderson	Oak	82–84	1.529	1.263	P	C
J. Price	Cin	83–84	1.615	1.500	P	C
M. Scioscia	LA	83–85	1.433	1.243	C	P
W. Boggs	Bos	85–86	1.481	1.370	P	C
G. Ward	Tex	84–86	1.322	1.075	C	C
P. Bradley	Sea	86–87	1.267	1.364	P	P
B. Butler	Cle	86–87	1.417	1.144	P	C
R. Darling	Mets	86–87	1.398	1.313	C	P
O. Hershiser	LA	86–87	1.667	1.375	P	C
C. Leibrandt	KC	86–87	1.400	1.172	P	P
G. Pettis	Cal	86–87	1.417	1.375	C	C
J. Acker	Atl	87–88	1.286	1.138	C	C
M. Moore	Sea	86–88	1.325	1.172	C	C
T. Teufel	Mets	86–89	1.750	1.255	C	P
B. Bonds	Pit	90–91	1.882	1.413	C	C
B. Bonilla	Pit	90–91	1.360	1.448	C	C
D. Drabek	Pit	90–91	1.467	1.450	P	P
W. Joyner	Cal	90–91	1.429	1.273	P	P
B. Santiago	SD	90–91	1.667	1.515	P	C

Sources: Dworkin (1981, pp. 191–95); *New York Times*, various issues 1982–84; *USA Today*, various issues 1985–91.

a. Player demand divided by team offer.

b. P = player won; C = club won.

c. J. Cruz repeated arbitration with Seattle each year during 1980–83. Because Seattle changed ownership in 1981, he is treated as repeating with the same ownership for 1980 and 1981 and as repeating with the same ownership for 1982 and 1983. Thus he is listed twice. In addition, the following seven players are excluded because they repeated arbitration either with two different teams or against two different owners: S. Balboni, E. Farmer, D. LaPoint, K. McReynolds, J. Morris, D. Petry, and L. Smith.

MKTSIZE is a binary variable that equals 1 when a team operates in a small market. The anticipated sign on this coefficient is positive, because we theorized that the club and the player have differing perceptions of the worth of said player in a small market. The player uses the universe of all players at his position as an estimate of his intrinsic value. The small-market team values that player relative to the particular market in which it operates. Therefore the relative spread should be greater for a small-market team. A small-market team is a team ranked in the bottom ten of the twenty-two major league cities both in the major media markets (according to Nielsen) and size of the standard metropolitan statistical area and one that did not have a national cable Superstation (such as Atlanta) or a major radio contract (such as St. Louis). Thus, excluding Atlanta and St. Louis, the universe of small-market teams for our study includes Cleveland, Cincinnati, Kansas City, Milwaukee, Minnesota, Pittsburgh, San Diego, and Seattle.

COLLUSION is a binary variable equal to 1 for the years when collusion has been ruled and 0 otherwise. The collusion rulings correspond to the arbitration cases heard during 1986–88. Because the initial collusion ruling (September 1987) did not deter collusion in the subsequent year, the behavior of the players is assumed to remain unchanged (that is, skeptical about whether there is free play in the market) until monetary damages are awarded (September 1989). Because of this expected behavior on the part of the players, the arbitration cases heard during 1989 are also assumed to belong to the collusion period. This coefficient is anticipated to be negative. This may be interpreted as the perceived lack of an alternative market or of the free play of market forces. It will therefore narrow the relative spread by lowering expectations.

Empirical Results

To determine whether the arbitration process assigns outcomes in an offsetting manner, we tabulated the outcomes for those players repeating the process with the same team. The observed frequency tables and associated statistics are presented in figure 2-1, for both the period 1982–91 and since the inception of baseball's salary arbitration procedure (1974–91), subject to the data limitations discussed above. First, the chi-

Figure 2-1. *Outcomes for Players Experiencing Arbitration Twice*

1982–91[a]

		Second arbitration outcome		
		Player won	Club won	Total
First arbitration outcome	Player won	5	7	12
	Club won	3	8	11
	Total	8	15	23

1974–91[b]

		Second arbitration outcome		
		Player won	Club won	Total
First arbitration outcome	Player won	8	14	22
	Club won	6	9	15
	Total	14	23	37

a. Pearson chi-square = 0.5242; $DF = 1$; ($p > 0.46$).
b. Pearson chi-square = 0.0501; $DF = 1$; ($p > 0.82$).

square test of the independence of the second outcome and whether the first outcome was won by the player or the club is not significant: $p > 0.46$ for 1982–91 and $p > 0.82$ for 1974–91. This result, that the second outcome is not dependent on the first outcome, is not consistent with the offsetting view of arbitration. Further examination of figure 2-1 reveals the procedure may also not represent a random walk. By summing the diagonal cells, one can observe that of the thirty-seven cases seventeen (46 percent) are players who either won both hearings or lost both hearings between 1974 and 1991. However, the percentage of players receiving the same outcome in both rulings increased to thirteen of twenty-three (57 percent) in the 1982–91 period (top diagram) from only four of fourteen (29 percent) in the 1974–81 period (calculated as the residual).[23]

To investigate whether the players behave in a manner predicted by the offsetting concept (that is, players who win the first arbitration case will not repeat the process), the proportion of players who had won the first ruling and elected to repeat was determined. From figure 2-1, twelve of the twenty-three players (52 percent) who repeated the process during 1982–91 won their first arbitration ruling, whereas twenty-two of the thirty-seven players (59 percent) who repeated during 1974–91 won their first ruling. The offsetting concept is not supported; that is, a majority of the players repeating the process won the first ruling.

Finally, a chi-square goodness-of-fit test was used to estimate if the likelihood of repeating the process is different for those players who win the first ruling, given the population of player and club wins in all arbitration rulings. Since 1974 players have won 145 and clubs 176 of the 321 arbitration rulings. Comparing this population of rulings with the outcomes of those repeating the process (using the chi-square goodness-of-fit test), it appears that since the inception of the salary arbitration process winning the first ruling does have an effect on whether a player repeats the arbitration process. First-time winners repeat salary arbitration more often than first-time losers; that is, twenty-two of the thirty-seven players repeating arbitration won the first ruling. This proportion of first-time winners is statistically significant from that expected by chance ($p < 0.10$). However, when one considers just the period 1982–91, this finding, that first-time winners repeat more often than first-time losers, does not reach statistical significance ($p > 0.25$).

Because the offsetting concept of baseball's salary arbitration procedure was not supported by the testing of arbitration outcomes, the regression results were used to differentiate between the parity and conservative concepts. These results are presented in table 2-4. Although we provide results for the complete time period, we focus our analysis on the period 1982–91.

The REPEAT1 and REPEAT2 processes both narrow the relative spread by approximately 8 percent. This narrowing of the spread for the second

23. This upward trend appears to continue in a more recent time too. Examination of the outcomes for players repeating with the team between 1987 and 1991 reveals that nine of fourteen (64 percent) received the same decision both times in arbitration.

Table 2-4. *Regression Results*[a]

Variable	1982–91	1974–91
Intercept	0.420 (12.82) ***	0.428 (17.38) ***
REPEAT1	−0.078 (−2.00) **	−0.045 (−1.54)
REPEAT2	−0.076 (−1.89) *	−0.025 (−0.72)
YEARS	−0.013 (−1.59)	−0.017 (−2.79) ***
MKTSIZE	0.054 (2.89) ***	0.044 (2.75) ***
COLLUSION	−0.089 (−4.95) ***	−0.109 (−7.25) ***
$\bar{R}^2$	0.17	0.20
F	9.15 ***	16.27 ***
DF	201	302

* Significant at < 0.10.
** Significant at < 0.05.
*** Significant at < 0.01.
a. The numbers in parentheses are t-statistics.

arbitration ruling by both first-time winners and first-time losers is not consistent with the conservative view of the arbitration process. In the conservative view only first-time losers would narrow the spread.[24] The *YEARS* variable has a negative coefficient but is statistically insignificant. The lack of significance of this variable, coupled with the significance of the repeat variables, indicates that, on average, *REPEAT1* and *REPEAT2* do not converge to the market solution simply because of getting closer to free agency. Figure 2-2 displays the relationship of the average relative spread between the final demands and final offers for all those in salary arbitration with the average relative spread of the players repeating the process during 1982–91.

As anticipated, *MKTSIZE* has a positive coefficient and is statistically significant (table 2-4). The small-market teams, on average, have a 5 percent larger spread. *COLLUSION* narrows the spread by 9 percent,

24. Supplementary analysis of the spreads using just those players who repeated the arbitration process strengthens this perception. Paired t-tests reveal that for 1982–91 both first-time winners, $t(1,11) = 3.45$, $p < 0.01$, and losers, $t(1,10) = 2.71$, $p < 0.05$, narrowed their spreads the second time, whereas during 1974–91 first-time winners, $t(1,21) = 2.84$, $p < 0.01$, narrowed their spreads but first-time losers did not, $t(1,14) = 1.06$, $p > 0.30$.

Figure 2-2. *Difference in Relative Spread for Players Repeating Arbitration, 1982–91*

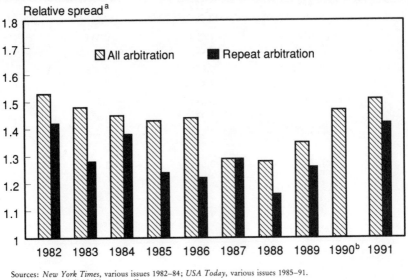

Sources: *New York Times*, various issues 1982–84; *USA Today*, various issues 1985–91.
a. Player demand divided by team offer.
b. No players repeated arbitration in 1990.

supporting our contention that lack of free play in the market lowers player expectations.

The overall explanatory power of this regression as measured by $\bar{R}^2$ is relatively low at 17 percent. The importance of the independent variables as a group, however, is supported by the significance of the F statistic. Three of the four independent variables are dichotomous in nature, which limits their ability to vary incrementally with the dependent variable. Thus the low $\bar{R}^2$ is not particularly surprising.

A concern with this particular estimation of the equation relates to the dichotomous nature of the small-market variable. This variable is probably more appropriately included as a continuous variable. However, the difficulties with operationalizing this variable continuously are myriad. The only precise measure of the market size would be accurate revenue records. The extent to which teams are privately held and do not fully disclose accurate financial records makes the reliability of any available measure questionable.

Conclusion

The results generated by our empirical tests provide strong evidence that players going through Major League Baseball's salary arbitration procedure for a second time behave differently than first-time entrants. This type of learning behavior following an arbitration experience was not unexpected. The specific impact of repeated arbitration on player behavior, however, is noteworthy. Players who reenter arbitration are likely to lower significantly the relative spread between their final salary request and the final offer of their team. This supports the view that players see the arbitration decision as a parity judgment. In other words, the decision is one in which the arbitrator selects a true market value for the player's services and selects the final position closer to that amount. Thus a player can try to improve his chances for success by making a final salary demand that will lead to a narrower spread between his demand and his team's offer. The economic implications of the spread-lowering impact of arbitration repetitions is that the arbitrator's decision will more closely approximate the true market value of a player's worth. Suppose an arbitrator decides on a parity (that is, true market) value exactly halfway between the player and team positions. If the player's request is twice the team's offer, then the arbitrator's best option is a salary that is 50 percent off market value. However, if the spread between player and team is only 10 percent, the arbitrator's decision will be off the market value by only 5 percent. The policy implication of the evidence presented in this chapter is that greater access to salary arbitration and more repeated use of arbitration will lead to player salaries that more closely reflect market values.

This research also opens possibilities for additional explorations. One class of extensions centers around finer tuning of the estimation. In this chapter we focused on a narrow set of variables as independent determinants of salary spread, namely, player repetition of arbitration, team market strength, collusion, and player experience. Other factors have been excluded, such as the importance of agents and the impact of team repetition.[25] Behavior of salary spread in arbitration might also be affected by factors such as player race and player position as a proxy for the variance of expected future performance. Research on the impact of ar-

---

25. The first arbitration experience of the Milwaukee Brewers was in 1991 with Jim Gantner. It involved one of the largest spreads ever.

bitration on other aspects of the business of baseball is also in order. For instance, how does an early arbitration experience affect behavior in future filings for arbitration, as opposed to actually going to arbitration? Furthermore, to what extent does the arbitration experience, with its reputation for having a negative effect on player–team relations, affect future free agency behavior? Research of this sort needs to be carried out before making a normative judgment about the value of arbitration to Major League Baseball.

References

Alba, Joseph W., and J. Wesley Hutchinson. 1987. "Dimensions of Consumer Expertise." *Journal of Consumer Research* 13:411–54.

Ashenfelter, Orley, and David E. Bloom. 1983. "The Pitfalls in Judging Arbitrator Impartiality by Win-Loss Tallies under Final Offer Arbitration." *Labor Law Journal* 34:534–39.

———. 1984. "Models of Arbitrator Behavior: Theory and Evidence." *American Economic Review* 74:111–24.

The Baseball Encyclopedia: The Complete and Official Record of Major League Baseball. 1990. Macmillan.

Chi, Michelene T. H., Robert Glaser, and Marshall J. Farr. 1988. *The Nature of Expertise.* Hillsdale, N.J.: Lawrence Erlbaum Associates.

Dworkin, James B. 1981. *Owners versus Players: Baseball and Collective Bargaining.* Boston: Auburn House.

———. 1986. "Salary Arbitration in Baseball: An Impartial Assessment after Ten Years." *Arbitration Journal* 41:63–69.

Erekson, O. Homer, James W. Moser, and S. Schwartz. 1989. "Evenhandedness in Arbitration: The Case of Major League Baseball." *Eastern Economic Journal* 15:117–27.

Farber, Henry S. 1980. "An Analysis of Final-Offer Arbitration." *Journal of Conflict Resolution* 24:683–705.

Gibbons, Robert. 1988. "Learning in Equilibrium Models of Arbitration." *American Economic Review* 78:896–912.

Hammond, K. R., D. A. Summers, and D. H. Deane. 1973. "Negative Effects of Outcome-Feedback on Multiple-Cue Probability Learning." *Organizational Behavior and Human Performance* 9:30–34.

Harrell, Adrian M. 1977. "The Decision-Making Behavior of Air Force Officers and the Management Control Process." *Accounting Review* 52:833–41.

Hogarth, Robin M., and Hillel J. Einhorn. In press. "Order Effects in Belief Updating: The Belief-Adjustment Model." *Cognitive Psychology.*

Jennings, Kenneth M. 1990. *Balls and Strikes: The Money Game in Professional Baseball.* Praeger.

Scully, Gerald W. 1989. *The Business of Major League Baseball.* University of Chicago Press.

Stevens, Carl M. 1966. "Is Compulsory Arbitration Compatible with Bargaining?" *Industrial Relations* 5:38–52.

CHAPTER THREE

Bargaining Power and Major League Baseball

Paul L. Burgess and Daniel R. Marburger

M AJOR LEAGUE Baseball's collective bargaining agreement defines three levels of player bargaining power. Most players with less than three years of major league experience ("ineligibles") are bound to a single team and are not free to negotiate contracts with competing clubs. Players with roughly three to six years of service ("arbitration-eligibles"), though still bound to one club, may opt to have their salaries arbitrated via final-offer arbitration. A third level of bargaining power belongs to players ("free agent–eligibles") who may negotiate freely with other teams. Players in this category must have at least six years of major league service. Not surprisingly, salary distributions in Major League Baseball correlate strongly with the bargaining power afforded the individual players.[1]

This chapter examines salary differences between the ineligible and arbitration-eligible players. Owing to the bargaining power inherent in this option, final-offer arbitration may reduce the monopsony power of clubs and, as a result, raise the salaries of arbitration-eligible players. Because players in both of these categories are bound to one team, any salary differential between the two groups is likely to be attributable to eligibility for final-offer arbitration. Using time series data on all arbitration-eligible players during the 1987 and 1988 seasons, this chapter presents evidence that hitters, starting pitchers, and relief pitchers obtain salary increases of 86 percent, 89 percent, and 58 percent, respectively, on gaining the right to final-offer arbitration.

1. Chelius and Dworkin (1980); Hill (1985); Hill and Spellman (1983); Marburger (1991); Raimondo (1983); Sommers and Quinton (1982).

Institutional Bargaining Power

The institutional bargaining power of major league baseball players has undergone significant transitions over the past twenty years. During the first hundred years of its existence, baseball used the reserve clause to restrict the mobility and bargaining power of players. The reserve clause enabled clubs to retain complete control over the players as property. For this reason, players were not permitted to negotiate with other clubs throughout their professional careers.

In 1973 the collective bargaining agreement between the clubs and the players' union was modified to allow for the implementation of final-offer arbitration. Under final-offer arbitration, both the player and the club submit offers to an independent arbitrator, who selects one of the two submissions as binding. Eligibility for the process is based on the player's years of major league experience. Until 1987 players with at least two years of major league service were eligible for this procedure. From 1987 through 1990, the requirement was raised to three years. Beginning in 1991, 17 percent of the players with between two and three years of experience also became eligible to participate in arbitration.

Players must apply for arbitration between January 15 and January 25 of the year in which they are eligible. Although players may withdraw from the process within seven days of the exchange of final offers, clubs may not. Hence arbitration-eligible players may compel the clubs to an arbitrated settlement.[2] All hearings are conducted during the following month, between February 1 and February 20. Arbitrators must submit their decisions, without explanation, within twenty-four hours of the hearing. Arbitration awards are for one-year contracts only and do not include bonuses of any kind.

The following criteria have been identified in the 1973 Basic Agreement as admissible evidence in arbitration hearings: (1) the player's contribution during the past season, including overall performance and special qualities of leadership and public appeal; (2) length and consistency of the player's career contribution; (3) the record of the player's past compensation; (4) comparative baseball salaries; (5) recent club performance; and (6) the existence of any physical or mental defects in the player. Evidence presented at the hearings may not include the financial position of either the player or the club, the cost of representation, offers made before arbitration, or salaries in other occupations or sports.

2. Final-offer arbitration may also be offered to free agent–eligible players. Under these circumstances, however, participation is not compulsory.

In 1975, two years after the introduction of final-offer arbitration, a landmark grievance arbitration decision invalidated the reserve clause and declared that players without a contract were free to negotiate with other teams. This decision ultimately led to the institution of the third level of bargaining power, free agency. Under free agency, players with six or more years of experience are free to negotiate with other clubs.

Prior Literature

Since the 1970s, researchers have examined the effects of arbitration and free agency on bargaining power in Major League Baseball. More general theoretical discussions about the nature of final-offer arbitration provide an important backdrop for understanding the process as applied to baseball.

Final-Offer Arbitration

Stevens first developed a theory of final-offer arbitration. He saw it as a means of encouraging negotiations between bargaining agents in the absence of a right to strike.[3] To reduce the incentive of arbitrators to split the difference between the offers in determining a settlement, arbitrators are obliged to select one of the two submitted offers as binding.

According to Farber's theoretical model, arbitrators formulate a notion of the appropriate award and then select the offer nearest this figure.[4] Given a set of arbitrator preferences, utility-maximizing bargaining agents submit offers that balance their desire for more favorable, extreme settlements against the probability that a given offer will be selected. Gibbons,[5] in response to evidence that the submitted offers convey information to the arbitrators,[6] amended Farber's assumption of arbitrator preference exogeneity by developing a sequential learning model in which arbitrators infer the bargaining environment from the submitted offers. Further, Farber and Katz suggested that arbitration procedures generate a contract

3. Stevens (1966).
4. Farber (1980).
5. Gibbons (1988).
6. Bazerman and Farber (1985); Bloom (1986); Farber (1980).

zone regardless of whether the case goes to arbitration.[7] For this reason, they explain, negotiated settlements change by the same amount as arbitrated settlements.

Bargaining Power

Numerous studies linking bargaining power to salary levels in Major League Baseball have appeared in economic literature. Using data from the reserve clause era, both Scully and Medoff measured the extent of monopsonistic exploitation by estimating the marginal revenue products of players and comparing them with salaries.[8] Chelius and Dworkin compared the salaries of arbitration-eligible players with those of ineligible players.[9] The study was guided by the hypothesis that final-offer arbitration eliminated the ability of owners to discriminate on the basis of the opportunity costs of players and would therefore reduce the disparity among players' salaries. The study used data from before the establishment of free agency. In the free agency era, several studies contrasted the salaries of free agents with those of non–free agents.[10] Not surprisingly, the researchers found that competitive bidding significantly increases free agents' pay. Marburger sought to update the work of Chelius and Dworkin to reflect baseball's current economic environment.[11] He theorized that the existence of competitively determined salaries would exert upward pressure on the salaries of arbitration-eligibles. Because arbitrators are permitted to consider comparative baseball salaries, free agent–eligible salaries are likely to play a role in determining the arbitration award. Given the obvious impact of free agency on players' salaries, it is likely that final-offer arbitration has a significant effect on bargaining power.

Methodology

To measure the bargaining-power effect of final-offer arbitration, we developed a sample of all arbitration-eligible players during the 1987–88

---

7. Farber and Katz (1979).
8. Scully (1974); Medoff (1976).
9. Chelius and Dworkin (1980).
10. Hill (1985); Hill and Spellman (1983); Raimondo (1983).
11. Marburger (1991).

seasons from information in the *Sporting News*.[12] The time series data include players who advanced from ineligibility to arbitration eligibility as well as those who moved into consecutive years of arbitration eligibility. The 1987–88 seasons are particularly relevant for this study because the three-year eligibility requirement became effective in 1987. Hence three-year players in the 1987 season entered their second year of eligibility and three-year players in 1988 were eligible for the first time. For this reason, this sample can isolate the bargaining-power effect of arbitration eligibility from salary increases owing to experience.

The bargaining-power effect of arbitration eligibility is measured by regressing the percentage change in salary against unit changes in the set of arbitration criteria previously discussed.[13] Because measures of contribution differ between hitters and pitchers, separate models for each group are estimated. Further, because the importance of various measures of contribution may differ between starting and relief pitchers, separate pitching models are also estimated.

Hitters

The model for hitters is

$$(1) \quad PCTSAL = \alpha_0 + \alpha_1 CHRUNS1 + \alpha_2 CHRUNS2$$
$$+ \alpha_3 CHFLD1 + \alpha_4 CHFLD2 + \alpha_5 CHEXPR2$$
$$+ \alpha_6 CHPCT + \alpha_7 MULT + \alpha_8 ARB88$$
$$+ \alpha_9 FIRST + \epsilon_1.$$

The dependent variable *PCTSAL* refers to the percentage change in the player's salary over the prior season. *CHRUNS1* refers to the change

12. Murray Chass, "Baseball's Bonus Beauties: '87 Pay Buoyed by Special Clauses," *Sporting News*, November 16, 1987, pp. 48–49; and "Salaries: The Future Is Now," *Sporting News*, January 2, 1989, pp. 56–65.

13. Numerous variations of the models described were also estimated. These models included the use of percentage rather than unit changes in the independent variables and the use of other proxies for team and individual performances. Relatively little variation in the size of the bargaining-power transition coefficient existed across models. The specification reported in this chapter represents the model with the best overall fit.

in the player's hitting performance over the two previous seasons.[14] *CHRUNS2* is the difference in performance two to three seasons before the hearing. *CHFLD1* and *CHFLD2* refer to similar changes in the player's fielding percentage over these same periods of time. Because the careers of some players in the sample span only three years, these are the only career-consistency proxies available for the entire sample.

To capture salary changes attributable to experience, *CHEXPR2*, the change in experience–squared over the previous two seasons, is also included in the model.[15] *CHPCT* refers to the change in the club's winning percentage over the two previous seasons.[16]

The sample consists of first-time arbitration-eligible players (all of whom became eligible in 1988), players eligible in consecutive seasons (consisting of all of the 1987 observations for players with single-year contracts and some of the 1988 observations), and players with multiyear contracts. To control for the players' eligibility characteristics, several dummy variables were created. *MULT* is a dummy variable equal to 1 for arbitration-eligibles who played under multiyear contracts. Unlike for players with single-year contracts, increases in pay for these players were prenegotiated.[17] *ARB88* is a dummy variable equal to 1 for 1988 arbitration-eligibles who were not in their first year of eligibility. Finally, the key variable of interest, *FIRST*, is a dummy variable equal to 1 for first-time eligible players. By controlling for 1988 filers (via *FIRST* and *ARB88*) and players with multiyear contracts, the benchmark consists of 1987 players with single-year contracts, none of whom would be in his first year of eligibility.

The results appear in table 3-1. As shown in the table, the only significant decision criteria are the offensive performance measures *CHRUNS1* and *CHRUNS2*. With regard to the effect of final-offer arbitration, the dummy variable *FIRST* is positive and significant with a coefficient of 0.86. This suggests that hitters can expect an 86 percent increase in salaries simply by gaining final-offer arbitration eligibility.

14. Hitting performance is measured as the player's runs produced, which is defined as runs plus runs-batted-in minus home runs.

15. Because the independent variables constitute a first-differencing of the arbitration criteria, the difference in experience would equal 1 for all observations. By squaring the players' experience, changes in salaries owing to experience may be captured.

16. The only criterion not directly measured is the mental or physical defects of the player. To the extent that such defects may affect playing time or performance, these effects may be captured in the contribution proxies, which are weighted by playing time.

17. All independent variables for players with multiyear contracts are based on seasons before the initial year of the contract.

Table 3-1. *Bargaining-Power Effect of Final-Offer Arbitration: Hitters*[a]

Independent variable[b]	Coefficient
Constant	1.43
	(5.23)*
CHRUNS1	0.0079
	(5.77)*
CHRUNS2	0.0036
	(3.12)*
CHFLD1	−0.0013
	(−0.415)
CHFLD2	0.003
	(0.978)
CHEXPR2	−0.007
	(−0.184)
CHPCT	0.0002
	(0.331)
MULT	0.003
	(0.020)
ARB88	−0.081
	(−0.707)
FIRST	0.864
	(6.35)*
$\bar{R}^2$	0.488

*Significant at 0.01 level.
a. Numbers in parentheses are *t*-statistics.
b. The dependent variable is *PCTSAL*.

Pitchers

Because the contributions of pitchers are different from those of hitters, a separate model must be estimated for pitchers. However, because the role of starting pitchers differs from that of relief pitchers, the same model is estimated separately for starting pitchers and relief pitchers.

In measuring pitching contributions, *CHPIT1* and *CHPIT2* refer to unit changes in the pitchers' effectiveness over the past three seasons, and *CHSV1* and *CHSV2* represent changes in the number of saves earned over the same period.[18] The complete pitching model is

18. The pitching effectiveness measure used in this study is (innings pitched/adjusted earned run average). The measure weighs a pitcher's effectiveness by the number of innings pitched. As constructed, the measure is an increasing function of performance. The adjusted ERA is the pitcher's ERA divided by the average league ERA. The adjustment is necessary because the existence of the designated hitter in the American League tends to inflate earned run averages relative to those of National League pitchers.

Table 3-2. *Bargaining-Power Effect of Final-Offer Arbitration: Pitchers*[a]

Independent variable	Starting pitchers' coefficient	Relief pitchers' coefficient
Constant	1.71	1.19
	(6.46)*	(4.20)*
CHPIT1	0.0037	0.0036
	(6.40)*	(2.96)*
CHPIT2	0.0018	0.0009
	(3.07)*	(0.937)
CHSV1	0.093	0.025
	(0.747)	(2.64)*
CHSV2	0.157	0.013
	(2.75)*	(1.25)
CHEXPR2	−0.024	0.023
	(−0.718)	(0.646)
CHPCT	−0.0005	0.0007
	(−0.767)	(0.945)
MULT	−0.249	−0.293
	(−0.869)	(−0.640)
ARB88	−0.122	0.017
	(−0.877)	(0.114)
FIRST	0.894	0.583
	(4.44)*	(3.35)*
$\bar{R}^2$	0.611	0.432

*Significant at 0.01 level.
a. Numbers in parentheses are t-statistics.

$$(2) \quad PCTSAL = \beta_0 + \beta_1 CHPIT1 + \beta_2 CHPIT2 + \beta_3 CHSV1$$
$$+ \beta_4 CHSV2 + \beta_5 CHEXPR2 + \beta_6 CHPCT$$
$$+ \beta_7 MULT + \beta_8 ARB88 + \beta_9 FIRST + \epsilon_2.$$

The results of the pitchers' models appear in table 3-2. For the starting pitchers, CHPIT1, CHPIT2, and CHSV2 are positive and significant. The bargaining-power transition variable, FIRST, is also positive and significant, with a coefficient of 0.89. This suggests that starting pitchers earn salary increases of 89 percent on gaining the right to final-offer arbitration.

In comparison, CHPIT1 and CHSV1 are positive and significant for relief pitchers. With regard to salary increases owing to bargaining power, the coefficient for FIRST is 0.58 and significant. Hence relief pitchers can expect to earn salary increases of 58 percent by gaining the right to an arbitrated settlement.

Perhaps the most interesting observation from these results is the relatively small impact arbitration eligibility has on relief pitchers' salaries relative to those of hitters and starting pitchers. The difference is probably attributable to contrasts in the elasticity of demand for these players. Although there are "star" relief pitchers who are regularly called on to earn saves, most of baseball's lowest-quality pitchers are relegated to relief roles. Lesser players who obtain large salary increases through final-offer arbitration may jeopardize their employment opportunities because clubs may wish to substitute younger, lower-cost players for their services. Given that arbitrated salaries are not guaranteed, these players may be less willing to exploit final-offer arbitration salary opportunities and may settle for more moderate increases in compensation.

Conclusion

Final-offer arbitration serves not only as a means of encouraging negotiations between players and clubs, but also as a device to reduce monopsony power. Time series data for the 1987–88 seasons were used to measure the extent to which arbitration eligibility raised players' salaries. We found that obtaining the right to final-offer arbitration increased the salaries of hitters, starting pitchers, and relief pitchers by 86 percent, 89 percent, and 58 percent, respectively.

An interesting observation in light of the substantial impact arbitration eligibility has on salaries is that the owners were ruled to have been guilty of colluding to suppress the mobility of free agents during the period studied. To the extent that the collusion held salaries down, there may have been some spillover effect on the arbitration-eligible players. This implies that the impact of final-offer arbitration, though clearly sizable, may be understated.

References

Bazerman, Max H., and Henry S. Farber. 1985. "Arbitrator Decision-Making: When Are Final Offers Important?" *Industrial and Labor Relations Review* 39:76–89.

Bloom, David E. 1986. "Empirical Models of Arbitrator Behavior under Conventional Arbitration." *Review of Economics and Statistics* 68:578–85.

Chelius, James R., and James B. Dworkin. 1980. "An Economic Analysis of

Final-Offer Arbitration as a Conflict Resolution Device." *Journal of Conflict Resolution* 24:293–310.

Farber, Henry S. 1980. "An Analysis of Final-Offer Arbitration." *Journal of Conflict Resolution* 24:683–705.

Farber, Henry S., and Harry C. Katz. 1979. "Interest Arbitration, Outcomes, and the Incentive to Bargain." *Industrial and Labor Relations Review* 33:55–63.

Gibbons, Robert. 1988. "Learning in Equilibrium Models of Arbitration." *American Economic Review* 78:896–912.

Hill, James R. 1985. "The Threat of Free Agency and Exploitation in Professional Baseball: 1976–1977." *Quarterly Review of Economics and Business* 25:68–82.

Hill, James R., and William Spellman. 1983. "Professional Baseball: The Reserve Clause and Salary Structure." *Industrial Relations* 22:1–19.

Marburger, Daniel R. 1991. "Bargaining Power and Salary Structures in Major League Baseball." Arkansas State University, College of Business Working Paper.

Medoff, Marshall H. 1976. "On Monopsonistic Exploitation in Professional Baseball." *Quarterly Review of Economics and Business* 16:113–21.

Raimondo, Henry J. 1983. "Free Agents' Impact on the Labor Market for Baseball Players." *Journal of Labor Research* 4:183–93.

Scully, Gerald W. 1974. "Pay and Performance in Major League Baseball." *American Economic Review* 64:915–30.

Sommers, Paul M., and Noel Quinton. 1982. "Pay and Performance in Major League Baseball: The Case of the First Family of Free Agents." *Journal of Human Resources* 17:426–36.

Stevens, Carl M. 1966. "Is Compulsory Arbitration Compatible with Bargaining?" *Industrial Relations* 5:38–52.

Part II

The Impact of Fans

CHAPTER FOUR

The Role of the Fan in Professional Baseball

Philip K. Porter

I N THE study of professional baseball, as in the study of all sports, the role of the fan as an input in the production process has not been given its rightful place. Player skill, an obvious input, has been accorded most of the attention.[1] Researchers have also examined coaches, organizational structure in professional sports leagues, property rights and incentives for performance, and even officials and the impact of game play refereeing.[2] Fans, however, are always treated as observers whose interests determine the demand for games. Demand feedback, as an influence on supply decisions, is ignored. That is, although fans attend games, bet on the outcome,[3] and reward university sponsors with contributions and enrollment applications,[4] they are not believed to influence the way the game is played.

This chapter investigates the fan's contribution to winning in the sport of baseball. The demand for baseball provides the wherewithal to acquire players, but this by itself does not determine a team's quality. Equilibrium quality, as measured by winning percentage, should be independent of the level of demand. Teams with larger annual revenues are no more prone to winning than others.[5] This is because teams with loyal fans,

---

1. The tradition began with Scully (1974).
2. On coaches, see Porter and Scully (1982); organizational structure, El-Hodiri and Quirk (1971); property rights and incentives, Lehn (1982); officials and refereeing, McCormick and Tollison (1984).
3. There is a large literature on betting. For an example, see Asch, Malkiel, and Quandt (1984).
4. See, for example, Coughlin and Erekson (1984); McCormick and Tinsley (1987).
5. That winning attracts fans is undisputed. That is, the level of quality positively influences *quantity demanded* at a constant price. The *level of demand* is defined here as attendance when winning percentage is 50 percent. This proves to be an insignificant predictor of winning percentage.

evident in high season ticket sales and attendance and a large media audience, earn rents over protracted periods. The advantage is locational in nature. The team might be in a large market or spatially separated from other competition for fan support, or it might have been blessed with die-hard fans (or have created them through marketing). These rents accrue to the franchise and do not reward player talent.

The role of the fan is at the margin of revenue. Ceteris paribus, when the revenue response to wins is elastic, fans punish the owner of a team that loses and reward the owner of a team that wins. These fans are intolerant of poor quality. With highly elastic revenue, the owner who does not field a winning team loses revenue. These losses cannot be exactly offset by winning in a subsequent season. Volatile revenue implies risk. Increased risk demands a risk premium, which erodes the rents that accrue to the owner when attendance and media audience are stable. When the revenue response is less elastic, the reward for the owner's consistent provision of quality is lessened. Seen in this light, fans have a large stake in determining the quality of the team, not by being loyal, but by being fickle. The more elastic the attendance response to wins, the greater the incentive of the owner to field a winning team.

There are at least two interesting corollaries to this train of thought. First, the owners' long-standing contention that the reserve clause (restricting player movements among clubs) might reduce competitive balance among teams in the league may be right, but the owners are giving the wrong reasons. They contend that the teams in the large markets, with greater economic clout, would corner the market for scarce player talent. My research suggests that teams in the most fickle markets tend to corner the scarce talent, that is, that the highest-quality teams will go where the greatest demand for high quality exists. Second, the owners are incorrect in asserting that a team's ability to compete, given high player salaries, requires a large market (an argument that supported an expansion team for Miami over Washington, D.C., or Memphis). There is indeed a minimum viable market size, for total revenue must cover player salaries and operating costs. Beyond this, however, the entry fee that could be charged to an expansion team (the rents the present franchise owner can capture from a prospective expansion owner) is higher in the larger market (presuming a larger average attendance and media audience). But, without knowledge of the fans' demand for quality, predictions of the competitive viability of the team are unfounded.

This chapter first presents contrasting individual and joint profit-maximizing models. In each of these models the marginal revenue product of talent, not the absolute level of revenue for the team, determines the level of talent employed. Then these models are tested using evidence from the last twenty-five years of Major League Baseball. I find that winning is not significantly correlated with absolute revenue, except as this is correlated with the responsiveness of fans. Fan response is a much better explanatory variable.

The Profit-Maximizing Models

Team revenues come from private sources—gate receipts, broadcast sales to local media, and concession sales—and jointly shared sources—national television contracts negotiated by the league. The shared component is unresponsive to individual team performance. The team's location dictates the proximate population and the size of the media market from which it draws its home attendance and its media audience and hence its private revenues. The revenues from these sources are responsive to the team's winning percentage.[6] Thus, $R^i = R + R^i(W)$, where R is the shared component of team revenue and the function R^i captures the locational differences as well as differences in fan responsiveness to performance.

The winning performance of any team, W, is a function of the talent hired by the team and the talent of the team's opponents. Assuming a player's (and hence a team's) performance is randomly distributed, the expected performance is a positive function of the differential of team i's and component j's talent, $W = W(T^i - T^j)$, where talent, T, is a one-dimensional variable that summarizes the multiple dimensions of baseball talent. Such a measure simplifies the exposition that follows without detracting from its validity. If the player talent pool, T, is fixed, the team's talent differential relative to the $n - 1$ league opponents is $T^i - (T - T^i)/(n - 1) = (nT^i - T)/(n - 1)$.[7] Cost per unit of talent is assumed to be exogenous to the individual team. When teams openly compete for talent, per-unit cost equals the marginal revenue product of talent and serves to ration talent among teams. When teams collude, the

6. Media revenues, which are typically contractually fixed during any season, will change in future contracts based on the size of the audience.

7. This formulation assumes that each team plays each opponent an equal number of times or, alternatively, that the remaining talent is evenly distributed among the opponent teams. This formulation would be modified, but would not change the general conclusions of the following analysis, if the distribution of talent between leagues differs because there is no interleague play during the regular season.

cost per unit of talent is assumed to be high enough to provide the same talent pool, and this talent is allocated so as to maximize joint profits of the teams. Interestingly, under these assumptions there is no change in the distribution of talent between the collusive and the competitive settings.

With collusion, the league attempts to maximize joint revenues and resist competition for scarce talent that raises wages. The prevailing wage per unit of talent will not approach the marginal revenue product of a unit of talent. The collusive wage rate per unit of talent, w, may be as low as the highest opportunity cost among players and still ensure that the best players are available. To avoid other dimensions of competition between teams, roster limits have been institutionally set so that the binding constraint is limited talent and not the cost of talent. The relevant Lagrangian for the talent-constrained, joint profit-maximization problem is

$$(1) \quad nR + R^1 \{W[(nT^1 - T)/(n - 1)]\} + \ldots$$
$$+ R^n\{W[(nT^n - T)/(n - 1)]\} + \lambda(T - \Sigma T^i).$$

First-order conditions for an interior solution for the maximization of joint revenues are

$$(2) \quad MR^i \cdot MP^i = (n - 1)\lambda/n \text{ for all } i,$$

where $MR^i = dR^i/dW^i$ is the marginal revenue of winning and $MP^i = dW^i/d\tau^i$ is the marginal product of relative talent, $\tau^i = (nT^i - T)/(n - 1)$, in the production of winning performance. That is, the collusive league allocates talent so that the marginal revenue product of relative talent across teams is equal. Team revenues are divided between the players who receive wT^i and the owner or owners who capture the residual $R + R^i (W) - wT^i$.

With competition among the teams for scarce talent, the individual team attempts to maximize its profit, given by

$$(3) \quad R + R^i \{W[(nT^i - T)/(n - 1)]\} - \omega T^i \text{ for all } i.$$

In the process of competitive bidding for talent, the wage paid per unit of talent, ω, is increased. So long as the marginal revenue product of talent on any given team exceeds its wage, bidding continues to increase wages. In this market, wages serve the allocation function presumably undertaken by some collective mechanism when collusion is present. The first-order conditions for an interior maximization of equation 3 are

$$(4) \qquad MR^i \cdot MP^i = (n - 1)\omega/n \text{ for all } i.$$

With competitive bidding for talent, the wage bill for each team is ωT^i and the residual claimed by the owner is $R + R^i(W) - \omega T^i$.

Equations 2 and 4 allocate player talent in the same pattern across teams where λ, the shadow price of talent, is its marginal revenue product, equal to ω in equation 4. Not surprisingly, the fixed component of shared revenues R, does not influence the allocation of talent when individual or joint profit maximization is the objective. Similarly, neither total revenue nor profit of the team is present in the allocation formula. Inframarginal returns are allocated to the accounting profits of the owner and constitute a return for the owner's entrepreneurial inputs and rents on the locational advantage of the team and the monopoly position of the league.[8] When the league colludes in hiring and distributing player talents, the lower salary costs for each team ($w < \omega$) are captured as a rental return to the monopsony power of the league.

According to equations 2 and 4, a large population base or media market for a team will not directly influence its choice of talent. Instead, the revenue response to changes in the winning performance of the team determines the allocation of talent. Differentiating either equation set yields

$$(5) \qquad dT^i/dMR^i = \frac{-(n - 1)MP^i}{n \sum_{i=1}^{n} MR^i(dMP^i/dT^i)},$$

which is positive because the marginal product of talent is a decreasing function of talent ($dMP^i/dT^i < 0$). As the revenue response to winning performance, MR, increases, the owner is induced to acquire more talent to enhance team performance.

This model is illustrated in figure 4-1 for a two-team league. If the talent on the two teams were equal, they would each expect to win 50 percent of their games. Revenues for team 1 would be $R_1(50)$, and revenues

8. Inframarginal returns are $\int_0^{T^i} R\{W[(nt - T)/(n-1)]\}dt - wT^i$.

Figure 4-1. *Profiles of Team Revenue: Two Patterns of Fan Response to Winning*

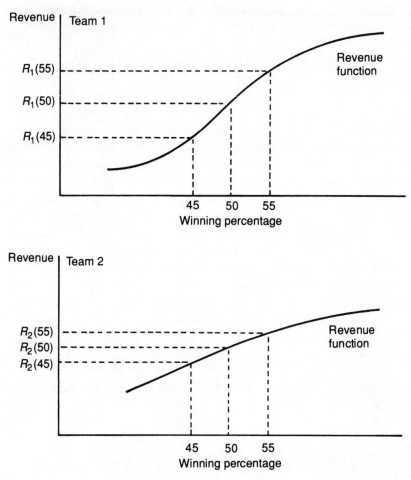

for team 2 would be $R_2(50)$. Talent costs for the two teams would be $wT_1 = wT_2$. The right to own a franchise in this league has value if total revenue, $R + R^i(W)$, exceeds wT. The sales price of a franchise is the discounted present value of the net revenue flow $R + R^i(W) - wT$, appropriately discounted for risk. A new owner in the league, therefore, must allocate $R + R^i(W) - wT$ annually to cover the cost of purchasing the franchise and to compensate for the riskiness of the investment. Existing owners fare no better. Even if the franchise was purchased at a low price, $R + R^i(W) - wT$ must be retained by the owner to cover the opportunity cost of not selling. Thus, if $R_2(50) > R_1(50)$, a greater share of the revenue of team 2 must be allocated to its owner because of the greater investment in team 2 relative to team 1. No additional revenues for player salaries remain after amortizing the value of the franchise.

Given the revenue functions depicted in figure 4-1, the teams will not, however, choose to employ the same talent. At a 50 percent winning performance, a performance increment is more valuable to team 1 than to team 2. The more talented players are more valuable at the margin to the first team, which would win a competitive bidding war or would offer some form of compensation in a collusive allocation of talent. The more elastic response of the fans to the performance of team 1 greatly rewards the team for winning, whereas the less elastic response of the fans of team 2 lessens the penalty for losing. Team 1 will continue to acquire additional talent at the expense of team 2, lowering the marginal product of talent and marginal revenue of winning on team 1 (and raising them on team 2) until the marginal revenue products of talent are equal across teams (equations 2 and 4).

Test of Competing Theories of Winning

An alternative hypothesis to the individual or joint profit-maximizing hypotheses presented above is the win-maximizing hypothesis. The belief that winning, not profits, is the owners' objective underlies the arguments of league officials in most professional sports that some form of the player reserve clause is necessary to prevent owners with higher revenues from acquiring the lion's share of the talent pool.[9] The gist of this argument is that teams with large media markets and home game attendence in, for example, New York, Los Angeles, or Chicago, would use their revenue advantage to dominate teams in Minnesota, Milwaukee, and Cincinnati. This conclusion is based on a simple syllogism that winning is all that matters and that the wherewithal to acquire winning talent derives solely from the operating revenues of the sport franchise. As sports franchise owners are generally wealthy individuals with other sources of income, the win-at-all-cost attitude should imply that the teams whose owners had the greatest income (from all sources) would dominate teams with

9. Balfour and Porter (1991) provide a history of the reserve clause in professional sports and a test of the hypothesis that competitive balance is promoted by restricting player movement.

less affluent owners. Nonetheless, it is possible that absolute (rather than marginal) revenues matter in the allocation of talent.

If winning performance is a consumption good for the owner or if winning pays dividends in other nonbaseball areas, a hybrid of the two hypotheses emerges in which owners, to a different and unknown extent, overinvest in talent relative to the profit-maximizing models of the previous section. After reviewing the backgrounds and quotes of baseball club owners, Jennings concludes that owners "regard their baseball venture as a hobby."[10] Scully comments that "part of the reason that August Busch owns the Cardinals is that it increases the sales of his beers," and "superstations like WTBS (Atlanta Braves) and WGN (Chicago Cubs) have used sports programming to break into the national [broadcast] market."[11] To the extent that winning performance yields profits for ancillary business interests or utility to the owner independent of the profits from baseball operations, the narrowly defined profit-maximizing model of the previous section will underestimate the return to winning. If ancillary business opportunities are more likely in large population centers or if the higher revenues in these markets afford greater opportunities to consume winning, absolute revenues will appear to play a part in the explanation of performance.

I begin my analysis of the influence of revenue on performance with the realization that data on the revenue of baseball franchises are not readily available and, when they are available, they are not reliable. Some data have "leaked out" or been reported in court cases, but they are either inconsistent or have been subject to accounting trickery.[12] A good proxy for revenue, however, is season attendance.[13] Gate receipts and concession income are directly linked to attendance. In addition, fan interest that dictates media incomes specific to the team is highly correlated with attendance. Greater attendance at home games will mirror larger audiences for local television and radio broadcasts. Finally, attendance is unambiguously measured, and attendance figures are readily available for all teams.

One cannot casually disentangle the two theories. A simple correlation between attendance (as a proxy for revenue) and performance (winning

10. Jennings (1990, p. 75).

11. Scully (1989, p. 133).

12. Scully (1989, chap. 7) presents team revenue data obtained from a court case for three different years and most teams. Even if this were enough for my present data needs, the measures are subject to accounting manipulation and are generally unreliable, as he points out.

13. A simple correlation of attendance and team revenue statistics available for three years (see note 12) yields coefficients of determination from 0.694 to 0.799.

percentage) would be positive under either theory of winning. If greater revenue is used to purchase more talent, the correspondence between winning and revenue is direct. If a more elastic response forces the profit-minded owner to provide better performance, the correlation between winning and revenue is of the same sign. Because revenues respond to winning performance, ceteris paribus, the teams that win more will have greater revenues. Moreover, if these teams are those with the more elastic revenue response, winning will have a greater impact on their revenues. Only the causality under the two theories of winning is different. Under one theory, teams win because they have greater revenues. Under the other, teams have greater revenues because they win.

Complicating the analysis is the economic principle that attendance responses will be greatest where there are more alternatives. In New York, Los Angeles, and Chicago, and to a lesser extent in other franchise markets, there is more than one baseball team. In addition, large cities provide more nonbaseball substitutes. These factors increase the elasticity of attendance with respect to performance. Consequently, attendance response is likely to be positively correlated to population and media market size.

To disentangle these effects, I begin my analysis by estimating the attendance function for a generic team. Attendance, win-loss record, and population of the standard metropolitan statistical area were gathered for all twenty-six major league teams.[14] OLS regression analysis reveals that attendance, *ATTEND*, across all teams is positively influenced by area population, *POP* (measured in thousands of persons), and team performance as measured by the percentage of all games won in the present year and in the previous year, WIN_t and WIN_{t-1}. Previous season performance is included because of its effect on preseason ticket sales. The results (with t-statistics presented in parentheses below the coefficient estimates) are

(6) $ATTEND = -2,476,777.3 + 55.47POP + 41,250.69WIN_t + 45,761.29WIN_{t-1}.$
(-2.31) (1.67) (2.35) (2.81)

$$R^2 = 0.484; F = 6.87$$

14. Baseball data were obtained from various sources, including the *Baseball Encyclopedia*, *Baseball Register*, and the league offices. Data on area population are from the *Statistical Abstract of the United States* and *Canada Year Book*, various years. These data are collected from several Census Bureau sources that use city-specific information, such as the number of new utility connections or phone lines, to interpolate population between census counts. When no information was available, I made a linear interpolation.

Across all teams, an increase in proximate population of 1,000 persons would be expected to increase season attendance by 55, while a 1 percentage-point increase in games won (typically less than one game) would increase attendance this year by 41,250 and next year by 45,761.

Equation 6 is used to find predicted attendance for each of the twenty-six teams based on their current population base and the assumption of winning 50 percent of their games in each year. This measure of attendance is independent of the nature of the fans of the individual team and the historical performance of the team. Predicted attendance is a measure of the appeal to a given number of average fans of an average team with average talent. As such, it is a proxy for the base revenue generated by the team's location that can, nonetheless, be allocated, all or in part, to the acquisition of talent.

To capture the particular responsiveness of the fans of each team, I used historical data on the attendance, performance, and population base of the team. Twenty-six equations of the general form shown in equation 6 were estimated with team-specific data for the twenty-five-year period 1966–90.[15] The resulting estimated coefficients of WIN_t and WIN_{t-1} for each team are presented in table 4-1. In only four of the models (Baltimore, Boston, Cleveland, and Toronto) were neither of the coefficient estimates statistically significant at the 10 percent level or less.

The total response, shown in the last column of table 4-1, is the sum of the coefficients of WIN_t and WIN_{t-1}. It is the appropriate measure of fan response to winning for several reasons. First, it is interpreted as the additional attendance a team could expect in the present and subsequent years as a result of a 1 percentage-point increase in the team's winning performance. Second, multicollinearity is likely to be a problem in these models because there is positive serial correlation of winning performance by a team.[16] Although the coefficient estimates are unbiased in the face of multicollinearity, when one of the coefficients is underestimated by the sampling procedure, the other tends to be overestimated, and vice versa. Because the individual coefficients are unbiased, the total effect is unbiased, and, in the total, the counterbalancing effects of over- and underestimation tend to offset one another. Finally, because of multicollinearity, little importance should be attached to the relative magnitude of the two coefficients.

Two independent measures, "predicted base attendance," *PATTEND*

---

15. The strike year 1981 was eliminated.
16. Scully (forthcoming).

Table 4-1. *Estimated Response of Baseball Attendance to Changes in the Percentage of Games Won*

League and team	WIN$_t$	WIN$_{t-1}$	Total response
American League			
Baltimore	12,063.424	− 4,494.980	7,568.444
Boston	19,290.314	17,504.579	36,794.893
California	41,902.980**	35,138.602**	77,041.582
Chicago	38,718.772***	22,811.549***	61,530.321
Cleveland	6,192.090	− 1,618.203	4,573.887
Detroit	39,741.006***	17,864.600***	57,605.606
Kansas City	30,563.256**	39,439.656***	70,002.912
Milwaukee	30,966.196***	39,250.520***	70,216.716
Minnesota	62,445.413***	31,223.360**	93,668.773
New York	32,453.400*	47,793.602***	80,247.002
Oakland	22,639.259***	8,693.774	31,333.033
Seattle	20,191.436*	7,781.979	27,973.415
Texas	29,168.407***	5,911.209	35,079.616
Toronto	− 4,908.882	− 14,525.125	− 19,434.007
National League			
Atlanta	45,488.601***	22,436.892***	67,925.493
Chicago	37,648.903***	22,964.132***	60,613.035
Cincinnati	40,064.021***	40,257.699***	80,321.720
Houston	39,812.197***	19,068.196	58,880.393
Los Angeles	47,502.857***	40,016.778**	87,519.635
Montreal	65,378.025***	12,728.740	78,106.765
New York	33,315.905***	41,089.457***	74,405.362
Philadelphia	53,521.976***	26,989.550	80,511.526
Pittsburgh	37,770.110***	10,864.110	48,634.220
St. Louis	64,360.076***	29,209.552***	93,569.628
San Diego	36,324.385***	32,337.601***	68,661.986
San Francisco	45,105.933***	7,446.333	52,552.266

*Statistically significant at the 90 percent confidence level.
**Statistically significant at the 95 percent confidence level.
***Statistically significant at the 98 percent confidence level.

(estimated from equation 6), and "predicted total response to improved performance," *PRESPOND* ("total response" in table 4-1), for the twenty-two teams with meaningful models were tested for their capacity to explain a team's winning percentage in the fifteen years since free agency, *AVEWIN15*, and in the twenty-five years of the sample *AVEWIN25*.[17] These results are presented below in equation form with the *t*-statistics presented in parentheses below the coefficient estimates.

17. The four teams removed from the sample were Baltimore, Boston, Cleveland, and Toronto, all in the American League. It is tempting to say that these teams had such inelastic responses that they were not significantly different from 0 and that they should be included. To eliminate them is to bias the sample by the choice of teams with more elastic

(7a) $AVEWIN15 = 37.270 + 3.850 \times 10^{-6} PATTEND + 6.695 \times 10^{-3} PRESPOND$
          (5.24)   (1.13)   (2.11)

$$R^2 = 0.274; F = 3.59; N = 22$$

(7b) $AVEWIN25 = 40.030 + 2.670 \times 10^{-6} PATTEND + 5.912 \times 10^{-3} PRESPOND$
          (5.12)   (0.71)   (1.70)

$$R^2 = 0.179; F = 2.08; N = 22$$

The seemingly low explanatory power of these two models should not be troubling. The independent variables were estimated and are therefore subject to sampling error in their measurement. When the independent variables are subject to measurement error, the OLS estimators and the F statistic have a downward bias. Furthermore, this bias is more acute in small samples.[18] Nonetheless, the t-statistics for the variable $PRESPOND$ in the fifteen- and twenty-five-year $AVEWIN$ models would prove to be significant at the 94 percent and 97 percent confidence levels, respectively, were there no bias. The downward bias of the test statistics increases confidence in the significant explanatory power of fan response.

The statistical significance of the coefficients of $PRESPOND$ in equations 7a and 7b makes a strong case for the profit-maximizing hypothesis. Team performance is strongly correlated with the observed response of the team's fans to its performance. Teams with less responsive fans are seen to win fewer games, and teams with more responsive fans win more games. A large attendance base contributes less to explaining wins, presumably because it represents revenues allocated to locational rents so that they are not available to pay for talent. This conclusion is true of the era of free agency as well as the longer period encompassing the era of the reserve clause. Nonetheless, the win-maximizing model cannot be completely dismissed. The positive coefficient of $PATTEND$ in equations 7a and 7b, subject as it is to a downward bias, leaves some room to

---

responses. However, with the exception of Boston, these teams had at least one negative coefficient estimate and total estimated effects that were clearly outliers with respect to the rest of the sample. Although the coefficients were all of the predicted sign and the total effect appears reasonable, for Boston the model had no explanatory value ($F = 0.50$). The small variance of the independent variables WIN and POP for Boston appears to provide little evidence of what fans would do were Boston's performance to change.

18. Judge and others (1980, pp. 513–16).

speculate that baseball is an "expensive hobby" for wealthy owners who, despite their investments and the lure of greater profits, play to win.

Conclusions

It is not uncommon to hear a professional sports franchise owner praise fan loyalty and promise fans a winner or lament the absence of a loyal core of fans and threaten to move the franchise. This chapter puts these comments in a different light. The owner is right to praise the loyalty of his team's fans. Their loyalty, to the extent it builds a steady attendance base and media audience, is captured by the owner as a rental return to the franchise location. The absence of a loyal core of fans may well be reason to move the franchise. If a larger core of loyal fans can be found elsewhere, the owner will realize a capital gain.

However, it is less likely that a loyal core of fans will get a winner than it is that a fickle groups of fans will get a winner. When fans demand a winner and express their distaste for losing by staying away from the games, the owner is more likely to hire the talent it takes to produce a winner. When fans are willing, out of loyalty or for another reason, to attend the games even when the home team is losing, they are more likely to be presented with a losing team. But fickleness is a two-edged sword. Without a loyal core of fans the franchise is likely to be worth more in an alternative location.

When representatives of Major League Baseball state that some franchise locations are too small to support a major league team, they would more rightly say they are too small to pay the franchise fees the league demands. Because the current team owners capture the locational rents associated with expansion through the franchise fee, they are interested in the base attendance from which that value is drawn. This analysis suggests a small-city team will be a winner when the franchise fee is low enough to enable a smaller absolute attendance to cover this fee and keep the team in business, if the fans are highly responsive to the team's performance.

References

Asch, Peter, Burton G. Malkiel, and Richard E. Quandt. 1984. "Market Efficiency in Racetrack Betting." *Journal of Business* 57:165–75.

Balfour, Alan, and Philip K. Porter. 1991. "The Reserve Clause in Professional Sports: Legality and Effect on Competitive Balance." *Labor Law Journal* 42:8–18.

The Baseball Encyclopedia. Various years. Macmillan.

Coughlin, Cletus C., and O. Homer Erekson. 1984. "An Examination of Contributions to Support Intercollegiate Athletics." *Southern Economic Journal* 51:180–95.

El-Hodiri, Mohammed, and James Quirk. 1971. "An Economic Model of a Professional Sports League." *Journal of Political Economy* 79:1302–19.

Jennings, Kenneth M. 1990. *Balls and Strikes: The Money Game in Professional Baseball.* Praeger.

Judge, George G., and others. 1980. *The Theory and Practice of Econometrics.* Wiley.

Lehn, Kenneth. 1982. "Property Rights, Risk Sharing, and Player Disability in Major League Baseball." *Journal of Law and Economics* 25:343–65.

McCormick, Robert E., and Maurice Tinsley. 1987. "Athletics versus Academics? Evidence from SAT Scores." *Journal of Political Economy* 95:1103–16.

McCormick, Robert E., and Robert D. Tollison. 1984. "Crime on the Court." *Journal of Political Economy* 92:223–35.

Porter, Philip K., and Gerald W. Scully. 1982. "Measuring Managerial Efficiency: The Case of Baseball." *Southern Economic Journal* 48:642–50.

Scully, Gerald W. 1974. "Pay and Performance in Major League Baseball." *American Economic Review* 64:915–30.

——. 1989. *The Business of Major League Baseball.* University of Chicago Press.

——. Forthcoming. "Momentum in Sports." In *Advances in the Economics of Sports*, edited by Gerald W. Scully. JAI Press.

Statistics Canada. *Canada Year Book*, various years 1965–90.

U.S. Department of Commerce. *Statistical Abstract of the United States*, various years 1965–90.

CHAPTER FIVE

Price Setting in
Professional Team Sports

David J. Salant

Most professional sports franchises, indeed many so-called amateur sports teams, are run as profit-seeking enterprises. Economic analysis suggests that profit-maximizing firms, especially those with monopoly power, should set ticket prices so that the extra revenue from the last ticket sold equals the extra cost associated with selling it, that is, marginal revenue equals marginal cost. For sports teams, which operate in arenas and stadiums with limited capacity, this can, but will not necessarily, lead to sellouts. However, according to traditional economic analysis, a profit-seeking enterprise should never price its product so low that a profitable secondary resale market develops. Simply put, if a team can increase profits by raising prices when there is excess demand for its tickets, such as occurs when teams are fortunate enough to be in the World Series, then why does it not do so?

Not only are prices for World Series and other playoff and championship game tickets set well below what seems to be short-run profit-maximizing levels, but so are tickets to many regular season games in many sports. On the surface, many teams' ticket prices seem to fall far short of their profit-maximizing levels.

This chapter surveys ticket price theory and policy in Major League Baseball and other professional team sports leagues. I seek to explain ticket-pricing policy in professional sports, especially where it seems most irrational. I start by briefly describing the nature of the ticket-pricing decision facing a professional sports franchise and reviewing earlier work

I would like to thank Philip Porter, Glenn Woroch, and especially Richard Cothren for their helpful comments. Responsibility for all remaining errors is, of course, mine. The opinions and views expressed herein are solely the opinions and views of the author, and do not necessarily reflect the opinions, views or policy of GTE Laboratories Incorporated or its affiliates.

on the subject. I then look at some of the ticket-pricing practices of professional sports teams and suggest a new explanation of them.[1]

The Ticket-Pricing Decision Problem

Professional sports franchises provide entertainment in different forms: through television, radio, news about a championship season, and live games. In the market for live viewing rights for a game, there is typically only one team playing in a city, and, therefore, it has a substantial amount of monopoly power. A few teams face competition from another team playing the same sport in their city, such as the Yankees and Mets in New York City and the Dodgers and Angels in the Los Angeles area, but even in these cases the teams generally have different fans and often play on different nights in different parks and leagues. Thus they still retain considerable monopoly power.

On the surface, the ticket-pricing decision facing each team is a variation of the classic monopoly problem analyzed long ago by Cournot. Cournot examined how the proprietor of a mineral spring that "possess(es) salutary properties possessed by no other" could make the most of the property.[2] Cournot supposed that the demand for the mineral water, like the demand for the summer elixir of baseball tickets, is a downward-sloping function of the price charged.

According to earlier studies, demand for baseball tickets is a downward-sloping function of price.[3] That is, demand for tickets can be expressed as

$$(1) \qquad\qquad Q = Q(p,z),$$

where Q is the number of tickets demanded, p is price, and $Q(p,z)$ is demand, which depends on a vector of other factors, z (such as city

---

1. Becker (1991) has recently provided a different explanation of persistent shortages. His explanation derives from the assumption that individual willingness to pay to see a game (or go to a restaurant or see a play) is higher the greater the number of others who are also watching the same game. For televised professional sports, the number watching a game includes both those at the game and television viewers. Therefore it is unclear that Becker's explanation is sufficient to generate the upward slope in demand needed to explain ticket-pricing practices.

2. Cournot (1929, p. 56).

3. For example, Noll (1982); Scully (1989).

Figure 5-1. *Monopoly Profit Maximization*

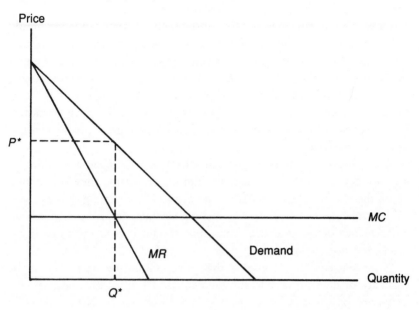

population and team performance), as well as price. The profit from ticket sales is

$$(2) \qquad \pi(p) = pQ(p,z) - C[Q(p,z)],$$

where $C(Q)$ is the part of team costs that varies with attendance. $C(Q)$ includes the cost of printing and selling tickets, as well as stadium costs for cleanup and ushers.

A baseball monopoly that seeks to maximize the profits from ticket sales should, following Cournot, set ticket prices so that marginal revenue equals marginal cost. This is equivalent to

$$(3) \qquad p(1 - 1/\varepsilon) = \Delta C/\Delta Q,$$

where $\varepsilon = -(\Delta Q/\Delta p)(p/Q)$ is the elasticity of demand and $\Delta C/\Delta Q$ is the marginal cost of an additional ticket.[4] The optimal ticket price is illustrated in figure 5-1. Stadium capacity can create a shortage at the

4. To see this, note that $\Delta\pi/\Delta p = Q + (p - \Delta C/\Delta Q)\,\Delta Q/\Delta p$. Setting $\Delta\pi/\Delta p = 0$ implies $p[1 - (-\Delta p/\Delta Q)Q/p] = p(1 - 1/\varepsilon) = \Delta C/\Delta Q$.

price that maximizes profits from ticket sales. In such a case the team should set price so that demand, $Q(p,z)$, equals capacity.[5]

Only when team owners care substantially about attendance should they not apply equation 3 for setting ticket prices. Owners do care about attendance because having more fans at the game creates more of an air of excitement at the park. However, it seems unlikely that, when almost every team averages over 25,000 in attendance per game, the additional excitement generated by extra people, especially given team performance, is sufficient to make attendance, apart from profits, an important consideration.[6]

Even when team owners are not profit maximizers and are willing to sacrifice some profits for a higher winning percentage, they still should apply the classic rule, as put forth in equation 3, in setting ticket prices. Ticket price has no effect on win-loss percentage.[7] Improvement in team performance increases demand and thus should lead to increased ticket prices and not vice versa.[8]

Note that equation 3 implies that prices should be set such that the elasticity of demand is at least 1 (and equal to 1 when the marginal cost of increasing the number of people at the game is 0). Noll and Scully have found that prices tend to be set such that the point estimates of elasticity of demand are less than 1.[9] This suggests that team owners do not maximize profits.

Both Noll and Scully have argued that these findings can be explained by the fact that the cost of a ticket is only a fraction of the cost of going to a game; other costs include transportation, parking, and concessions. The estimated elasticities underestimate demand elasticities by excluding the full costs of attending a game. Although the estimated elasticities are underestimates, the relevant elasticities for maximizing profits are the ones being estimated because team revenue is the average ticket price

5. Note too that in Major League Baseball the home team splits gate receipts with the visiting team. The split differs in the two leagues; in the American League the home team keeps 80 percent of gate receipts; in the National League the home team keeps about 90 percent of gate receipts. Letting α denote the home team share of gate receipts, equation 2 becomes $\pi(p) = \alpha p Q(p,z) - C[Q(p,z)]$, and equation 3 becomes $\alpha p(1 - 1/\varepsilon) = \Delta C/\Delta Q$. Sharing of gate revenues does not materially affect this analysis.

6. Scully (1989).

7. Some might argue that the crowd affects team performance. Thus ticket price through demand could indirectly affect performance. In this analysis, I assume this effect is negligible.

8. Noll (1982); Scully (1989).

9. Neither Noll (1974) nor Scully (1989) could reject the hypothesis that prices are set at levels where demand is elastic, as the confidence intervals would include 1.

times the number of tickets sold, not the average cost of going to the game times the number of tickets sold.[10]

Two other factors bear on team ticket pricing. One is that not all seats are the same. Teams generally sell different types of tickets. For instance, the Boston Red Sox sell field box seats (for $14 in 1988), roof boxes ($12), box seats ($11), reserved grandstand ($9), and bleacher seats ($6 on the day of the game and $5 in advance). The estimated demand elasticities are for some "average" seats and "average" prices. However, the last seats sold within each section are usually the worst seats in the section, and, as Noll pointed out, his estimated demand elasticities may be biased.[11]

The other important factor about ticket sales is that some seats are sold as part of season ticket packages, other seats are sold well in advance, and the remaining seats are sold shortly before the game. Those who purchase season tickets make their purchase in advance, obtain priority in seat selection, often renew subscriptions, and retain or improve seating priority from one season to the next. Season ticket purchases can have a pronounced effect on ticket pricing, as is discussed below.

Further, note that equation 3 implies that variations in the parameters, z, that affect demand from city to city and team to team, such as population, win-loss percentage, and other competition, should mean ticket prices also vary. In particular, ceteris paribus, more successful teams in large cities should face different (and probably higher) demand and charge higher prices than do less successful teams in small cities. Data from Scully and others do not confirm this.[12]

Ticket Pricing in Professional Team Sports

Ticket prices in baseball and other professional team sports indicate that professional sports teams often and persistently fail to set ticket prices high enough. According to a *Boston Globe* article, ticket agents were

---

10. To see this, let p denote the ticket price and $P = x + p$ denote the cost of attending a game. Further suppose marginal costs are 0. Then profits, $pQ(P)$, are maximized where $p[1 - (-\Delta Q/\Delta P)^{-1} Q/p] = p[1 - (-\Delta Q/\Delta p)^{-1} Q/p] = 0$. In other cases teams share parking and concession revenues with local stadium authorities. If $P = P_1 + P_2$, where P_1 is the ticket price and P_2 is the team's share of concessions, then the first-order conditions for a profit maximum are $P[1 - (-\Delta Q/\Delta P)^{-1} Q/P] = 0$; and as $-(\Delta Q/\Delta P)^{-1} Q/P < -(\Delta Q/\Delta P)^{-1} Q/P_1$ (because $P = P_1 + P_2$), a profit-maximizing team could then be setting ticket price where the observed elasticity, $-(\Delta Q/\Delta P) P_1/Q$, is at least 1.

11. Noll (1974).

12. Scully (1989, p. 106).

charging anywhere from a 50 percent premium to over ten times the nominal ticket price for Red Sox games in 1989.[13] And tickets at Fenway to games between the Red Sox and Yankees are typically available only to season ticket holders.

Boston is not the only city where baseball tickets can be hard to get. According to the *New York Times*, one agent was typically selling tickets to Mets games that had a face value of $11.50 for $25.00.[14] The same article also mentioned that Cubs fans have an especially difficult time getting tickets. In the *Los Angeles Times* classified ads, the asking price of Dodgers tickets is as much as $65 each, which is well above their face value.[15]

Franchises in the other major team sports—football, basketball, and hockey—also usually have monopoly power and also seem to fail to maximize gate receipts. In the National Football League (NFL) over 97 percent of all seats were sold during the 1972 season, and ticket sales varied little in the following four years.[16] According to Noll, by 1970 roughly two-thirds of NFL games were virtually sold out.[17]

Among the most difficult football tickets to come by are those to Giants games. Their top ticket price of $26 in 1990 was less than the $35 top price for the Buffalo Bills and not much more than the Bills' $20 minimum price.[18] Yet the Bills often have had trouble selling out (especially toward the end of the season, when blizzard conditions are not uncommon).

According to one report, a travel agency was paying New York Giants players $850 apiece for tickets to the last Super Bowl that had a face value of $150.[19] A ticket agent was quoted elsewhere as saying that players could earn $5,000 by selling their allotment of four Super Bowl tickets.[20] Another agent was quoted as saying he paid the owner of a luxury box $1,100 each for tickets to the Super Bowl held the previous year in Miami.

13. Kevin Paul Dupont, "Red Sox Tickets Getting Scarcer," *Boston Globe*, June 18, 1989, p. 97.

14. Gerald Eskenazi, "Getting a Good Seat: A Shutout before the Game," *New York Times*, May 31, 1989, p. D24.

15. *Los Angeles Times*, June 8, 1991, p. G2.

16. Siegfried and Hinshaw (1979).

17. Noll (1974).

18. Joe Sexton, "Madison Sq. Garden Planning $70 Seats to Pay for Face Lift," *New York Times*, October 20, 1990, p. 45; and *Buffalo Bills Media Guide*, 1990.

19. "Giant Players Accused of Ticket Scalping," *The Latest News*, January 25, 1991, p. 20.

20. Eskenazi, "Getting a Good Seat."

The Boston Celtics have sold out almost every game since Larry Bird joined the team. According to their ticket office, there is a waiting list of over 4,000 names for season tickets. One of the same ticket agents that handles Boston Red Sox tickets, Front Row, has quoted prices starting at around $45 for unobstructed $21 balcony seats. (Tickets for Celtics games against the Bulls or Lakers start much higher.) As of 1989, the price of the top Celtics ticket ($32) was less than that of the top tickets to many other teams that do not draw nearly as well.[21]

The Portland Trailblazers have sold out every game since 1977.[22] Their ticket prices are higher than average and were raised between the 1988–89 and 1989–90 seasons. Nevertheless, the over twelve years of sellouts suggests that, for many years, capacity constraints were strictly binding and the team failed to maximize annual gate receipts. Many other teams always sell out; they include the Washington Redskins and Denver Broncos in the NFL and the Montreal Canadians and Toronto Maple Leafs in the National Hockey League (NHL). Such persistent sellouts strongly suggest that those who set ticket prices care little about profits, know little about economics, or have other economic motives.

Analyses of ticket pricing in Major League Baseball by Noll and Scully have found that ticket prices are set where demand is inelastic.[23] Although they argued that this is not inconsistent with profit-maximizing behavior, they cannot reject the hypothesis that demand is elastic.[24] Their findings can be interpreted as suggesting ticket prices are too low.

Major League Baseball franchises now sell for more than $100 million. It seems almost inconceivable that ticket prices are set too low despite all the evidence indicating that higher prices could allow teams to earn more money in the short run. Either team owners permit continued and widespread mismanagement, or other factors lead teams to set ticket prices at such levels.

One explanation often given of ticket-pricing decisions is that for many owners the team represents a hobby and is not their main source of income. This seems to be an unsatisfactory explanation of ticket shortages for at least three reasons. One is that the great value of franchises makes it unlikely that they would be operated purely as hobbies. Another, more

21. Michael Hurd, "Most Teams Hike Ticket Prices," *USA Today*, September 19, 1989, p. 9C; *Sport, Inc.*, January 23, 1989.

22. Eskenazi, "Getting a Good Seat."

23. Noll (1974); Scully (1989).

24. The standard errors were too large for them to reject this hypothesis. See p. 81 above.

significant, reason is that many teams are owned by large, publicly traded corporations, for example, the Chicago Cubs in Major League Baseball and the Boston Celtics and New York Knicks in the NBA. It is unlikely that their management would want or be able to consistently set prices too low. Third, with changes in team ownership, the expected changes in ticket-pricing policy do not occur. Washington Redskins tickets, probably the most difficult to get of all regular professional sports regular season tickets, still have lower than average prices despite ownership changes.

How Ticket Prices Are Set: A New View

For many teams, a large, if not primary, source of gate receipts is season ticket sales. In 1989 the Cubs sold almost 15,000 season tickets. The Boston Red Sox have virtually no season tickets available other than bleacher tickets. The Mets and Yankees sell over 20,000 season tickets each, and the Giants and New York Jets sell over 74,000 season tickets each. For many teams, most of the season tickets are purchased by corporations.[25] Any explanation of ticket-pricing policy in professional team sports should therefore consider, if not stress, the demand for season tickets and the manner in which season ticket purchase decisions are made.

Purchase of a season ticket is not the same type of purchase for a fan as that of a ticket to an individual game. Season tickets are typically purchased well in advance of the season and renewed from season to season. Season ticket subscriptions are frequently purchased by corporations and ticket agencies.[26] The decision to purchase a season ticket is usually based on longer-term considerations than the decisions to see individual games.

Those purchasing season tickets decide that they want to go, or have the option to go, to games over a long period of time, usually more than just one season. Further, through purchasing season tickets, their holders receive specific seats, usually among the better seats at the ballpark, as well as a place on a waiting list for improved seats in the future.[27]

25. Eskenazi, "Getting a Good Seat." According to this same article, approximately 80 percent of season tickets were purchased by corporations.

26. The Boston Red Sox sell 450 season tickets that they know of to ticket agencies. This represents about 36,000 tickets out of a total of slightly more than 2,000,000, or a bit less than 2 percent of their sales. Dupont, "Red Sox Tickets Getting Scarcer."

27. I was told by the Red Sox ticket office that it would take an additional five years before I would be allowed to upgrade my own season tickets.

In contrast, tickets to individual games are usually purchased during the course of the season, possibly on the day of the game. Those purchasing a ticket to only one game will have a great deal more information about the value of the ticket than did season ticket holders, who had to buy their tickets long before the season started. Further, the quality of the seats, especially within a given price category, will be lower for tickets purchased on a game-by-game basis.

Nevertheless, non-season tickets, although for lower-quality seats, usually sell for the same price per game as season tickets. Except for special promotions, season tickets almost never cost more than non-season tickets. Most promotions involve either large blocks for a single game or giveaways that benefit season ticket holders as well.

Besides purchasing the best, if not the most, tickets, season ticket holders purchase a package of tickets that includes (1) priority in seat selection; (2) an option for playoff and World Series tickets, should the team make the playoffs; and, perhaps most important, (3) the right to renew seat priority and playoff and World Series tickets for the following season. The price charged for this package then determines the price per seat for game-by-game purchases. In maximizing income from ticket sales, a team should therefore consider demand for both season tickets and tickets for individual games.

The value of, and hence demand for, season tickets depends largely on expectations about the value of the options for priority seating for playoffs and future seasons. This value depends in turn on a number of factors. One is the possibility of getting World Series tickets.

This option for World Series tickets can enhance the value of season tickets. A season ticket holder will not derive any value from having first rights to World Series tickets if these ticket prices are set high. Because the face value of World Series tickets is usually well below market value, anyone who has rights to purchase those tickets at face value would probably wish to do so, even if only to resell them for a profit.[28] Therefore the value of the option for World Series tickets depends not just on the probability of the team making the World Series, but also on how much such tickets are likely to be worth over and above the price the team charges for them.

---

28. Although reselling or "scalping" tickets for a substantial premium above face value is illegal in many states, many tickets are sold under the counter by ticket agents or through informal channels. These laws can always be avoided by ticket agents in adjacent states where the scalping laws from the state where the game is played do not apply because states cannot regulate interstate commerce.

Similarly, the value of having a priority for good seats for regular season games depends on two factors: the value of those seats and the amount the season ticket holder expects to have to pay for them in the future. Therefore a season ticket holder will renew a subscription at a price greater than their value in a bad season, that is, one in which the team is not performing well, if it is expected that the team will improve and the tickets will become more valuable and if it is also expected that the team will not raise ticket prices to compensate for improved team performance. If the team raises ticket prices when the team has a good year, then season ticket holders would have less of an incentive to buy their tickets before seasons when the team is not expected to be strong. Part of the value of the season ticket is getting a "bargain" at some later time when the team is good.

For example, suppose some fans value tickets during bad years at $5.00 each and at $10.00 each during good years. If the team is equally likely to have a good year as it is to have a bad year, then such fans would, if they are risk neutral, be willing to pay $7.50 on average for those tickets. And if fans are risk averse, then they would be willing to pay a premium to avoid risk, such as $8.00 or even $8.50, to be guaranteed those seats every year.

If the fans would rather pay $8.50 a ticket every year rather than $5.00 in bad years with 0.5 probability and $10.00 in good years, then both the team and the fans are better off if the team charges anywhere between $7.50 and $8.50 a ticket every year. The team can and does sell its season ticket holders insurance and collects a premium, as much as $1.00 in the above example, as a risk premium for the insurance. The fans are better off too, in that they can buy tickets at the same price every year rather than having to pay $5.00 half the time and $10.00 the other half.[29]

This example assumes there is only one type of season ticket purchaser, one who prefers to avoid risk, which enables the team to make more money when it keeps ticket prices stable than when it raises and lowers ticket prices from year to year depending on expectations about the team. Typically the value of tickets to the fan varies with team performance and across fans. Some "loyal" fans might have a constant willingness to

---

29. An example of a utility function that gives approximately these numbers is as follows. Suppose fans' utility is $(9 - p)^2$ in bad years, where p is the price paid for the ticket, and utility in good years is $(14 - p)^2$. Then fans would be indifferent between buying tickets for $5.00 in bad years and $10.00 in good years, and getting tickets for slightly less than $8.50 (actually about $8.37) every year. In this example, the fan will attend games in both good and bad years. Not all fans do.

pay, and other "high rollers" might have valuations that vary considerably with their expectations about how hot the team is. When there is a large contingent of risk-averse, loyal fans, then the above example indicates that a team would wish to offer its fans the type of insurance that comes with a stable ticket-pricing policy.

But the above example can readily be modified to allow for a case in which the team has different types of fans, including "high rollers" who are not risk averse. What matters is the proportion of the two types of fans and that the risk-averse fans' valuation of tickets is on average higher than that of risk-loving high rollers.

To see this, consider a variation of the above example in which there are two types of fans, high rollers, who are fickle, and loyal fans. Further suppose, as above, that each loyal fan will pay $8.50 a ticket for the assurance of tickets to all the games. Suppose that initially the team sold 25,000 season tickets for $8.50 each, yielding revenue of $212,500 per game. If the team gets hot with high rollers who will each spend $12.50 a seat for some fraction, x, of games, then the team may or may not wish to raise ticket prices. When the team can sell $N = 25,000x$ tickets at $12.50 in good years and 25,000 tickets at $5.00 in bad years, the team is better off maintaining its original pricing policy whenever $x < 0.4$. This example illustrates that considerable excess demand can develop before the team would wish to raise ticket prices.

In the above example there are loyal, risk-averse fans who are willing to pay a premium to have guaranteed access to seats. In this case a team can make more money by keeping prices stable from year to year and game to game than if it charged different prices in each year or for different games.[30] When season tickets are sold in this fashion, shortages are likely to develop during good years. When the team is good, there will be more fans who want tickets at the going price, $8.50, than there are likely to be seats. There are also likely to be bad years when there will be a lot of no-shows.[31]

Before or during seasons when fans and sports commentators expect a team to improve, shortages are likely to develop unless ticket prices are

30. Many teams charge different prices for different games. In professional football, preseason tickets usually cost less than regular season tickets. In college sports, conference game tickets often cost more than those for nonconference games. For example, according to their team price lists, the Virginia Tech Hokies charge more for Metro Conference basketball games than for nonconference games, and the price for Boston College football games varies depending on the opponent.

31. When a team is performing poorly on the field and at the gate, it can always discount tickets through special promotions and other giveways.

increased. Yet raising ticket prices in good years will not always pay, because the value of the season ticket priority will decrease. This means that season ticket holders would be more likely to drop their subscriptions in bad years and when it looks as if team performance is likely to deteriorate. Just as random redistribution of seats for season ticket holders would reduce their value, frequent increases and decreases in ticket prices in response to changes in team fortune would also affect demand.

Season ticket holders have an implicit contract with the team, one part of which usually gives the ticket holder rights to the same or better seats from one season to the next. Another part of the relationship between the team and their season ticket holders is a mutual understanding of how much ticket prices can reasonably be expected to vary. Changes in the terms of the relationship affect the value of the option that season tickets represent, and a team may be unwilling to raise ticket prices even when shortages and secondary markets develop.

When team popularity increases, that is, when there is an unanticipated shift in demand, teams face a dilemma. They can raise ticket prices and perhaps get increased short-run profits. But if they do so, they risk reducing the value season ticket holders place on their subscriptions such that they will drop their subscriptions as soon as team performance sags. For example, the NFL's Dallas Cowboys at one time were labeled "America's team," but they stopped selling out when they stopped winning. Apparently their season ticket prices are set so high that subscriptions rise and fall with team performance.

On the other hand, some teams have maintained stable prices even when there has been strong demand for season ticket subscriptions. This can lead to persistent shortages of tickets, which seems to be the situation for the New York Giants and Washington Redskins in the NFL, the Montreal Canadians and Toronto Maple Leafs in the NHL, and the Portland Trailblazers and Boston Celtics in the NBA.

A number of factors determine whether it pays for the team to maintain stable prices or let price vary in response to the changes in demand that follow changes in team performance. One is the percentage of tickets that can be sold at a premium as season tickets. The more fans there are who would pay a premium for season tickets compared with the average of prices in good and bad years, the higher the percentage of tickets that can be sold at a premium, and the greater the likelihood the team will wish to maintain stable prices.

Another factor is the fans' degree of risk aversion. The more risk averse fans are, the greater a premium the team can get for the price stability.

Recall too that season ticket holders effectively receive a discount compared with non–season ticket holders. This discount comes from the fact that season ticket holders get the first seats within any price class of seats. The discount or bonus for season ticket subscribers can reinforce the option value of a season subscription.[32]

Transaction costs create inertia and give added reason for fans to renew subscriptions after bad years and fail to sign up for new subscriptions after good years. This inertia can reinforce or counter the insurance motive to induce teams to depart periodically, and perhaps persistently, from short-run profit-maximizing prices. Fans are slow to renew subscriptions once they have dropped them. However, fans are also slow to drop their subscriptions in response to undesired variation in price or team performance. Persistence of shortages is especially likely when there has been an unanticipated change in the expected team performance or popularity.

Conclusions

There is substantial evidence that owners and managers of major league sports franchises fail to set ticket prices at levels that maximize their short-run profits from ticket sales. Whether their ticket pricing policy is economically irrational is hard to discern given the available data.

In this chapter I have offered an alternative explanation of team ticket-pricing practices, in which season ticket sales are an important factor. Team ticket-pricing practices can be explained as the team essentially selling its season ticket holders an implicit insurance contract in the form of a renewable option for seats of a given quality. This explanation, in turn, suggests patterns of ticket sales that may be observable. For instance, the percentage of tickets sold as season tickets and the pattern of shortages that appear and disappear as team quality fluctuates may be used to verify or refute this hypothesis.

Are prices for tickets to World Series games too low? This chapter argues that "bargains" for World Series tickets are part of the package or implicit contract that season ticket holders buy. High prices for World Series tickets, or large ticket price increases in good years, would break

32. Options to World Series tickets also add to the value of season subscriptions. Note that virtually all World Series and playoff tickets are sold to season ticket holders or set aside for VIPs. Teams offer different packages of season tickets. A single seat at Fenway can be sold or be included as part of a weekday or weekend package. Both holders usually get an option for playoff and World Series tickets.

the contract and reduce the value of this package in later years. In particular, reduced prices for World Series tickets add more to the value of season tickets than it costs the team in expected lost gate receipts for years it makes the series.

References

Becker, Gary S. 1991. "A Note on Restaurant Pricing and Other Examples of Social Influences on Price." *Journal of Political Economy* 99:1109–16.

Cournot, Augustin. 1929 (originally pub. 1838). *Researches into the Mathematical Principles of the Theory of Wealth*, trans. by Nathaniel Bacon. Macmillan.

Noll, Roger G. 1974. "Attendance and Price Setting." In *Government and the Sports Business*, edited by Roger G. Noll, 115–57. Brookings.

————. 1982. "Major League Sports." In *The Structure of American Industry*, 6th ed., edited by Walter Adams. Macmillan.

Scully, Gerald W. 1989. *The Business of Major League Baseball*. University of Chicago Press.

Siegfried, John J., and C. Elton Hinshaw. 1979. "The Effect of Lifting Television Blackouts on Professional Football No-Shows." *Journal of Economics and Business* 32:1–13.

CHAPTER SIX

Baseball, Bubble Gum, and Business

John A. Vernon

F OR MOST people, even highly experienced researchers, about all the National Archives of the United States and the national pastime—baseball—seem to have in common is the word *national*. After all, the one holds records relating primarily to the federal government and the other constitutes an almost totally private enterprise.

To presume, however, that Uncle Sam has nothing of interest relating to such a deeply rooted American cultural phenomenon as baseball is to be mistaken on two counts. First, it demonstrates a general ignorance of how often and how thoroughly the political, economic, and social conventions of the nation and the workings of the federal government have affected one another. Second—if that be so and the government is accountable to Congress, the courts, and ultimately to the public in whose name it rules—then it has had to carefully develop and maintain records relating to significant programs, policies, and activities. Thus for baseball researchers to forgo investigating what the National Archives has to offer could be a major mistake, robbing them of opportunities to examine interesting and relevant documents to be found nowhere else.

Warmup Tosses

This chapter examines an exotic—although easily researchable—group of records deposited in one of the fourteen National Archives records centers located around the nation. These documents pertain to a restraint of trade action filed before the Federal Trade Commission by one bubble gum card manufacturer against another in 1962. At that time, the Frank H. Fleer Corporation of Philadelphia was attempting to prove that Topps

Chewing Gum, Inc., through monopolistic practices, unfairly controlled the bubble gum player picture card industry.

In the years that followed, that issue—dominance in the sale of baseball cards—has been revisited often. Ever more companies have sought to break into what has become a dazzlingly lucrative market. As larger numbers of private collectors have competed with one another to acquire highly prized sets and individual items, the cards they seek have skyrocketed in value, providing more incentive for both manufacturers and collectors to pursue their respective interests aggressively.

Advertising posters, player endorsement contracts, prize lists, marketing surveys, sales promotions, and thirty years of baseball cards are but some of the items submitted in evidence in the 1962 case. Their unusual visual allure and intellectual content belie the notion that governmental records are always drab, humdrum, and irrelevant. Yet, like the more conventional documents found in most government files, these records also reflect the workings of the federal government and qualify as legitimate archival holdings.

The accumulation of records relating to Docket 8463 is admittedly not typical of archival holdings in the wide and colorful array of documents provided, nor in the exceedingly wide research purposes for which this body of records can be put. But it is also not atypical in including many documents received by the government in the course of conducting public business, not just those created by the government. In this instance, the Topps-Fleer conflict involved so many issues and took place over so prolonged a period of time that it resulted in much documentation being both generated and received by the Federal Trade Commission.

Of particular interest are the more than 750 government and defense exhibits, the latter including such unusual documents as bubble gum wrappers, cereal boxes, advertising agency storyboards, specialized flyers, and other promotional material. The *pièces de résistance* are the many baseball cards, coins, and buttons that date back to the 1930s. The presence of such visually appealing and emotionally evocative promotional items, supplemented by the many legal documents and more than 4,000 pages of testimony, found together in two letter-sized file drawers of materials, makes this aggregation the realization of a researcher's dream.[1]

The completeness of the coverage and the careful order in which they were assembled and maintained make the documents easy to use. So easy,

1. These records are in Docket 8463 (Boxes 1448–65), Docketed Case Files 1915–68, Records of the Federal Trade Commission, National Archives Record Group 122.

in fact, that any lover of baseball research cannot help but wish wistfully that comparable records relating more centrally to organized baseball's institutional infrastructure (for example, commissioners, league presidents, player and umpire unions, and individual ball clubs) could be as complete, well maintained, and available for scrutiny.

Encountering the Topps-Fleer materials for the first time, I was reminded that, although institutional records usually come into being to serve a particular, limited purpose—and that purpose is to reflect or facilitate institutional business—they can serve other broader purposes later on. The materials brought together for this case tell the story of a government agency's effort to prosecute particular legal actions falling under its jurisdiction. Under article I, section 8, of the Constitution, the federal government has the right and obligation to regulate interstate commerce. The Federal Trade Commission is its specified agent to that end.

But the records for Docket 8463 do more than document legal actions. They also provide the outsider with a good look at what the baseball picture card industry was like during its "infancy" in the late 1950s and early 1960s, before the industry became so complicated. Today the industry has a great number and range of competitor card companies, a variety of products offered with cards, diverse advertising methods, buyers' increased level of sophistication, and advances in photographic and printing techniques, as well as graphic design. The most important and biggest difference between the industry today and thirty to forty years ago, however, is the potential to realize large profits.

The docket records go far to explain how a well-organized, enterprising company gets the jump on its competition in a wide-open industry. In the process, they provide a juicy slice of American popular culture not usually found in bureaucratic files. The records not only demonstrate their makers' promotional ingenuity but furnish a chronicle of popular consumer tastes in one significant collecting area over an important period of time.

The Game

This history of the controversy surrounding baseball cards in many ways reflects the national pastime and how it is viewed.

Player Introductions

Baseball cards seem to have existed almost as long as the game itself. They date back to at least the 1880s when they were sold with tobacco products. Certainly most Americans today are familiar with them. These cards have usually been colorful cardboard rectangles physically embodying the fondest dreams of generations of American youth who have hoped that they too might some day play major league baseball. Until that time arrives, the kids want to identify with famous players of their day. They do so through the purchase of baseball cards with the players' images on them. In a child's world, the cards have often served as the secular equivalent of religious icons or relics with presumed magical qualities. Perhaps the talent and good fortune of the player pictured would rub off on the possessor of the card if he or she was a true believer.

Business firms were quick to try to cash in on this hero worship. Early on, companies realized that one of the best ways to make a successful sales pitch to adolescents was to get famous players to endorse products. The companies thus began to aggressively compete with one another for player testimonials.

Exhibit items from Docket 8463 indicate that companies that sell edibles likely to be consumed by youngsters—products such as potato chips, bread, milk, ice cream, hot dogs, candy, soft drinks, and flavored gelatin—are among the most interested and successful in putting out baseball cards to accompany and be associated with their products. But by the 1930s manufacturers of chewing gum in particular saw the player cards' special potential as reliable promotional vehicles for selling gum to kids and began in earnest to supply such cards with their wares. Nevertheless, not until the early 1950s did any company issue card sets complete with all players, not just the stars. When that happened, the market for baseball cards began to take off. Among the early gum picture cards submitted in evidence in the Topps-Fleer controversy are those made by Goudey Gum in the 1930s and National Chicle Company, Leaf Brands, and Bowman Gum in the 1940s.

Getting the Sign

By the late 1950s and early 1960s, Topps Chewing Gum Company of Brooklyn, New York, had emerged as the acknowledged leader in card sales, with or without accompanying products. Using such marketing research tools as surveys and questionnaires conducted among readers of *Boys Life* and *Life* magazines, Topps, like the catcher in a baseball game giving a signal to the pitcher indicating what to deliver to the batter, could accurately decide the best pitch to make to the consumer.

The 1950s were the perfect time for an enterprising and well-run company like Topps to enter the baseball picture card market. There was a continuing influx of new and exciting players, many of them blacks or Latin Americans. Expansion, both in number and locations of major league franchises, caused more and more people to become fans, attending games and rooting for their teams. Also, television viewership increased mightily as many more games were being broadcast. Now the individual players could be seen in action.

Perhaps most important of all, an unprecedented crop of youngsters, affluent and impressionable "baby boomers," were growing up and now wanted to see, hear, and read about their heroes. And, of course, that meant they would welcome having baseball cards to collect, trade, or flip. Topps, through such pioneering tactics as signing almost all players featured on its cards to exclusive, long-term contracts, could assure that its card sets would be highly prized and sought out because of their completeness.

Many of the materials submitted in evidence for Docket 8463 testify to the thoroughness of Topps's approach, its sagacity, and its desire to "cover all the bases." They include an interoffice memorandum analyzing team signing possibilities and several expense account chits submitted by Topps scouts during spring training when they were sizing up the new prospects and trying to get established players and veteran superstars in the fold once more.

Topps also used minor league coaches, trainers, and managers to solicit player signatures on its contracts. Finally, Topps sponsored player proficiency awards for minor leaguers and selected rookie all-star teams to ingratiate themselves with teams and players. As a consequence, few players with major league potential were overlooked.

Some players, such as Stan Musial and Robin Roberts, got more lucrative deals than others, and some players, such as Brooks Robinson, opted for gifts listed in annual gift catalogs in lieu of cash when their contracts were up for renewal. Also contained in these records are numerous player contracts. One of the more compelling is the 1956 contract signed by young Donald Drysdale, a minor, and witnessed by his father.

Winding Up

Topps had been the first company to make available a complete card set that provided the photographic likeness of each major leaguer on one side of the card and a brief biography and summary of his playing statistics on the other. Once Topps realized how popular that approach was, it standardized card size and format. Cards were now small enough to put in shirt or back pockets, large enough to contain pertinent information, eye-catching enough to be noticed, and sturdy enough for repeated handling through inventory review, trading, and flipping. Now that the card itself seemed perfect for the intended market, Topps advertised heavily, taking advantage of its momentum to effectively "wind up" as would a baseball hurler in anticipation of making a winning pitch.

Delivering the Pitch

In baseball or business, "delivering the pitch" amounts to almost the same thing. An object, whether a thrown baseball or an advertising contract, is represented as being attractive enough to trigger an enthusiastic and spontaneous response in those to whom it is directed. Thus the preparations for doing that had to be carefully planned and coordinated.

Massive sales campaigns utilized advertising agency storyboards to lay out, panel by panel, how a commercial message should be presented on television or radio. Promotional plans called for the integrated use of public and trade press releases. Advertising flyers went out wholesale, intended for both a general and a retail audience. Finally, huge color posters featuring famous players and eye-catching and impressive store displays were placed strategically in grocery stores and retail outlets to announce card availability. Topps and other business colossuses such as General Foods Corporation, Jello Gelatin, and Armour and Company spared no expense in their efforts. They engaged such high-priced advertising firms as Benton and Bowles and Young and Rubicam to ensure that they delivered the best pitch possible.

Protecting the Lead

Whether in baseball or business, once one side gains an advantage over another, it attempts to convert this temporary "lead" into permanent control. By 1956, Topps had become so dominant that it had been able to buy out its chief competitor, Bowman Gum.

According to documents from Docket 8463, in 1959 the Topps Corporation reported gross revenues of $13,884,500, of which baseball card sales amounted to slightly over $6 million—well over 40 percent. Such figures clearly show why Topps had a vested interest in attempting to play "hardball" with any would-be competitors for what it regarded as its rightful province, the bubble gum card market.

As the 1962 Topps hearing transcripts reveal, most players (two being Charles M. "Charlie" Lau and Richard H. "Dick" Williams, both of whom later came to be regarded as cerebral baseball people) had little idea of the terms or duration of contracts. And the few requests made by players like Bobby Shantz to receive copies of the contract were refused by Topps. Thus 98 percent of the more than 400 big leaguers were bound exclusively to Topps for use in marketing its bubble gum.

Similarly, Topps had signed more than 1,500 minor leaguers to contract binders. In the 1950s the going rate was $5, "steak money." When and if the youngsters made it to the majors, then they would receive additional payments from Topps. In the meantime, the company had "shut out" its rivals, at least in the confectionary products field, from obtaining enough player signatures to compete effectively.

Rhubarb

For latecomers who tried to compete in the signing sweepstakes in the late 1950s and after, Topps's virtual monopoly on the players meant trouble. While trying to gain entry into the market, the Frank H. Fleer Corporation of Philadelphia was reduced to using the images of long-retired players not under contract to Topps, such as Joe Tinker, Frank Chance, and Babe Ruth. It also put out a series of cards detailing Ted Williams's baseball and nonbaseball exploits, including his wartime service, fishing, relaxing, and posing with his daughter.

Fleer agents attempted to lure other players who either were no longer willing to be signed by Topps or who were in the minors and appeared so marginal in talent that Topps had not bothered to sign them for the $5. Astonishingly, one of these was Maury Wills, the National League's most valuable player in 1962, who stole 104 bases that year. Wills, having first signed with Fleer in 1958, for a time served as the company's main player-recruiter to get other players to sign with Fleer rather than with Topps. Fleer actively sought to gain players by indicating that it was willing to sign them to a nonexclusive contract—that is, the players then could sign with another gum company as well. Numerous letters compared Fleer's signing policies with Topps's allegedly less forthright approach. These were sent to all players, urging them to check with their major league union player representatives or with Frank Scott, a player agent and head of the union.

Topps fought back, raising payments and sending to its clients question-and-answer sheets regarding contractual information. The company retained most players' allegiance. Fleer's frustration became acute. In a desperate maneuver intended to get around legal strictures regarding players' signings in association with confectionary products, the company began selling "cookies" with the cards. The cookies were made with such low sugar content that they did not technically qualify as confectionary products. Few kids "bit." They disliked the cookie, Fleer's cards, or both. Not that Topps's thin slabs of low-grade gum supplied in its nickel pack were good. But Fleer's cookies tasted even worse.

Finally, Fleer had had enough. It charged that Topps had used unfair tactics and had such a stranglehold on player signings that its control of the market constituted a monopoly. Thus in 1962 it turned to the Federal Trade Commission (FTC) for help.

The Umpire's Decision

Formally titled "United States of America Before Federal Trade Commission: In the Matter of Topps Chewing Gum, Inc., A Corporation," Federal Trade Commission Docket 8463 contains the official documents belonging to the FTC's three-year examination of the Fleer-Topps confrontation over the issues involved. Two legal documents are attached to the case: one, the complaint filed by the FTC on January 30, 1962, against Topps, and the second, the company's answer. Together these indicated the legal parameters of the case and its basic issues.

The original complaint consists of eight "paragraphs." Paragraphs 1 through 3 identified the respondent (Topps), its line of business, and the FTC's authority to rule on the issues. Further, paragraph 3 noted that Topps was the largest manufacturer of bubble gum in the United States, having annual sales of about $14 million in an industry with total annual sales in the United States by all manufacturers of approximately $30 million.[2]

Paragraph 4 alleged restraint of trade on Topps's part, and paragraph 5 clarified that this was possible through the use of highly sought-after

2. "Complaint," Box 1448, folder 8463-1-1-1/9, pp. 1, 2.

picture cards. The most popular was three and a half by two and a half inches in size, with a photograph or picture of a major league player on one side and his brief biography on the other. Paragraph 5 further suggested that youths "engaged in collecting these cards will only purchase bubble gum which is packaged or accompanied with a baseball picture card."[3]

Paragraph 6 indicated that Topps was able to maintain an unfair advantage over Fleer and other would-be competitors through the use of exclusive contracts with almost all major league players (allegedly 414 of 421) and "practically all minor league players having a major league potential." This was achieved as a result of Topps's primacy in the industry and its use of exclusive contracts with the players. The FTC went on to charge that the players received no copies of the contract and that payoffs to player agents and others, together with threats of legal action against Topps's rivals, had "thereby foreclosed and prevented said competitors from selling their products, including bubble gum, to substantial markets."[4]

Paragraphs 7 and 8 summed up the FTC's position toward Topps. Its unfair business tactics resulted in a virtual monopoly over the manufacture and sale of cards, thus making it possible to victimize those members of the public who sought to purchase such cards.

The FTC therefore required Topps to appear before it on April 9, 1962, to respond to the complaint. If Topps chose not to respond or attend the hearing, an order would be issued to stop the company from re-signing players to contracts of more than one year's duration, signing new players to multiyear contracts, or failing to provide copies of contracts to all signees.

In reply, Topps Chewing Gum, Inc., conceded nothing more than it was indeed a corporation engaged in the production and manufacture of bubble gum packaged with player cards. It denied that it had profited from inappropriate business practices. Topps also put forth five "affirmative" defenses in its own behalf. It argued:

1. That its player card contracts signed with individual professional ballplayers were not a matter involving interstate commerce—thus they could not be construed as restraint of trade;

2. Because players' pictures could be secured elsewhere, the corpo-

3. "Complaint," p. 2.
4. "Complaint," p. 3.

ration's picture card series was only an additional source, of no real consequence except to collectors;

3. Cards were only promotional devices to sell gum, and Topps's competitors were also free to sell bubble gum through whatever "sales aid" they might wish;

4. Topps's "exclusive" picture card contracts pertained only to a limited area—the sale of confectionary items with cards; cards sold with other products or alone were not affected; and

5. Because other card and bubble gum companies continued to exist and compete with Topps in selling their products, the contention that a condition of monopoly or restraint of trade in the industry existed was baseless.[5]

Although the corporation asked that the complaint be dismissed, the FTC asked attorneys for both companies to bring evidence for their positions and appear at a formal hearing on the matter.

Umpire's Original Decision: Out!

More than two years later, on August 7, 1964, Hearing Examiner Herman Tocker ruled against Topps, observing that children and collectors were especially fond of baseball player picture cards, so the Topps argument that it did not overwhelmingly control either the picture card or bubble gum industry was disingenuous. Organized baseball and its most proficient players were so popular with many boys and girls that they would buy products only associated with the game or endorsed by favorite players as "vicarious entry into and participation in the game."[6] Single cards had little individual value, but complete sets of cards did. They were much in demand, and therefore, in his mind, constituted part of interstate commerce.

In the billion-dollar confectionary industry Topps's sales did amount to only about 1 percent of the industry's. Yet the company, through its player contracts, held exclusive rights to the ballplayers' pictures. "Thus about 99 percent of that entire industry is foreclosed from access to every current baseball trading card subject due to a Topps' contract."[7] Further, Topps, through financial and other inducements, sought to extend con-

5. "Answer," Box 1448, folder 8463-1-1-1/9.
6. "Initial Decision," Box 1448, folder 8463-1-1-1/9, p. 22.
7. "Initial Decision," p. 106.

tracts first signed by the players starting out in the minor leagues. Tocker then dismissed the notion that other cards and card sets were of comparable value to Topps's own issues. Cards available elsewhere, in nonconfectionary items, were not as prized "because of the relatively large expenditure necessary to obtain the few, inferior, one-sided cards which may come on a cereal box or a box of gelatin dessert."[8]

Topps's actions in signing almost all players in the majors and minors to exclusive contracts meant in practical terms that no other companies could effectively compete. This made for a near-monopolistic and potentially dangerous situation that Topps could exploit. Tocker stated:

> Although it actually has not done so, by reason of its control of baseball trading cards, it has the power to increase or decrease at will the price of cards when sold alone or the price of combination packages of gum or cards. . . . It could, if it so chose, withhold from the market all baseball trading cards as separate articles of commerce and thus reserve them for use solely in the promotion of the sale of its own bubble gum in the form of a combination product of baseball cards and bubble gum, even to the extent of depriving persons engaged in the vending machine business of the opportunity to vend such cards in their machines.[9]

Tocker concluded that Topps was therefore guilty of violating the Sherman Antitrust Act, section 2, in its domination of the baseball picture card market. These card sales represented a substantial portion of interstate commerce. Tocker thereupon ordered Topps to cease entering into contracts for more than two years' duration on or after November 1, 1964; to cease enforcing after October 31, 1966, contracts already signed; to refrain from entering into renewals or extensions before the original contract was a year old; and from "entering into, or enforcing any extension or renewal of, any such contract for or during a period in excess of two years from the date on which it is or has been extended or renewed."[10] Also, players henceforth had to receive copies of any contracts they signed with Topps and could sign with other companies if they so wished after their current contract expired.

8. "Initial Decision," p. 108.
9. "Initial Decision," p. 109.
10. "Initial Decision," p. 112.

Umpire's Decision Reversal: No, Safe!

Predictably, Topps, through its attorneys, filed notice of appeal. Finally, after delays and maneuverings, on April 30, 1965, the FTC commissioners themselves, in an eleven-page opinion with one dissension, dismissed the original complaint, largely reversing Tocker's previous decision.

They stated that Topps's "monopoly" extended only to cards sold in conjunction with bubble gum, not to cards sold alone or with other nonconfectionary products. Accordingly, the picture cards were only promotional tools, nonessential in the sale of bubble gum. The commissioners noted that Topps's major brand of bubble gum, "Bazooka," went unaccompanied with cards, and Fleer, despite its failure to successfully enter the baseball card market, through other promotional means still managed to retain its status as the second biggest bubble gum manufacturer.

Thus, Fleer had failed to prove that "current baseball picture cards are so unique and indispensable a promotional technique in the bubble gum industry that a firm denied use of the technique cannot compete on fair and equal terms."

They cited other promotional techniques to sell bubble gum, such as football cards, "Beatles" cards, "Spook Theater" cards, and cards featuring famous baseball players no longer active, and concluded that Fleer "has not shown that its market position is attributable to baseball picture cards."[11]

Having decided that children bought the cards for the gum rather than the gum for the cards, the commission indicated that there was nothing "inherently unfair" about the firm's use of exclusive contracts and efforts to sign all the players it wished because Fleer could attempt to do the same thing and, "given the large influx of new players into the minor leagues every year, it should not take Fleer or some other firm long to shake [Topps's] hold." Thus the matter of *Topps* v. *Fleer*, Docket 8463, was officially closed.[12]

11. "Opinion of the Commission: United States of America Before Federal Trade Commission: In the Matter of Topps Chewing Gum, Inc., A Corporation," p. 9.

12. "Opinion of the Commission," p. 10. The following exhibit items provide further information on case particulars: marketing surveys, RX 68, RX 144; promotionals, RX 144, RX 153, RX 154; player gift lists, CX 35, CX 42, CX 51-C, RX 87; a Topps employee expense account, CX 57N; Drysdale's initial Topps contract, CX 231A; the Topps agreement, CX 382D; and the Fleer alternative, RX 106, CX 278B, CX 364A, CX 378A and B.

Extra Innings

Closed temporarily, that is. In 1975 Fleer renewed the struggle with Topps by filing suit in a federal court, again charging restraint of trade. This time the players' union, the Major League Baseball Players Association, was included as well because it continued to grant Topps preferred status. In 1980, a federal judge agreed that Topps was indeed in restraint of trade and allowed Fleer and Donruss Company to compete in marketing cards with gum. Donruss, a subsidiary of General Mills, in 1963 had put out a product called, disgustingly enough, "Little Leaguer Chewing Tobacco Bubble Gum." The same idea was picked up later by ex-big leaguer Jim Bouton when he began to market "Big League Chew." In the mid-1980s Donruss and another gum company, Leaf Brands, merged.

Given the high stakes and its long-standing preeminence in the field, Topps appealed the decision. In 1981 the U.S. Court of Appeals provided an answer more to Topps's liking. Donruss, Fleer, and others could continue to sell cards, but not alone or with gum.

Thus the matter lurches on, with Topps still trying to sign exclusive contracts and still maintaining the lion's share of the market although challenged occasionally by other companies such as Fleer, Donruss, Score, and Upper Deck.[13]

For the last ten or fifteen years, the collecting market has exploded, and for the most part there seems to be room enough for anyone to issue cards novel enough for ravenous collectors to feed on. In 1972 Topps printed approximately a half million cards; sixteen years later, it is estimated that Topps printed approximately 2.4 billion (and 4 billion the following year).[14]

A more sobering phenomenon today than an apparent glut of trendy baseball cards is how the industry has begun to overshadow its parent, baseball. In 1987 Major League Baseball set an all-time attendance record of 52 million fans, who paid $350 million for their tickets. That figure seems healthy enough, but a comparable amount of money was spent in the same year for merely the resale of cards, and twice that amount was spent on new card issues.[15]

All of this interest in cards has spawned a number of collateral businesses. There are now thousands of retail card stores, and many more

13. Good historical discussions of the periods surrounding the 1960s Topps-Fleer battle are found in Clark (1982); Sullivan (1983); and Kirk (1990).

14. Boyd and Harris (1973, p. 18); Kirk (1990, pp. 58–59).

15. Zoss and Bowman (1989, p. 16).

dealers are buying and selling cards through the mail. Card companies print specialized baseball-style business cards, Olympic Games participant cards, minor league cards, Little League cards, umpire cards, and even sportswriter cards. In addition, there are card-collecting shows, card-rating manuals, card catalogs, and card investment clubs. Topps itself has even gone public, beginning in 1987 to sell stock in the corporation.[16]

Collectors' habits have gradually been altered. Cards now are increasingly likely to be collected by adults or economically precocious kids, both of whom may be more interested in the statistics on cards as an indicator of real or potential financial worth. Romantic young hobbyists have been displaced by materialists who consider the collections of various cards the equivalent of stock portfolios. Cards of stars are likely to be held and hoarded today not so much for respect or admiration of the player's talent as for how much a card with his name on it is currently worth and therefore how much profit can be realized later.[17] The new beginning of the old song "I Love You for Sentimental Reasons" goes "I Love You for Commercial Reasons."

Of course, despite the understandable nostalgia for the good old days when the pure of heart collected, an element of commercialism always existed—even then. The desire to make money from the game's popularity was made explicit in the Topps case for the card makers, baseball's administrative cadre, and probably the majority of its players—for that matter, even for many of the juvenile "collectors."

Even in the 1950s and 1960s and even among baseball's most ardent young aficionados, cards were regarded as the equivalent of money, a commonly recognized medium of exchange suitable for trading, hoarding, or flipping. Thus baseball picture cards served two related purposes. They made money for grown-up businessmen and served as money for children. Then, as now, cards have served as both recreational and commercial instruments, and it has been hard to separate the two.

16. Kirk (1990, p. 68); Zoss and Bowman (1989, p. 20).

17. See in the popular literature: David P. Garino, "If You Never Made a Buck Out of Baseball, Take a Look at These Bubble-Gum Cards," *Wall Street Journal*, August 6, 1979, p. 28; Manuel Schiffres, "Investment Update: Here's Another Way to Play Baseball," *Changing Times* (April 1991), p. 20; David S. Krause, "Baseball Cards Bat .425," *Money* (June 1988), pp. 140–47; Jack McCallum, "The Memory Business: Big Bucks Take the Joy out of Collecting Baseball Cards," *Sports Illustrated*, August 1, 1988, p. 86; and Judd Tulley, "Ballpark Figures," *Portfolio* (July 1989), pp. 17–19, 72. See also Zoss and Bowman (1989, pp. 20–25).

Hot Stove League

The records of this case, Docket 8463, show how two superficially disparate institutions—baseball and business—were intimately connected and developed a symbiotic partnership based on mutual respect for the dollar and how it could be made. The advertising posters, prize lists, depositions, and marketing surveys all speak of merged cultural values. The common denominator in the two worlds, baseball and business, was a competitive spirit for gaining profit.

Business competition for player endorsements of products has been just as intense as any rivalry taking place on the diamond. Topps rose to the top and maintained its forty-year dominance by playing its own brand of "hardball" with its rivals. In its own special sphere of activity it has been at least as successful as the Yankees, Dodgers, and Cards combined have been in their own!

The places of venue, boardroom versus playing field, and mode of dress, three-piece suits versus players' uniforms, admittedly have differed, but attitudes and methods appear strikingly similar. So much so that the careful reader of the case materials may want to ponder once again which activity—baseball or business—can really be considered the "national pastime." As these records demonstrate, Americans possess an eager appetite for both.

These same records suggest that institutional records are not always dry reading and devoid of interest to all but the devotees of the arcane. They illustrate the workings of the federal government and provide in-depth information about the baseball picture card industry in an early but crucial time in its development. Most important, they serve to demonstrate in the most immediate and familiar sense facets of the wider culture and the values that make it up. They contribute not only to nostalgia for a game and its performers but also to a more balanced perception of the game and its relationship to our society.

These records relate to actions and individuals frozen in time. Although the players who appear on cards never grow old—as long as the cards on which they are pictured exist—researchers do. At least researchers usually learn or gain insight from their experience. It is hoped that present-day baseball researchers will not continue to think exclusively in terms of conventional sources—newspapers, periodicals, and books, supplemented by a few oral interviews—as the only legitimate sources for information on the game they love. Archival records—those relating to institutions—need to be considered too. Therein may lie previously un-discovered connections between the subject of research and the business of that institution.

Of course, the next step for future baseball historians is to demand that more such materials be preserved for use and made available for research by the powers of the game. Otherwise, research in certain directions, particularly those that pertain primarily to baseball's administrative apparatus (for example, the teams' front offices and scouting operations, commissioner and league president policies, player, manager, and owner investigations), will be delimited. Until that time the most informed judgments about such matters can be only tentative at best. Access to the original written record is necessary for making definitive judgments about institutional transactions.

References

Boyd, Brendan C., and Fred C. Harris. 1973. *The Great American Baseball Card Flipping, Trading, and Bubble Gum Book.* Little, Brown.

Clark, Steve. 1982. *The Complete Book of Baseball Cards.* Grosset and Dunlap.

Kirk, Troy. 1990. *Collector's Guide to Baseball Cards.* Radnor, Penn.: Wallace-Homestead Book Co.

Sullivan, George E. 1983. *The Complete Book of Baseball Collectibles.* New York: ARCO Publishing.

Zoss, Joel, and John Bowman. 1989. *Diamonds in the Rough: The Untold History of Baseball.* Macmillan.

Part III

Pay, Performance, and Competitive Balance

CHAPTER SEVEN

Salaries and Performance: Beyond the Scully Model

Andrew Zimbalist

THE EXPENSIVE settlement of Collusion I, II, and III, as well as the proviso in the 1990 Basic Agreement calling for triple damages in future collusion cases, has sent player salaries skyrocketing again for 1991 and presumably after. Average major league salaries rose from $591,498 in 1990 to $848,499 in 1991, an increase of 43.4 percent.[1] The pre-1991 season contracts include more than 124 players with salaries of $2 million or more and 32 players with salaries of $3 million or more, as well as the first $5 million annual salary. Even baseball's prodigal prince, Jose Canseco, has raised his eyebrows in disapproval of Roger Clemens's four-year $21.5 million contract: "He should definitely be paid the highest of all the pitchers, but that much for going out every four or five days, I just don't buy it."[2]

I wish to thank Donald Coffin, Lawrence Kahn, Jim Quirk, Pete Bavasi, Kevin Ryan, Gerry Scully, and Liz Savoca for helpful comments. This chapter draws from material presented in Andrew Zimbalist, *Baseball and Billions: A Probing Look inside the Big Business of Our National Pastime* (Basic Books, forthcoming), chap. 4.

1. Ira Berkow, "Where Bam-Bam Fits In," *New York Times*, April 10, 1991, p. B5. Also see Murray Chass, "Money, Money and More Money," *New York Times*, November 21, 1991, p. B18. The average salaries are based on all players on the twenty-five-man roster plus the disabled lists on August 31 of each year. The increase, in fact, is overstated because contracts signed before the 1990 season were structured to minimize the impact of an anticipated work stoppage during the season on player salaries, that is, with lower salaries in 1990 and higher salaries in subsequent years. Pete Bavasi, president of Sportsticker and former executive of the Padres, Indians, and Blue Jays, argues that the salary explosion has less to do with a rational owner response to institutional change and more to do with the departure of Commissioner Peter Ueberroth. Bavasi credits Ueberroth with having maintained "salary discipline" among the owners. Letter to author, March 22, 1991. Also see John Helyar, "How Peter Ueberroth Led the Major Leagues in the 'Collusion Era,' " *Wall Street Journal*, May 20, 1991, p. A1.

2. Quoted in "Henderson's Absence Offsets Canseco's Attempt at Levity," *USA Today*, February 28, 1991, p. 3C.

More philosophically, Bob Tewksbury, pitcher with the St. Louis Cardinals, opines: "As a fan of the game, I'm worried about the state of baseball. I mean, what's the incentive to do well? The salaries, it seems like, are just based on service time. Don't get me wrong. The personal side of me says, 'Hell, if these guys can go out and make millions of bucks, I can do it, too. All the better.' But I really think something has to be done. . . . You hear about people losing their houses and losing their jobs. Then you look at what is happening in baseball, and it's hard to figure out."[3]

The labor market issues raised by the work of Rottenberg, Gregory, and Andreano and first answered by Scully are again being seriously explored.[4] The 1990 Basic Agreement provides for the establishment of a study committee inter alia to investigate the relationship among pay, performance, and competitive balance. Owners from baseball's "small markets" are sending out a collective SOS, claiming that they cannot afford to pay baseball's new salaries and hence face losing their stars to "big-market" franchises. At an awards dinner at Fairfield University in Connecticut on February 21, 1991, Baseball Commissioner Fay Vincent echoed these fears: "Baseball is poised for a catastrophe and it might not be far off. The major markets will continue to attract players and they'll win. What will happen to the smaller markets like Seattle?"[5] Vincent went on to argue for a form of revenue sharing among teams.[6] Others argue for salary caps or greater restrictions on arbitration or free agency. But is the current system really broken, and does it require fixing?

An important part of the answer to this question resides in the relationship between pay and performance. The seminal empirical work on this question was Gerald Scully's article in the *American Economic Review*.[7] A variation of Scully's methodology was used in the arbitration hearings before Thomas Roberts and George Nicolau in Collusion I,

---

3. Quoted in "Growing Salaries Worry Tewksbury," *Baseball America*, April 25–May 9, 1991, p. 2.

4. Andreano (1965); Gregory (1956); Rottenberg (1956); Scully (1974).

5. "Vincent Financial Plea," *New York Times*, February 23, 1991, p. 46 (early ed.).

6. A substantial part of the revenue differential among clubs is properly understood as economic rent and should not affect the allocational decisions of profit-maximizing owners. If integrated into the analysis, the extent of optimal revenue sharing for promoting competitive balance would be reduced. For an interesting discussion of this point, see Philip K. Porter, chap. 4, in this volume.

7. Scully (1974).

II, and III.[8] Scully presented an updated version of his 1974 two-equation model in his book *The Business of Major League Baseball.*[9]

Scully's model posits, first, that team winning percentage is determined by batting and pitching performance and, second, that overall team revenues are determined by team winning percentage, after controlling for the size of the team's geographic market. Thus the dollar value of a player's incremental contribution to team revenue (net marginal revenue product) can be indirectly estimated by identifying the effect of the player's performance on winning percentage and then of winning percentage on revenue.

Clearly, the model does not provide either a precise or a nuanced measure of a player's value. It does not take into account, for instance, the charisma contributions of certain star players such as Reggie Jackson or Dave Winfield, the contributions of base-stealing artists such as Rickey Henderson or Vince Coleman, the psychological or strategic contributions of players such as Tony Peña or Don Baylor, or the fielding contributions of others such as Ozzie Smith or Don Mattingly, nor does it take into account the negative effects of poor fielding, bad baserunning, or contentious or self-absorbed personalities. Yet if the model is properly specified, it can on balance capture the most important contributions of the great majority of ballplayers and provide a reasonable standard for gauging the equity of absolute and relative levels of pay.

Although Scully's two-equation model is not econometrically elegant, it is as reliable as any existing empirical or subjective procedure for estimating players' worth. Scully's 1974 article was also useful for the compelling evidence it provided of exploitation of players in the pre–free agency era. For his past contributions, we owe Scully a debt of gratitude. Both his 1974 and 1989 efforts, however, are flawed, the latter fatally so.

Scully's 1989 Model

Scully suggests the following two-equation model,

8. Roberts actually employed a modified Scully-type model as one of three empirical estimates in computing damages. Nicolau heard testimony based on a Scully-type model, but he did not use it in calculating damages.
9. Scully (1989).

(1) $$PCT = 0.00109\ SLG + 0.00065\ K/BB$$
$$(2.53)$$

(2) $$TR = -1{,}877.2 + 31{,}696.1\ PCT + 3.31\ POP;$$
$$R^2 = 0.69,$$

where PCT is team winning percentage, SLG is team slugging percentage (batting performance), K/BB is the team's strikeout-to-walk ratio (pitching performance), TR is team total revenue, and POP is the population of the metropolitan area.[10] The model is tested for the year 1984. Scully provides only the information shown in the equations above, where the number in parentheses is the t-statistic of SLG and it is not known whether the first equation was tested with or without a constant term. Although the omissions are problematic, I shall focus on the substantive questions I have regarding Scully's 1989 method.

First, Scully asserts that slugging percentage and strikeout-to-walk ratio are the best performance predictors of team winning percentage.[11] This is not true of Scully's original 1968–69 data set,[12] nor is it true for 1984 or for any year between 1984 and 1990. Regressions running PCT on SLG and K/BB have significantly lower R^2s than those using practically any other set of reasonable performance indicators. Indeed, for 1984 and 1984–89 regression results (presented in table 7-1), the percentage of explained variance in Scully's specification is less than one-half that when PCT is run on earned run average (ERA) and $PROD$.[13]

The reason for this is not difficult to discern. Slugging percentage is a good indicator of offensive performance, but it excludes one major component of offensive contribution, namely, walks. This omission can be

10. Scully (1989, pp. 154–55, 205). Scully does not indicate clearly whether or not he divides SMSA population by two in those cities with two teams (Chicago, Los Angeles, and New York). Although this practice is frequently followed, as I shall show below, it is not justified. That is, teams do not split cities and to be a fan of one team is not mutually exclusive of being a fan of the other team in the city (the Brooklyn Dodgers and New York Yankees of the early 1950s to the contrary.)

11. "But, the slugging average for hitters and the strikeout-to-walk ratio for pitchers have been and remain the best single predictors of player quality." Scully (1989, p. 154).

12. When winning percentage is run on slugging percentage and the strikeout-to-walk ratio for 1968–69, $\overline{R}^2$ is 0.593; when it is run on production and ERA for 1968–69, $\overline{R}^2$ is 0.858. I thank Kevin Ryan for sharing these results.

13. $PROD$ or "production" is equal to slugging average (SLG) plus on-base percentage (OBP).

remedied by adding on-base percentage (*OBP*) to slugging percentage, yielding the synthetic indicator "production," or *PROD*.[14] Strikeout-to-walk ratio, however, appears to be an indirect and relatively poor indicator of pitching performance, inferior to opponents' on-base average, which, in turn, is inferior to the old standby, earned run average. Strikeout-to-walk ratio will correlate well with performance for strikeout pitchers like Roger Clemens or Nolan Ryan but not so well for the more numerous control pitchers like Tommy John or Mike Boddicker. *ERA* is superior to opponents' on-base average because it indirectly captures additional components such as team fielding, opponent slugging, and base stealing.[15] Thus the best predictors of team winning percentage (*PCT*) for each year, as well as the pooled regression during 1984–89, were *PROD* and *ERA*, as reported in table 7-2.

Second, although Scully's total revenue equation is more on the mark, I believe it is also mispecified. Most important, Scully does not include the lagged win percentage, *PCT* (− 1), as an explanatory variable.[16] Because fans' interest in a team is clearly affected by the team's previous-year performance, a player's contribution in any one year will influence team revenue in at least two years. In table 7-3, the statistical significance of this lagged relationship is robustly demonstrated. Lagged values of *PCT* greater than one year, however, are not significant. Scully also omits at least two other significant variables in his equation: whether the team is in the National League or American League and the city's per capita income.[17]

Further, Scully seems to follow the common, but unjustified, practice of dividing in half the population of those cities with two major league teams (that is, New York, Chicago, and Los Angeles).[18] This practice

14. I first encountered this indicator in Thorn and Palmer (1989).

15. It is arguable that one drawback of *ERA* relative to the strikeout-to-walk ratio is that *ERA* includes more components not strictly related to the individual player's performance. Good team fielding, for instance, can lower a pitcher's *ERA*. On the other hand, a consistent and effective pitcher can improve team fielding, and even the strikeout-to-walk ratio is affected by team elements, for example, the catcher's strategy and handling of a pitcher. Further, the more effective is team defense, the more the pitcher's arm is preserved to increase future strikeouts and reduce future walks.

16. In an earlier treatment of total revenue, Scully (1989, chap. 6) includes *PCT* (− 1), but he excludes it in his marginal revenue product estimates without explanation.

17. Of course, the coefficients will be biased only to the extent that the omitted variables are correlated with the included independent variables. The correlation is high in the case of *PCT* and *PCT* (− 1).

18. I say "seems" because Scully notes he adjusts for two-team cities only once, in an earlier chapter and in a different empirical exercise (1989, p. 95).

Table 7-1. *Alternative Determinants of Team Winning Percentage*[a]

Independent variable and summary statistics	1984 equations				1984–89 equations			
	(1)	(2)	(3)	(4)	(1)	(2)	(3)	(4)
Constant	0.24 (1.93)	0.29 (0.94)	-0.03 (-0.17)	-0.002 (-0.001)	0.25 (5.99)	0.61 (5.71)	-0.06 (-0.79)	-0.02 (-0.48)
SLG	1.59 (4.79)	…	1.09 (2.70)	…	1.83 (15.4)	…	0.88 (5.38)	…
K/BB	…	…	0.06 (1.40)	…	…	…	0.12 (7.19)	…
PROD[b]	…	…	…	1.22 (5.24)	…	…	…	1.38 (17.8)
ERA	-0.09 (-4.38)	…	…	-0.10 (-4.73)	-0.12 (-18.2)	…	…	-0.12 (-20.1)
OBP[c]	…	3.35 (4.04)	…	…	…	2.82 (10.5)	…	…
OOBP[d]	…	-2.76 (-3.65)	…	…	…	-3.21 (-12.6)	…	…
$\bar{R}^2$	0.58	0.50	0.29	0.62	0.72	0.59	0.34	0.77
N	26	26	26	26	156	156	156	156

a. Numbers in parentheses are *t*-statistics. In this and subsequent tables, *t*-statistics equal to or greater than 2.34 (1.65) are significant at the 0.01 (0.05) level for regressions with N = 156, and those equal to or greater than 2.50 (1.71) are significant at the 0.01 (0.05) level for regressions with N = 26. Numbers are rounded.
b. *SLG* plus *OBP*.
c. On-base average.
d. Opponents' on-base average.

Table 7-2. *Best Determinants of Team Winning Percentage*[a]

Independent variable and summary statistics	Equations						
	1984	1985	1986	1987	1988	1989	1984–89[b]
Constant	−0.002	−0.111	−0.105	−0.108	0.056	−0.630	−0.024
	(−0.01)	(−0.72)	(−0.92)	(−0.57)	(0.43)	(−0.39)	(−0.48)
PROD	1.221	1.483	1.574	1.419	1.331	1.467	1.380
	(5.24)	(6.98)	(9.01)	(5.40)	(7.43)	(6.05)	(17.8)
ERA	−0.096	−0.116	−0.134	−0.106	−0.130	−0.123	−0.119
	(−4.73)	(−8.90)	(−9.66)	(−6.04)	(−9.09)	(−7.85)	(−20.1)
$\bar{R}^2$	0.62	0.82	0.83	0.67	0.83	0.75	0.77
N	26	26	26	26	26	26	156

a. Numbers in parentheses are t-statistics. Coefficients are rounded off to nearest thousandth. All coefficients are significant at the 0.01 level, and none of the constant terms is statistically significant.
b. Pooled regression, used in two-equation model.

Table 7-3. *Determinants of Total Revenue*[a]

Independent variable and summary statistics	Equations								
	1984	1985	1986	1987	1988	1989	1984–89[b]	1984–89	1984–89
Constant	-163E+5	-229E+5	-280E+5	-402E+5	-454E+5	-610E+5	-492E+5	-620E+5	-533E+5
	(-1.33)	(-1.79)	(-2.19)	(-3.04)	(-2.98)	(-2.44)	(-7.71)	(-8.99)	(-8.26)
PCT	233E+5	486E+5	284E+5	227E+5	418E+5	344E+5	286E+5	318E+5	290E+5
	(1.83)	(3.87)	(1.72)	(1.35)	(2.21)	(0.92)	(3.38)	(3.34)	(3.33)
PCT(−1)	457E+5	271E+5	276E+5	383E+5	200E+5	424E+5	370E+5	363E+5	348E+5
	(4.17)	(1.65)	(1.94)	(2.18)	(0.89)	(1.39)	(4.34)	(3.73)	(3.94)
POP	1.64	1.65	2.12	2.17	2.77	3.97	2.40	...	...
	(5.20)	(4.06)	(4.46)	(4.79)	(5.15)	(4.33)	(10.2)		
POP2	...	...	...	...	...	...	...	4.31	...
								(7.05)	
POP3	...	...	...	...	...	...	...	...	3.64
									(9.45)
YCAP[c]	-112	232	1177	1873	2070	2608	1740	2339	1924
	(-0.22)	(0.39)	(1.91)	(2.93)	(2.95)	(2.39)	(5.42)	(6.72)	(5.91)
NL[d]	131E+4	238E+4	295E+4	451E+4	513E+4	138E+4	321E+4	358E+4	320E+4
	(1.00)	(1.48)	(1.56)	(2.25)	(2.05)	(0.32)	(3.04)	(3.01)	(2.94)
TREND[e]	...	...	...	...	...	...	231E+4	171E+4	210E+4
							(5.49)	(3.67)	(4.90)
$\bar{R}^2$	0.80	0.83	0.81	0.81	0.80	0.71	0.77	0.71	0.76
N	26	26	26	26	26	26	156	156	156

a. E+5 denotes add five zeroes. All numbers are rounded. Numbers in parentheses are *t*-statistics.
b. Pooled regression, used in two-equation model.
c. Per capita income in the standard metropolitan statistical area.
d. A dummy variable, equaling 1 when team is in National League, 0 when in American League.
e. Increments one digit per year, beginning at 1 in 1984.

implicitly assumes that fans in a city support either one team or the other but not both and that interest in one team does not enhance overall interest in baseball. In fact, having two or more teams in one city might deepen the baseball culture in the area and thereby increase the number of fans. Finally, teams' output is not homogeneous. For example, Yankee fans cannot watch Dwight Gooden pitch at Yankee Stadium or on Madison Square Garden cable network. Equations predicting either total revenue or attendance were tested using three population variables: *POP*, no adjustment for two-team cities; *POP2* (0.5 × *POP*), for two-team cities; and *POP3* (0.7 × *POP*), for two-team cities.[19] *POP3* was introduced to represent an intermediate state between mutual exclusivity of fan support and no symbiosis on the one hand, and no exclusivity and complete symbiosis on the other. In every case, the *t*-statistics on *POP* were higher than those on *POP3*, which, in turn, were higher than those on *POP2*.

Of all the explanatory variables in the total revenue equations, *POP* clearly is the most consistently significant during the six-year period. Using the pooled equation (1984–89), the coefficient on *POP* signifies that team revenue grows by $2.40 for every additional person living in the city. If we discount *PCT(−1)* by the average yield on one-year Treasury bills (T-bills) over the period and add the coefficients on *PCT* and discounted *PCT(−1)*, then each 0.001 increase in a team's winning percentage augments team revenues by $63,026. That is, a 0.001 increase in team winning percentage adds as much to team revenue as does a population increase of 26,260 people. Alternatively, because each win contributes 0.00617 points to the winning percentage, on average each additional victory brings the same increment to total revenue as 162,000 people in a city's population.

The significant coefficient on *YCAP* in the pooled regression shows a positive correlation between SMSA per capita income and team revenue. Higher income levels enhance an area's market and contribute to richer media contracts. The positive and significant coefficient on *NL* probably derives from the disproportionately favorable treatment of allocations from the major league central fund to National League clubs.[20] The pos-

---

19. Equations predicting attendance are not reported in this chapter. The quadratic modeling of population's impact with a dummy variable for two-team cities, as suggested by Sommers and Quinton (1982), did not improve the $\bar{R}^2$s. In a variety of linear specifications as well, the dummy variable for the two-team cities was never significant and in some functional forms it even was positive.

20. Through the 1988 season, revenues from the national media packages, after deductions for administrative expenses, were divided 50–50 between the two leagues. Because the National League had twelve teams and the American League had fourteen, the per-

itive coefficient on *TREND* simply reflects the strong upward trend in baseball revenues over the period.

The third problem is conceptual. In order to measure marginal revenue product, one first has to know what output is. What output does a ballplayer produce? Presumably, and consistent with the Scully model, a player produces walks, hits, and runs—intermediate outputs that contribute to final output, wins. If wins is the final output, then does a player who bats below the league average or the average for his position contribute to a team's winning percentage? Does a player who hits .230 or .180 without power contribute more to a team's winning than to its losing?[21]

Scully's computations of player marginal revenue product assume a counterfactual for batters of no hits. That is, he assumes that if the player being evaluated did not play, then his replacement would have been up the same number of times and would have had no hits (a zero batting or slugging average), or, adjusted to the *PROD* concept, the replacement would have had no hits and no walks. Because Scully's model excludes defensive performance (except for pitchers), it would be consistent to assume that without a given player there would be no replacement and the team's hitting performance would subtract both the number of at bats and bases of the player under evaluation. That is, a player's marginal revenue product would be the difference between the team's *PROD* with him in the lineup and the team's *PROD* in his absence, or how much the player added to the team *PROD*.[22]

Although there is some theoretical ambiguity as to which is the correct concept of a player's marginal revenue product, I prefer the latter. Consider an analogy to a factory that produces goods. In a manufacturing plant, if the marginal worker is not hired, the output of the factory does not decrease; rather, it stays constant. In Scully's treatment, if a player is out of the lineup (not hired), the team's hitting performance (*PROD*) falls (and markedly so). The limitation with my method is that it does not permit a direct, absolute measure of player marginal revenue product, as I shall discuss below.

---

team share for NL clubs was approximately 16.6 percent higher than for AL clubs. The formula was changed after the 1988 season to provide equal revenue to all clubs. The previous inequality is one of the reasons why the American League claimed it was entitled to share equally in the NL expansion sale of two franchises for $95 million each.

21. Various studies show no significant correlation between measures of defensive performance and salary. See, for instance, Hill and Spellman (1983, p. 7).

22. This would be the same as assuming that the player were replaced and his replacement batted the team average, in terms of either slugging or slugging plus on-base average (*PROD*).

The fourth and final weakness in Scully's 1989 treatment is that he employs gross, rather than net, marginal product.[23] The concept of net marginal product adjusts for the presence of certain complementary inputs that allow the player to attain his productivity and that the franchise experiences as auxiliary or collateral costs. A profit-maximizing employer will hire workers up to the point where the marginal factor cost (*MFC*) is equal to the gross marginal revenue product (*MRP*). The marginal factor cost, in turn, will equal the salary paid to the factor (the player) plus any necessary marginal auxiliary costs that accompany the factor.[24] Hence, the profit-maximizing condition can be written as:

$$(3) \qquad\qquad MFC = \text{gross } MRP, \text{ or}$$

$$(4) \qquad \text{Salary} + \text{marginal auxiliary cost} = \text{gross } MRP, \text{ or}$$

$$(5) \quad \text{Salary} = \text{gross } MRP - \text{marginal auxiliary cost} = \text{net } MRP.$$

The difficulty, of course, lies in identifying and quantifying marginal auxiliary costs. Certainly in the case of hitters the baseball bats a team purchases for a player are necessary auxiliary costs, as are the batting helmets, rosin bags, and uniforms.[25] Similarly, it can be argued that items such as batting cages, mechanical or batting practice pitchers, and the trainer and training room are all complementary factors that are not measured independently in the production function and should be considered auxiliary costs. It would also be appropriate to deduct marginal

23. This is something of a curiosity because in his seminal 1974 article Scully did use the concept of net marginal product. He does not explain why he abandons this approach in his 1989 book.

24. Of course, insofar as the owner's labor market circumstance emulates that of a monopsonist, the marginal factor cost will also include extra payments that the owner will make to other players. This would result in lower salaries. It seems reasonable to expect that in some instances paying more to one player will raise the salary demands (and, ultimately, the salary) of other players. If nothing else, baseball's salary arbitration procedure will ensure that this happens to some degree, but there is an interesting twist. Namely, if one owner raises the salary of a player, it may not only raise that owner's labor costs but it may raise the labor costs of fellow owners. This raises once again the question of the appropriate unit for and the modeling of the analysis of profit-maximizing behavior in sports leagues.

25. The player is responsible for his own glove and spikes, although in many cases their expense is covered as a minor part of an endorsement contract.

player development costs or the indirect cost of signing a free agent (usually the loss of a top-round draft pick in the June amateur draft).

The matter of quantifying player development costs has been hotly contended. Some owners, for instance, have maintained that development costs per player should be calculated by dividing the team's total annual minor league and scouting budget by the average number of major league ballplayers produced per year by the minor league system (roughly three). Because player development budgets often exceed $5 million, this calculation yields figures as high as $1.8 million per player, or roughly $300,000 per player per year for an average-length major league career.[26] These figures, however, are inflated because they ignore that the minor league systems generate fan support and modest revenue.[27] Farm systems also provide security for the major league club in the case of player injury. Further, as some have observed, there are many unnecessary expenses or inefficiencies in the player development system that should not be deducted from the players' contribution.[28]

Finally, as estimated above, the $300,000 figure represents average, not marginal, auxiliary cost per player per year. Under reasonable assumptions, the marginal auxiliary cost would be substantially less because the farm systems are already in place. Minimally, then, several downward adjustments would have to be made to the $300,000 figure. Nonetheless, the theoretical point remains: it is the net marginal revenue product that should be compared with player salaries. In the empirical analysis below, I shall assume somewhat arbitrarily that auxiliary costs amount to 10 percent of gross marginal revenue product.

New Estimates

Using the results from the pooled regressions in tables 7-2 and 7-3, a modified two-equation model can be applied to estimate player marginal revenue products during 1984–89. Specifically, for batters the coefficients on PCT and PCT (−1) discounted by the average short-term T-bill rate

26. See, for instance, Dave Nightingale, "The $1.8 Million Odyssey," Sporting News, June 18, 1990, pp. 7–8.
27. Actual revenue generation before the 1991 Professional Baseball Agreement was minor and limited to those few cases where the major league club owned the minor league franchise. With the new Professional Baseball Agreement, explicit revenue sharing from ticket sales will grow incremently from $750,000 in 1991 to $2 million in 1994.
28. Others have argued that star players on average require less training and should have lower auxiliary costs.

from the first pooled equation in table 7-3 are added together and multiplied by the coefficient on *PROD* from the pooled equation in table 7-2. This product is multiplied by the player's impact on team *PROD*. The result is then added to the average team salary, yielding the player's gross MRP, which is then diminished by 10 percent to arrive at net MRP. The accuracy of the final estimate thus is sensitive to the extent to which the average player is paid his MRP (to be discussed below.)

I begin by comparing the results of my method with those that would be obtained by the Scully method for various leading hitters on the 1989 Boston Red Sox (see table 7-4). I compare four estimates of marginal revenue product: (1) *Scully1*, where the counterfactual of a zero *PROD* for the replacement player is assumed and only *PCT* is included in the equation; (2) *Scully2*, where the counterfactual of a zero *PROD* is assumed and both *PCT* and discounted *PCT* (-1) are included; (3) *Zim1*, where the counterfactual of average team *PROD* is assumed and only *PCT* is included; and (4) *Zim2*, where the counterfactual of average team *PROD* is assumed and both *PCT* and *PCT* (-1) are included. As suggested above, I believe *Zim2* represents the correct specification.

In both *Zim1* and *Zim2*, the player's contribution is measured relative to the team average without the player. In both *Zim1* and *Zim2* net marginal revenue products are computed relative to average team salary. Hence they accurately represent absolute net marginal revenue products only if the team's average salary equals the net marginal revenue product of the team's average player. To the extent that the average player is under- or overpaid, *Zim2* will under- or overestimate the player's actual net marginal revenue product. An alternative to computing *Zim1* and *Zim2* on the basis of the actual average team salary would be to use a fixed percentage of team revenue divided by 25 as a proxy for the net marginal revenue product of the average player.

Naturally, my estimates share the same limitations as those inherent to the basic Scully methodology. That is, fielding prowess, ability to advance runners, runners left on base, contribution to team spirit, intimidation factors, and star attraction to fans are not considered. Statistically, the results are based on two point estimates, each with its own standard errors, and hence should be regarded only as ballpark figures.

In table 7-4, when the Scully method is applied to the correctly specified equation with both *PCT* and discounted *PCT* (-1), the resulting estimates are inordinately large by any standard. For example, Wade Boggs's 1989 MRP is estimated to be $8,350,000, and Rich Gedman's is estimated to be $4,001,000, even though he batted only .212. The basis

Table 7-4. *Player Performance and Salaries, Boston Red Sox, 1989*[a]
Thousands of dollars

Player and service[b]	PROD (batting average)	Scully1 (gross MRP)	Scully2 (gross MRP)	Zim1 (net MRP)	Zim2 (net MRP)	Actual salary	Coefficient of exploitation[c]
Rice (15)	.620 (.234)	1,515	2,360	358	210	2,360	0.09
Boggs (7)	.879 (.330)	5,195	8,350	1,356	1,811	1,775	1.02
Reed (2)	.769 (.288)	3,842	6,175	681	726	175	4.15
Burks (2)	.836 (.303)	3,193	5,132	909	1,093	275	3.97
Evans (17)	.860 (.285)	4,275	6,871	1,128	1,445	1,100	1.31
Greenwell (4)	.813 (.308)	4,491	7,219	933	1,131	550	2.06
Barrett (7)	.638 (.256)	2,056	3,305	251	34	775	0.04
Gedman (9)	.565 (.212)	2,489	4,001	164	-104	1,150	-0.09
Team average (all players)	.754 (.277)	...	...	...	...	668	...

a. These estimates are based on the coefficients from the pooled regressions, 1984–89. If the 1989 single-year regressions are used, the disparities between Scully's estimates and mine (and actual salary) are even greater. For instance, using 1989 regressions, *Scully2* for Rice would equal $3,019,677 and for Boggs, $10,353,178; *Zim2* for Rice would equal $115,742 and for Boggs, $2,065,963.

b. The number of years appearing on the major league roster before 1989 season. This figure will differ from the official major league service calculation, which determines eligibility for salary arbitration and free agency.

c. *Zim2* divided by actual salary. Hence values greater than 1 denote exploitation; values below 1 denote overpayment. The greater the value above 1, the greater the exploitation; the lower the value below 1 (including negative numbers), the greater the overpayment.

for these exaggerated figures is Scully's untenable counterfactual of a 0 slugging or *PROD* average.

My estimates, though more reasonable, do not correspond closely with player salaries either. To predict actual salary, one would want to consider major league experience, lifetime performance, whether the player was a free agent or eligible for salary arbitration, and whether the player was a record holder or all-star team member, along with other factors. My intention here, however, is not to predict salaries but to see how well performance and pay are correlated in any given year.

My results of comparisons of estimated MRPs and salaries for hitters during 1986–89 are summarized in tables 7-5 and 7-6.[29] Discussion of these results must begin with the caveat that 1986, 1987, and 1988 have been found to be years of ownership collusion over free agent salaries. The collusion cases further established that the adverse effects on player salaries went beyond 1988. Evidence presented before arbitrators Roberts and Nicolau, as well as accounts elsewhere, make it clear that the most overt collusion took place before the 1986 season, following the September 1985 owners' meeting and at the initiative of Lee MacPhail and Commissioner Peter Ueberroth.[30] Responding to the suit brought by the Players Association, the owners' collusive practices became more indirect and diluted in 1987 and 1988.

The correlation between estimated MRPs and salaries for hitters is presented for each year between 1986 and 1989 in table 7-5, controlling for years of major league service. Effectively, there are three labor markets for major league ballplayers: for those under the reserve clause without salary arbitration rights, hereafter called apprentices (basically those with less than two years of major league service); for those under the reserve clause with salary arbitration rights,[31] called journeymen (basically those with two to five years of major league service); and for those free agents

29. My sample includes all hitters according to 1990 team rosters. Because some of these players did not play in previous years, the sample size decreases for each preceding year. Only players for whom complete data were available in a particular year were included.

30. Helyar, "How Peter Ueberroth Led the Major Leagues"; Kuhn (1988, pp. 170–72); Major League Baseball (1985, 1988, 1989, 1990a, 1990b).

31. Salary arbitration was begun before the 1974 season and was extended to any ballplayer with two years of major league service and without a contract for the next year. In the 1985 bargaining agreement between the owners and the players, it was agreed that the eligibility for salary arbitration would be raised to three years of major league service beginning with the 1987 season. The 1990 agreement changed eligibility requirements once again, beginning with the 1991 season, by granting eligibility rights to 17 percent of the players with between two and three years of experience. My measure of major league service does not correspond precisely with the official measurement.

Table 7-5. *Regressions for Salaries and Marginal Revenue Products*[a]

Year and category	N	Dependent variable[b]	Constant (thousands)	Service[c] (thousands)	Marginal revenue product	$\overline{R}^2$
1986						
All	211	Sal 86	−32.4 (−0.83)	82.2 (14.6)	0.0001 (0.35)	0.50
	231	Sal 87	−92.9 (−2.32)	75.1 (12.9)	0.331[d] (9.04)	0.57
<2 years	42	Sal 86	62.2 (3.81)	9.5 (0.91)	−0.0000 (−0.062)	0.02
	58	Sal 87	69.6 (3.22)	19.4 (1.39)	0.017[d] (0.96)	0.02
2–5 years	99	Sal 86	−399.4 (−4.67)	133.0 (7.09)	0.190 (6.44)	0.52
	103	Sal 87	−479.6 (−4.58)	159.3 (7.00)	0.340[d] (9.23)	0.60
>5 years	70	Sal 86	400.5 (2.14)	26.8 (1.51)	0.251 (3.08)	0.14
	70	Sal 87	333.7 (1.50)	30.4 (1.44)	0.404[d] (4.14)	0.22
1987						
All	246	Sal 87	−156.2 (−3.61)	82.6 (14.7)	0.201 (6.71)	0.54
	257	Sal 88	−100.2 (−2.39)	78.2 (13.7)	0.318[e] (10.1)	0.55
<3 years	71	Sal 87	43.0 (2.36)	23.7 (3.10)	0.003 (0.31)	0.09
	92	Sal 88	−0.2 (−0.01)	62.4 (4.59)	0.055[e] (2.81)	0.23
3–5 years	81	Sal 87	−740.4 (−4.30)	182.1 (5.39)	0.271 (7.73)	0.53
	85	Sal 88	−532.0 (−3.00)	159.9 (4.57)	0.375[e] (10.3)	0.60
>5 years	94	Sal 87	319.5 (1.88)	38.7 (2.41)	0.235 (3.76)	0.17
	93	Sal 88	428.2 (2.26)	26.1 (1.46)	0.387[e] (5.59)	0.26
1988						
All	278	Sal 88	−157.2 (−3.27)	78.6 (13.1)	0.267 (7.17)	0.49
	306	Sal 89	−60.4 (−1.35)	71.9 (12.4)	0.385[f] (10.2)	0.51
<3 years	70	Sal 88	−56.4 (−1.65)	61.0 (4.57)	0.055 (3.61)	0.35
	94	Sal 89	−120.5 (−2.39)	100.1 (4.80)	0.164[f] (5.33)	0.38

Table 7-5 *(continued)*

Year and category	N	Dependent variable[b]	Constant (thousands)	Service[c] (thousands)	Marginal revenue product	$\bar{R}^2$
3–5 years	88	Sal 88	−467.8 (−3.16)	139.5 (4.81)	0.207 (5.81)	0.39
	90	Sal 89	−492.3 (−2.40)	160.6 (3.97)	0.475[f] (9.45)	0.54
>5 years	120	Sal 88	269.9 (1.66)	32.3 (2.14)	0.417 (5.54)	0.24
	122	Sal 89	443.6 (2.76)	23.6 (1.57)	0.422[f] (5.68)	0.23
1989 All	277	Sal 89	−82.3 (−1.5)	78.7 (12.1)	0.242 (5.88)	0.42
	280	Sal 90	31.9 (0.57)	65.5 (10.1)	0.499[g] (12.3)	0.52
<3 years	51	Sal 89	40.6 (2.17)	25.5 (3.46)	0.003 (0.26)	0.20
	53	Sal 90	76.9 (2.03)	46.9 (3.10)	0.036[g] (1.56)	0.21
3–5 years	92	Sal 89	−337.2 (−1.73)	124.0 (3.22)	0.222 (5.07)	0.28
	92	Sal 90	−61.2 (−0.22)	96.9 (1.84)	0.520[g] (8.64)	0.45
>5 years	134	Sal 89	470.8 (2.93)	26.6 (1.83)	0.325 (4.20)	0.15
	135	Sal 90	340.4 (2.39)	33.4 (2.61)	0.562[g] (8.39)	0.38

a. Numbers in parentheses are *t*-statistics.
b. Salary and year.
c. The number of years a player's name appeared on the major league roster before the season in question. It does not correspond precisely with the official designation of major league service and hence only roughly indicates whether a player was eligible for salary arbitration (after two years of major league service in 1986 and after three years of service from 1987–90) or for free agency (after six years of major league service).
d. Marginal revenue product in this equation is for 1986.
e. Marginal revenue product in this equation is for 1987.
f. Marginal revenue product in this equation is for 1988.
g. Marginal revenue product in this equation is for 1989.

with no reserve restrictions, called masters (basically those with six or more years of major league service).

For the regressions including all hitters, there is a significant correlation between salary and MRP for 1987–89. The correlation for 1986, however, is insignificant. This is probably a function of the overt collusion among the owners following the 1985 season. There may also have been some disincentive effects for those players who previously looked forward to their free agent bargaining in future seasons.

Table 7-6. *Relationship of Salaries to Marginal Revenue Products*

Year and category[a]	N	Average salary (dollars)	Average marginal revenue product (dollars)	Exploitation[b]
1986				
All	199	459,942	607,628	1.32
<2 years	35	78,786	361,580	4.59
2–5 years	95	322,210	644,612	2.00
>5 years	69	842,914	681,514	0.81
1987				
All	238	486,205	638,962	1.31
<3 years	65	96,708	563,573	5.83
3–5 years	80	351,781	670,492	1.91
>5 years	93	874,068	664,530	0.76
1988				
All	274	527,856	605,948	1.15
<3 years	67	125,044	552,673	4.42
3–5 years	87	339,407	524,415	1.55
>5 years	120	889,385	695,076	0.78
1989				
All	277	629,470	634,514	1.01
<3 years	51	102,471	421,534	4.11
3–5 years	92	420,337	661,643	1.57
>5 years	134	973,628	696,948	0.72

a. See note c, table 7-5.
b. Average marginal revenue product ÷ average salary. Values greater than 1 denote exploitation; values less than 1 denote overpayment.

If MRP were estimated exactly and labor markets functioned efficiently, then the expected results would be a 0 constant term, a 0 coefficient on service, and a coefficient of 1 on MRP. Many factors preclude such a result: imperfectly measured MRP, long-term contracts, minimum salaries, imperfect information, and non-profit-maximizing behavior.

Nonetheless, service and MRP together explain between 42 and 54 percent of the variance in salary, depending on the year. Since the coefficient on MRP is so far below 1 (indeed, in the current-year regressions it is always below 0.4, even for masters), it may be hypothesized that service is picking up some of the MRP. Specifically, my measure of MRP is based solely on on-field performance in the current year, but many players attract fans through stellar performances in previous years. Players with more years of service, the argument might go, have a larger following of loyal fans and, hence, bring more people to the ballpark and more viewers to the television. There is probably some validity to this perspective, but the extent to which service is picking up MRP must be modest. Fans, after all, hold their primary loyalty to teams, not players, and rising young stars can be every bit as exciting as declining old ones.

Generally, the significance of the coefficients on MRP rises appreciably in the lagged specifications. Surely it would rise even more were it not for long-term contracts. This result suggests the importance of imperfect information in the salary determination process. Where contracts permit, next year's salary is more closely correlated with this year's performance than is this year's salary. This result also is testimony to the variability and unpredictability of player performance from one year to the next. It thus provides an insight into the perplexing question of why the era of free agency has not corresponded with dominance by big-city teams. That is, the unpredictability of player performance, inter alia, makes it difficult to buy winning teams.

As expected, there is a strong positive correlation between salary and service for all players. That is, independent of MRP, salaries rise systematically with years of experience. The coefficient on service in the regression for all players is stable over the four years tested, ranging from 78.6 to 82.6. The interpretation of this coefficient is straightforward: in 1986, for instance, each additional year of service brought $82,200 in additional salary.

Within categories, it is not surprising that among apprentices, except for 1988, there is no significant current-year correlation between salary and MRP. Even in the exceptional case, however, the coefficient on MRP suggests salary rises only 5.5 cents for every $1 increase in MRP. Not only are apprentices under reserve, but their preprofessional or minor league records are not always reliable predictors of their proficiency at the major league level. In contrast to the finding reported in Scully, Hirschberg, and Slottje,[32] among journeymen there is a significant relationship between salary and MRP in each year (both current and lagged). Indeed, the *t*-statistics on MRP among journeymen are higher than among masters in every case.[33] It appears that salary arbitration does enforce a salary responsiveness to player performance, whereas long-term contracts among free agents attenuate the incentive linkage between salary and performance. Evidence shown in table 7-6, however, clarifies that, although a systematic link is established between pay and output among

32. Scully and others (1990).
33. The closer correlation between salary and MRP among journeymen than among masters suggests the testing of curvilinear forms in the regressions for all players. Semilog and quadratic forms were tested but were inconclusive.

Table 7-7. *Degree of Exploitation, by Player Category, 1986–89*

Player category	N	Exploitation[a] (percent of players)	High exploitation[b] (percent of players)
Apprentice	255	77.6	71.8
Journeyman	338	66.9	39.9
Master	418	38.5	11.2

a. *MRP/SAL* > 1.
b. *MRP/SAL* > 2.

journeymen, the reserve system for players with less than six years of service preserves the monopoly power of owners who are still able, on average, to pay journeymen below their MRPs.[34]

My estimates in table 7-6 suggest that players on average were paid less than their marginal revenue products in each year from 1986 through 1989, although by the last year the differential was trivial. This result is consistent with the arbitrators' findings of collusion for these years. The appearance of diminishing exploitation, however, is mostly due to a statistical idiosyncrasy in my procedure.[35]

On average, only players under reserve are exploited. Apprentices, without salary arbitration rights, were paid between roughly one-fourth and one-sixth of their net marginal revenue product. Journeymen, with arbitration rights and the imminent prospect of free agency, were paid on average between 50 and 64 percent of their MRP.[36] Masters were paid on average 23.6 percent above their MRP in 1986, 31.5 percent above their MRP in 1987, 28.0 percent above in 1988, and 39.7 percent above in 1989.

Table 7-7 provides a more detailed breakdown on the incidence of exploitation among the players by category. Considering the four years together, more than three-fourths of apprentices were paid below their MRP, and almost three-fourths were paid less than half their MRP. Roughly two-thirds of all journeymen were paid less than their MRP, but fewer than two-fifths were paid less than half their MRP. Finally, over 60 percent of masters were paid more than their MRP.

34. This finding also appears in Scully, Hirschberg, and Slottje (1990).
35. That is, the estimating equations covered all four years, 1986–89, so the resulting coefficients reflected the higher revenues in later years. Hence, the estimates for MRP in 1986 and 1987 are biased upward slightly and those for 1988 and 1989 are biased downward slightly.
36. Of course, as journeymen approach free agency their salary rises dramatically. According to data obtained by the author from the Players Association, in 1989 the average salary for players with zero years of service was $72,977, while it was $121,970 for players with one year of service, $219,114 for two years of service, $398,605 for three years of service, $687,052 for four years of service, and $892,405 for five years of service.

Evaluation of the Estimates

These estimates hinge on the average salary per team. To the extent that the average player on a team is under- or overpaid, my MRP estimates will be too low or too high. What can be said about average team salaries during 1986–89? Given collusion, it is likely that average team salaries were below the average player's marginal revenue product. That is, my MRP estimates are probably too low.

It is difficult to identify an independent standard to allow an assessment of the proximity of average salary and average MRP, but perhaps some sense of this can be inferred from considering the player salary share in team revenues. At the beginning of the 1990 Basic Agreement negotiations, the owners proposed that a salary cap be introduced at 48 percent of defined revenues. Defined revenues denoted all ticket and broadcast revenues; this excluded parking, concessions, and licensing income and amounted to roughly 82 percent of total revenue in 1989.[37] One can estimate, therefore, that 48 percent of defined revenues was equivalent to roughly 39.4 percent of total revenues, including benefits, or 35.3 percent of total revenues, excluding benefits, as shown in table 7-8. The actual average salary share in Major League Baseball, excluding benefits, was 35.3 percent during 1986–89, exactly the same share offered by the owners in the first round. As in all negotiations, the owners would undoubtedly have been willing to go above their opening gambit. This fact, together with the estimate that the salary share rose to 42.9 percent in 1991, when Major League Baseball's profits were healthy, suggests that the average salary was too low (below the average MRP) during 1986–89.[38]

Although the structure of the sports differ, some have suggested a comparison between the player salary share in baseball with that in basketball is appropriate. In basketball there is a 53 percent salary cap. However, there is no professional minor league system, and the 53 percent includes league retirement contributions.[39] In baseball, minor league player development costs approach 13 percent of total revenues. Major League

---

37. David A. Kaplan, "Yet Another Major Mess over Money," *Newsweek*, February 19, 1990, p. 60. Also see Murray Chass, "Owners Offer Revenue-Sharing Deal," *New York Times*, January 11, 1990, p. B12.

38. The 1991 estimated share is based on the active twenty-five-man rosters plus players on the disabled list on August 31, 1991. It excludes benefits.

39. Basketball also allows individual teams to exceed the cap if they are re-signing free agent players from their own team.

Table 7-8. *Salary Share of Team Revenues, Selected Years, 1974–89*

Year	Share (percent)
1974	17.6
1977	20.5
1978	25.1
1979	28.1
1980	31.3
1981	39.1
1982	41.1
1983	41.1
1984	40.3
1985	39.7
1986	40.0
1987	35.2
1988	34.2
1989	31.6

Sources: Scully (1989, p. 118); "Major Leagues Show Record Profit in '89," *USA Today*, November 28, 1990, p. 2C; and data from Players Association.

Baseball pension contributions come to an additional $55 million, or roughly 4 percent of Major League Baseball's total revenues. The baseball owners' proposed cap, then, would put the overall player compensation share higher in baseball than in basketball. Salary shares of total revenue in professional sports in 1990 (considering only the top level of play) were 30 percent in hockey, 33 percent in baseball, 41 percent in football, and 41 percent in basketball.[40]

It is also appropriate to recall that my estimates are based on official revenue figures provided by the teams. To the extent that teams carry more than one set of books or engage in transfer pricing or other strategies that understate their real revenues, my MRP estimates will be too low. The recent suit brought against Marge Schott, general partner of the Cincinnati Reds, by her limited partners heightens suspicions of such practices.

If my MRP estimates are reasonable, why would a franchise owner be willing to pay a player above his marginal revenue product? There are several possible explanations. Perhaps the most obvious is that owners can misgauge a player's worth. This could happen for a number of reasons, including poor judgment, unpredictability of performance (particularly when a change of venue is involved), or pride and competitive pressure. Once a player attains free agent status, the monopoly relationship is in

40. Anthony Baldo and others, "Secrets of the Front Office: What America's Pro Teams Are Worth," *Financial World*, July 9, 1991, pp. 28–43.

many senses reversed. The player under reserve competes with all major and minor league players for his job but can sell his services to only one owner. From the standpoint of an individual owner, however, a free agent often has unique skills fitted for the team's needs. In this case, the player is a monopolist selling his services to competing teams. Even under these circumstances it would still not be in the owner's interests to pay a player above his expected net MRP. Nonetheless, the competitive pressures of the market might well compel risk taking and lead to errors.

A second explanation is that a player's value to a given team may be more than his actual physical product. Winning, of course, is a function of one team's performance relative to the opposing team's performance. By hiring a star, a team is not only buying that player's hits and RBIs but is assuring that its opponents do not benefit from the same. My measure considers the player's value only in what he adds to his team, not what he takes away from the opposing team. The more a player's performance stands out relative to others at his position, the stronger will be this effect.[41]

Another explanation is that owners seek team stability, and in the post-1976 era this necessitates long-term contracts. For tax and other reasons these contracts are usually structured for higher pay in later years. Yet the average player reaches his peak performance years before his contracted salary peaks. Further, many have claimed that long-term contracts reduce a player's motivation to perform and increase his motivation to protect his valuable physical equipment. For instance, during his September 1985 upbraiding of team owners, Lee MacPhail, then head of the Player Relations Committee, claimed that players with contracts for three years or more experienced an increase of almost 50 percent in the amount of time spent on the disabled list compared with those with one-year contracts and an average decline of nearly 20 points in their batting average.[42]

A fourth explanation is that owners may not attempt to maximize profits. If owners are sportsmen, they may satisfice or even accept losses in order to assemble a winning team. A variation on this explanation is that owners may maximize joint profits rather than maximize on their

41. This effect will also be influenced by the degree of revenue sharing among teams and the competitive desire of each league to have a superstar in its league, if not on a particular team. The relationship is further complicated by the eventual onset of diminishing returns from adding star players to a particular team.

42. Cited in Helyar, "How Peter Ueberroth Led the Major Leagues." Also see Lehn (1990).

baseball operations alone. Baseball may be a vehicle to enhance other business ventures. The better a team performs, the more it promotes the individual or corporate owner, and, hence, the more it promotes other activities.

Finally, it may be argued that the worth of an aging star player is greater than his contributions on the field. Such a player may draw fans to the ballpark, whether or not he continues to lead the league in batting or home runs.

I began by asking whether the current system of labor relations in baseball is broken. The absence of data for 1990 and 1991 and the fact that empirical evidence is limited to collusion-affected years do not permit definitive conclusions. What is confirmed by my data is the weak correlation between salary and performance.[43] On the one hand, this points to inequity and inefficiency that cry out for rectification. On the other hand, this weak correlation, along with other factors, probably contributes to the maintenance of competitive balance in the game. If labor market inefficiency and exploitation are necessary to achieve competitive balance, then baseball's current structures are not optimal. Nonetheless, proposals for salary caps (as in basketball) or more extensive revenue sharing (as in football) will probably be rejected by the Players Association or by owners of big-city teams. Owners are currently too divided to challenge the players. It will likely take the catastrophe portended by Commissioner Fay Vincent to effect any significant institutional change.

References

Andreano, Ralph. 1965. *No Joy in Mudville: The Dilemma of Major League Baseball*. Cambridge, Mass.: Schenkman.

Gregory, Paul M. 1956. *The Baseball Player: An Economic Study*. Washington: Public Affairs Press.

43. The measure of performance used in this chapter is, of course, imperfect. Home runs enter slugging percentage as four times more valuable than singles. A single and a walk enter equally. Stolen bases and caught stealing do not figure in my measurement at all. Ryan (1991) has suggested a purer measurement based on Thorn and Palmer (1989). They ran computer simulations of over 100,000 baseball games and estimated the run values of every type of play. For instance, a single is estimated to be worth 0.47 runs, a walk 0.33 runs, a double 0.78 runs, a triple 1.09 runs, and a homer 1.40 runs. I used the "run value" performance measure and came up with similar estimates. The fit of my regressions was not improved.

Hill, James R., and William Spellman. 1983. "Professional Baseball: The Reserve Clause and Salary Structure." *Industrial Relations* 22:1–19.

Kuhn, Bowie. 1988. *Hardball: The Education of a Baseball Commissioner*. McGraw-Hill.

Lehn, Kenneth. 1990. "Property Rights, Risk Sharing and Player Disability in Major League Baseball." In *Sportometrics*, edited by Brian L. Goff and Robert D. Tollison, 35–38. Texas A & M University Press.

Major League Baseball. 1985. Arbitration Panel. Panel Decision 66. Grievance 83-1.

———. 1988. Arbitration Panel. Decision on Grievance 87-3.

———. 1989. Arbitration Panel. Present Status of the Disposition on Grievance 86-2.

———. 1990a. Arbitration Panel. Remedial Reward on Grievance 87-3.

———. 1990b. Arbitration Panel. Decision on Grievance 88-1.

Rottenberg, Simon. 1956. "The Baseball Players' Labor Market." *Journal of Political Economy* 64:242–58.

Ryan, Kevin. 1991. "Pay and Performance Research in Major League Baseball." Middlebury College, Department of Economics.

Scully, Gerald W. 1974. "Pay and Performance in Major League Baseball." *American Economic Review* 64:915–30.

———. 1989. *The Business of Major League Baseball*. University of Chicago Press.

Scully, Gerald W., Joseph Hirschberg, and Daniel Slottje. 1990. "A Test of the Efficient Labor Market Hypothesis: The Case of Major League Baseball." University of Texas, School of Management.

Sommers, Paul M., and Noel Quinton. 1982. "Pay and Performance in Major League Baseball: The Case of the First Family of Free Agents." *Journal of Human Resources* 17:426–36.

Thorn, John, and Pete Palmer with David Reuther, eds. 1989. *Total Baseball*. Warner Books.

CHAPTER EIGHT

Pay and Performance: Is the Field of Dreams Barren?

Rodney Fort

Sᴛʏʟᴠᴇsᴛᴇʀ sᴛᴀʟʟᴏɴᴇ reportedly received $20 million for *Rocky V*, Jack Nicholson $11 million for *Batman*, Arnold Schwarzenegger $10 million for *Total Recall*, Tom Cruise $8 million for *Days of Thunder*, and Bruce Willis $7 million for *Die Hard II*. Meryl Streep reportedly is paid $5 million per picture, and Cher, Sigourney Weaver, Jane Fonda, Sally Field, and Michelle Pfeiffer are in the $3 million to $5 million range. In another entertainment field, Janet Jackson recently contracted with Virgin Records: she received $15 million to sign, $5 million for the first record, and $6 million for records two and three (with performance clauses, the payment per record would be closer to $10 million). That these figures are not a cause for public concern is borne out by where they can be found: inside the entertainment section of the newspaper.

If the level of discussion about salaries in movies and popular music is a murmur, then it is a high-pitched scream in another entertainment area, Major League Baseball. At age 28, Boston Red Sox pitcher Roger Clemens became the highest paid player in baseball history. In 1991 he signed a four-year contract for $21.5 million, exceeding the historical record paid for an entire team by over $400,000, when Nelson Doubleday purchased the New York Mets in 1980.[1] Clemens's salary clearly is not in the same league as the incomes of the other entertainers listed above, yet the Major League Baseball salary level has elicited the following comments: "The current system (of escalation of players' salaries and lack of revenue sharing) is a prescription for disaster. But whether the disaster is just around the corner or will take place 10 years from now, I don't

---

1. Joseph Durso, "Group Led by Doubleday Buys Mets for a Reported $21 Million," *New York Times*, January 25, 1980, p. A1.

know."[2] "No rational person can view what's going on in baseball and not have concerns."[3] "No one foresaw what was coming in salaries. Not the players. Not the management. I always had thought I'd be an Oakland A for my whole career, that I'd end like Al Kaline or Brooks Robinson. That just isn't going to happen anymore. It's sad, bad for baseball, but it's the truth."[4]

Why baseball somehow is considered different from other entertainment fields and deserving of more concern is under discussion here. In this chapter I analyze salary determination, because the explosion in salaries is interesting in its own right, because it leads to new, interesting questions. The results of my salary determination study make it clear that the field of dreams continues to provide fertile soil for economists interested in a variety of labor and industrial organization questions.

The bulk of studies on the salary process in Major League Baseball has sought to determine its distributional impacts, for example, monopsony exploitation and racial discrimination, with little attention to the determinants themselves, especially over time. The exception is work on the effects of free agency on the process, although the effort was still aimed at determining whether player earnings more closely approximated marginal revenue products after players obtained free agency.[5] In a nonrigorous way, this chapter examines changes in the salary process over a broader time span. My aim is to provide a basis for more rigorous and thorough investigations into the behavior of the Major League Baseball salary process itself over time, including the periods of both the reserve clause and free agency.

In addition, the distribution of salary wealth in Major League Baseball receives brief treatment. Much work has been done about the distribution of salaries between owners and players,[6] under the reserve clause and after free agency, and between players of different races.[7] Little is known,

2. Deputy Commissioner Steve Greenberg, quoted in Dave Nightingale, "Baseball," *Sporting News*, December 31, 1990, p. 29.

3. Commissioner Fay Vincent, quoted in "Contracts Bug Vincent," *Spokesman-Review and Chronicle* (Spokane), February 12, 1991, p. C1.

4. Reggie Jackson, highest paid of the first crop of 1976 free agents at $3 million over five years, quoted in Leigh Montville, "The First to Be Free," *Sports Illustrated*, April 16, 1990, p. 114.

5. Cymrot (1983); Hill (1985); Hill and Spellman (1983, 1984); Raimondo (1983); Sommers and Quinton (1982).

6. El-Hodiri and Quirk (1971); Gwartney and Haworth (1974); Medoff (1976); Neale (1964); Rottenberg (1956); Scully (1974b, 1989).

7. Madura (1980); Medoff (1975, 1986); Mogull (1981); Pascal and Rapping (1972); Scully (1973, 1974a).

however, about the overall distribution of salaries among players. Always an interesting economic question is the degree of equality of the wealth distribution that results from any labor market. Looking directly at the salary distribution provides insight into competing predictions about the distributional effects of labor market institutions (such as union activity).

This chapter is based on a substantial data set, which covers salaries from 1965 to 1976 and 1986 to 1990. For the reserve clause period (1965–74), salaries are taken from a player sample dramatically different from those used in past studies. The data were collected by agents of the Internal Revenue Service and employees of the American League office, in connection with *Selig* v. *U.S.*[8] The data were painstakingly verified by the IRS because they were used in litigation.[9]

Salary Determination Revisited

I first apply an amended version of a well-established salary model to an extended time period to ascertain which determinants of the process are associated with the dramatic rise in Major League Baseball salaries. This information will provide a launching pad for future, more rigorous, analysis of the Major League Baseball salary process over time.

The Major League Baseball player labor market has been extensively studied and the connection between the performance of athletes and their salaries convincingly demonstrated. This chapter proceeds under the assumption that teams seek to maximize profits.[10] Evidence supports the proposition that most teams maximize profits, though a few are more aptly described as maximizing victories subject to a break-even constraint. Tom Yawkey's ownership of the Boston Red Sox from 1933 to 1976 fits this latter description.

The theoretical argument relating pay and performance can be summarized as follows. Following the rule in economics that actions are undertaken until the marginal benefits equal the marginal costs, the most

8. *Alan Selig* v. *U.S.*, 565 F. Supp. 524 (1983), 740 F.2d 572 (1984).

9. I thank Rich Hill at Central Michigan University for data from the immediate free agency period (1975–76) and Phil Porter at the University of South Florida for some of the more modern data.

10. Of course, this view must be modified in the case of "superstation" teams, which contribute to the overall profitability of a television production unit (most notably, Ted Turner's Atlanta Braves).

that profit-maximizing teams will be willing to pay players is their marginal contribution to team revenues, referred to as marginal revenue product (MRP). Certainly, the structure of input markets allowing, employers would like to pay less than MRP. The demand for baseball talent inputs, then, is derived from their contribution to team revenues, but salaries actually earned will depend on the level of competition for inputs. The greater the level of competition, the tighter the relationship between pay and MRP. When there is market power in inputs, players are paid less than their MRP. The stronger the market power over inputs, the larger is MRP over input price and the weaker the relationship between pay and performance.

Before 1974, the reserve clause generated monopsony power over all baseball players. Afterward, during the free agency period, Major League Baseball teams' monopsony power was preserved over players with less than six years of experience, especially players with less than three years of experience, because these players are ineligible even for salary arbitration. Other structural changes have had effects; however, nothing has had a greater impact on Major League Baseball salaries than the demise of the reserve clause. Free agency eventually had an effect on Major League Baseball salaries similar to that of the demise of "contract players" on the salaries of movie stars.

A Model of Salary Determination

There are two types of models of the salary process, the one just described, based on profit maximization, and one that can be referred to as the "Bill James model." The latter would be useful in the context of input payments if the goal of teams were to maximize wins. However, even if teams maximize wins, the profit constraint on their behavior limits the usefulness of such a model. To the extent that teams do not maximize wins, the Bill James model becomes less useful than profit-maximization models.

From the theory, profit maximizers pay, at most, a player's MRP, which is determined by two considerations, the player's marginal product (contribution to close contests and winning) and the price of output (revenue sources, including television, gate, and concessions). Thus salary at time t depends on performance up to time $t - 1$, that is, "last season." (A baseball season begins at the start of the baseball fiscal year, October 1, approximately the end of the preceding season.)

Gerald Scully's seminal work provides the benchmark model for analysis of Major League Baseball salaries.[11] The major explanatory variables include a measure of playing time, on-field performance, age, and experience. The playing time, performance, and experience variables are meant to capture the marginal productivity of the player, one of the components in the player's MRP.

Another important distinction in the salary process is between "stars" and other players. The stars' MRPs are dramatically different from those of other players.[12] Thus the relationship between pay and performance may be nonlinear. In Scully's original work, a log-log structure was used.[13] The benefit of this is that estimated coefficients are elasticities, but the shortcoming is that elasticities do not vary across playing time and performance levels. In a more recent work, Scully related the logarithm of salary to raw performance variables so that the elasticities vary with the independent variables.[14] In the work that follows, a particular type of log-log framework is applied so that the elasticities can vary.

All previous attempts at widening the repertoire of performance variables have reached the same conclusion: the variables are so highly correlated that, once a few are included, more variables provide little additional explanation. Typically, playing time seems to capture a large part of the performance explanation because a rational team will give the most playing time to players contributing most to the team.

Despite this, a few areas of improvement in the specification of the salary process that seem important have not been tried.[15] The first is distinguishing different types of hitters and pitchers. Relief pitchers play a distinct role from starting pitchers. Playing time gives undue weight to starters. Correcting for starting appearances by using the ratio of starts to total appearances should lower the value of starters relative to relievers. Second, less experienced, perhaps less talented players ("hopefuls" and "rookies") must be considered different from other players. A hopeful can be distinguished by lack of playing time and experience (less than five years on a major league roster and less than forty at bats in any season for hitters or less than thirty innings pitched in any season for pitchers). A rookie, then, is a nonhopeful who just completed his first

11. Scully (1974b).

12. To see this, one need only look at the impact on attendance of particular pitchers, such as Nolan Ryan during his 3,000-strikeout run in 1990.

13. Scully (1974b).

14. Scully (1989).

15. Fort and Noll (1984).

year in the majors. Although coefficient estimates are sensitive to these conventions, these players might be lost in the shuffle due to low levels of on-field performance, age, and experience.

Third, much can be learned by unfolding the intricacies of the relationship between age and experience. First, there is no reason to suspect age enters the process linearly (or linearly in logarithms). Age has more pronounced effects early and late in a player's career and less in the middle years. Furthermore, age and experience typically are closely related. Experience is thought to improve performance, especially early in a player's career; for two players of equal age, the player with more experience can be expected to perform better.

To handle the nonlinear effect, age is used in deviation from mean form, separating players of above- and below-average ages. In addition, the squares of these deviations from the mean age are included. To untangle the age-experience relationship, experience is represented by the residual of a regression of experience on age. Residual experience captures the independent effect of experience that is not explained by age.

A fourth consideration is that recent performance receives different weight than career performance. For variables that measure playing time, a substantial change from career averages can occur because of injuries that have a bearing on a player's long-run abilities. Poor players may get more playing time in a given season because of an injury to a regular in the starting lineup, or a starting regular may be out of the lineup temporarily because of injury.

Finally, the structure of free agency can be incorporated as follows. Players with less than three years of experience are ineligible for arbitration, whereas players with three to five years are eligible for arbitration. After six years, free agency is available. To control for this structure, dummy variables were defined to designate players in each category, that is, a variable equal to 1 for players with less than three years in the majors, as well as a variable for those non–free agents eligible for arbitration. In the dummy variable scheme, eligible free agents represent the omitted category.

Other variables were tried but were found lacking in empirical content. An attempt to model "banjo hitters" (high batting average, but low slugging percentage) based on underlying regressions of slugging on batting average was as unsuccessful as Scully's original dummy variable technique.[16] In the same way that recent departures from career playing time

16. Scully (1974b).

were developed, departures in on-field performance variables were un-revealing.

Results

A complete description of the derivation of all explanatory variables can be found in appendix table 8-A. Underlying regressions used in deriving the experience residual variables appear in appendix table 8-B. Tables 8-1 and 8-2 show the results of estimating the salary equation for 1965–74 and 1986–90.[17] Identifying two distinct periods, one before free agency and one after the effects of free agency have been sorted out, should facilitate the intertemporal comparison of the process.

Before turning to an intertemporal look at the salary determination results, it is worth examining the model's veracity. The model compares favorably with Scully's previous work, and the new variables just detailed provide additional insights. The playing time and performance variables always behave as expected, generally in a significant fashion. Once specified, the data make it obvious that the importance of starting pitchers in the salary process has been overblown. The lower the ratio of lifetime starts to lifetime total games, the higher the salary, indicating a bonus for relief pitchers, generally. Playing-time departures from historical averages have a predictable and statistically significant impact for hitters. For pitchers, the effects are not significant nearly as often, and a salary decrement for decreased playing time occurs twice as often as an increment for increased time. An interesting puzzle is the positive sign for decreased playing time in 1988. The remaining extensions are interesting primarily in intertemporal comparison, to which I now turn.

The intertemporal comparison will proceed in two parts, qualitative and quantitative (the latter requiring the calculation of elasticities), facilitated by the distance between the two time periods analyzed. Judging from tables 8-1 and 8-2, the qualitative effects of playing time are consistent over time, but performance variables are much more sporadic. Variables that capture playing-time departure from historical averages also are sporadically significant; sometimes such departures matter and sometimes they do not. Such variation in significance over time is some

---

17. The earlier sample uses all available salary observations, whereas the latter sample uses a randomly selected subsample of 200 players for each year.

evidence of the tenuous relationship between salary ("pay") and MRP ("performance") over time.

The decomposition of age picks off a recurrent effect, but primarily for the youngest players ($YOUNG^2$) and more often in the past than in the recent salary process (only one in the five most recent years, but in nine of the ten earlier years). When statistically significant, experience residuals influence earnings just as expected. The pattern over time is interesting. From 1965 to 1974 positive residuals earned their bonus, but negative residuals were not consistently penalized (negative and significant in 1966 and 1971–73). In the 1986–90 period (except in 1988), effects are revealed exclusively in salary decrements for players with less experience than their age would indicate. The disappearance of rewards to positive experience residuals after free agency begs structural explanations beyond the scope of this work. For example, players with less experience than their age would indicate would receive "reserve clause treatment" under modern structural arrangements concerning those not eligible for free agency. The absence of an experience bonus seems likely to be due to the escalation in salaries for experienced players in the free agency period.

Finally, distinguishing between types of players (hopefuls, rookies, players with no last year, and the arbitration-eligible non–free agents, in the more recent period) provides some interesting insights. In the 1965–74 period, hopefuls and rookies typically received a small salary increment relative to their peers and, toward the end of the period, players with no last year received a statistically detectable salary decrement. But in the 1986–90 period, the "bonus" for rookies disappears completely, and no effect for players without a preceding year is detected.

Discussion of the two types of players ineligible for free agency must be restricted to the 1986–90 period. As should be expected, relative to the eligible free agent population, other players receive salary decrements, and, just as predictably, lower decrements occur for the arbitration eligible. This discount does not appear in 1986, also the infamous year of collusion among Major League Baseball owners. Any connection between the two, however, would rely on an argument that the owners, while attempting to keep free agent salaries down, allowed the salaries of the institutionally "salary handicapped" to increase relative to other years. This strains credibility. An answer to this puzzle awaits further study.

Turning to a quantitative examination of the Major League Baseball salary process requires the computation of elasticities. The elasticities in tables 8-3 (the reserve clause period) and 8-4 (the free agency period) are

Table 8-1. *Determinants of Major League Baseball Salaries, 1965–74*[a]

Variable[b]	1965	1966	1967	1968	1969	1970	1971	1972	1973	1974
AT BATS	9.31	7.39	11.0	11.1	11.8	10.9	10.6	11.1	13.4	13.9
	(1.71)*	(2.21)*	(1.90)*	(2.04)*	(2.12)*	(1.42)*	(1.49)*	(1.57)*	(1.58)*	(1.67)*
SLUG	1.99	1.72	0.904	1.13	0.414	1.90	1.43	2.19	1.73	2.88
	(0.610)*	(0.646)*	(0.655)	(0.853)	(0.872)	(0.570)*	(0.491)*	(0.511)*	(0.535)*	(0.533)*
AT BATS+	3.07	2.10	-0.809	8.63	8.20	3.00	1.48	4.48	1.14	2.12
	(2.81)	(2.48)	(2.46)	(3.68)*	(4.26)*	(2.04)	(2.26)	(2.74)	(2.52)	(2.61)
AT BATS-	-10.8	0.356	-4.79	-5.85	-9.07	-4.35	-4.08	-3.99	-6.10	-11.5
	(3.55)*	(3.17)	(3.12)	(3.87)*	(4.74)*	(2.52)*	(3.06)	(3.75)	(2.42)*	(3.01)*
IP	9.32	10.	13.0	11.0	9.04	12.9	14.3	10.7	11.2	12.2
	(1.43)*	(1.84)*	(1.73)*	(2.46)*	(2.22)*	(1.58)*	(1.66)*	(1.82)*	(1.60)*	(1.78)*
SW	0.365	0.308	0.085	0.331	0.196	0.339	0.317	0.777	0.712	0.517
	(0.177)*	(0.201)	(0.189)	(0.242)	(0.250)	(0.160)*	(0.121)*	(0.185)*	(0.175)*	(0.174)*
STARTER	-0.299	-0.638	-1.19	-0.769	-0.739	-0.679	-1.24	-0.615	-0.811	-0.964
	(0.264)	(0.258)*	(0.244)*	(0.347)*	(0.289)*	(0.218)*	(0.285)*	(0.234)*	(0.233)*	(0.246)*
IP+	0.638	-0.190	2.51	-0.476	1.28	0.130	3.02	1.87	4.05	6.13
	(2.05)	(1.78)	(2.24)	(3.64)	(2.49)	(1.69)	(2.09)	(1.94)	(2.23)*	(2.02)*
IP-	-2.28	-5.61	-3.98	-2.37	-1.05	-4.55	-0.538	-5.56	-2.79	1.67
	(1.92)	(2.35)*	(2.53)	(3.39)	(2.80)	(2.69)*	(2.37)	(2.17)*	(2.31)	(1.91)
OLD	0.129	0.278	-0.268	-0.046	0.039	-0.042	-0.115	-0.005	0.333	0.135
	(0.166)	(0.196)	(0.154)*	(0.152)	(0.196)	(0.168)	(0.160)	(0.155)	(0.162)*	(0.142)
OLD^2	-0.006	-0.075	0.178	0.095	0.042	0.046	0.085	0.069	-0.103	-0.015
	(0.065)	(0.084)	(0.067)*	(0.065)	(0.074)	(0.070)	(0.066)	(0.067)	(0.065)	(0.055)

YOUNG	0.368	0.123	0.058	0.324	0.343	0.089	-0.020	0.116	-0.265	0.253
	(0.186)*	(0.194)	(0.156)	(0.177)*	(0.232)	(0.175)	(0.189)	(0.169)	(0.187)	(0.174)
YOUNG^2	-0.337	-0.200	-0.154	-0.282	-0.344	-0.151	-0.122	-0.182	-0.240	-0.253
	(0.079)*	(0.088)*	(0.076)*	(0.091)*	(0.107)*	(0.083)*	(0.093)	(0.081)*	(0.088)*	(0.083)*
EXPER. RESID +	0.141	0.139	0.233	0.238	0.231	0.234	0.173	0.128	0.092	0.172
	(0.056)*	(0.061)*	(0.057)*	(0.062)*	(0.058)*	(0.042)*	(0.049)*	(0.050)*	(0.052)*	(0.051)*
EXPER. RESID –	-0.086	-0.187	-0.062	-0.107	-0.071	-0.002	-0.171	-0.124	-0.134	0.022
	(0.066)	(0.077)*	(0.066)	(0.071)	(0.073)	(0.050)	(0.056)*	(0.053)*	(0.055)*	(0.052)
HOPEFUL	0.378	0.328	0.073	0.249	0.134	0.321	0.365	0.632	0.537	0.779
	(0.174)*	(0.187)*	(0.164)	(0.220)	(0.222)	(0.138)*	(0.133)*	(0.143)*	(0.142)*	(0.146)*
ROOKIE	0.533	0.662	0.332	0.640	0.615	0.692	0.676	0.823	0.920	1.26
	(0.202)*	(0.248)*	(0.248)	(0.240)*	(0.241)*	(0.151)*	(0.142)*	(0.170)*	(0.171)*	(0.218)*
NO LAST YEAR	-0.106	-0.055	-0.095	0.020	-0.132	-0.120	-0.121	-0.194	-0.201	-0.350
	(0.072)	(0.092)	(0.078)	(0.120)	(0.084)	(0.072)*	(0.071)*	(0.063)*	(0.071)*	(0.085)*
PITCHER	0.053	0.212	0.139	0.080	0.129	0.112	-0.029	-0.090	-0.094	0.353
	(0.068)	(0.120)*	(0.084)*	(0.114)	(0.099)	(0.077)	(0.077)	(0.076)	(0.084)	(0.094)*
Constant	9.72	9.90	10.1	9.93	10.2	9.82	10.2	9.85	9.90	9.53
	(0.201)*	(0.211)*	(0.186)*	(0.242)*	(0.243)*	(0.161)*	(0.159)*	(0.166)*	(0.175)*	(0.158)*
R^2	0.913	0.855	0.861	0.828	0.788	0.854	0.839	0.848	0.850	0.901
$\bar{R}^2$	0.899	0.828	0.841	0.797	0.764	0.837	0.821	0.833	0.836	0.889
DF	119	99	131	105	171	157	174	197	195	153
RSS	5.95	6.26	8.58	8.59	19.5	8.80	11.8	14.1	14.6	8.95

*Significant at the 0.05 level (2-tail for the constant and 1-tail for the remaining coefficient estimates).
a. Numbers in parentheses are standard errors.
b. See table 8-A for definitions.

Table 8-2. Determinants of Major League Baseball Salaries, 1986–90[a]

Variable[b]	1986	1987	1988	1989	1990
AT BATS	20.4	19.0	22.5	21.7	17.5
	(1.98)*	(1.78)*	(1.73)*	(2.07)*	(1.62)*
SLUG	0.872	0.194	2.68	1.93	2.63
	(0.897)	(0.328)	(0.332)*	(0.883)*	(0.695)*
AT BATS+	11.4	7.27	2.63	4.37	5.76
	(3.65)*	(3.07)*	(3.03)	(3.30)	(2.63)*
AT BATS−	−10.1	−7.49	−6.85	−16.9	−15.9
	(3.92)*	(5.05)	(3.80)*	(3.98)*	(1.73)*
IP	14.6	18.6	17.8	15.4	16.1
	(1.87)*	(2.60)*	(2.02)*	(2.24)*	(2.09)*
SW	0.773	0.312	1.03	1.05	0.860
	(0.242)*	(0.224)	(0.242)*	(0.226)*	(0.212)*
STARTER	−0.555	−1.19	−0.737	−0.716	−0.630
	(0.252)*	(0.328)*	(0.230)*	(0.284)*	(0.260)*
IP+	−1.04	4.27	4.76	1.62	2.43
	(2.70)	(3.11)	(2.86)*	(2.84)	(2.49)
IP−	−10.4	−2.49	8.32	−5.19	−3.89
	(1.77)*	(4.34)	(3.26)*	(3.02)*	(3.02)
OLD	0.251	0.448	0.068	0.169	0.162
	(0.211)	(0.246)*	(0.246)	(0.234)	(0.214)
OLD^2	−0.094	−0.212	−0.067	−0.086	−0.015
	(0.080)	(0.089)*	(0.105)	(0.087)	(0.083)
YOUNG	−0.390	0.116	−0.425	−0.485	0.012
	(0.250)	(0.287)	(0.238)*	(0.221)*	(0.235)
YOUNG^2	−0.026	−0.263	0.123	0.098	−0.118
	(0.123)	(0.141)*	(0.112)	(0.116)	(0.117)

EXPER. RESID+	0.036	0.097	−0.072	0.055	0.020
	(0.083)	(0.087)	(0.072)	(0.079)	(0.075)
EXPER. RESID−	−0.446	−0.287	0.040	−0.333	−0.156
	(0.102)*	(0.100)*	(0.067)	(0.091)*	(0.091)*
HOPEFUL	0.568	0.341	1.23	1.14	1.01
	(0.296)*	(0.198)*	(0.351)*	(0.272)*	(0.270)*
ROOKIE	0.084	0.299	0.118	−0.044	0.047
	(0.181)	(0.194)	(0.287)	(0.183)	(0.252)
NO LAST YEAR	0.098	0.192	0.160	−0.070	0.145
	(0.144)	(0.250)	(0.230)	(0.142)	(0.206)
PITCHER	−0.126	−0.075	−0.123	0.027	0.119
	(0.147)	(0.194)	(0.215)	(0.151)	(0.152)
Constant	11.6	11.7	11.0	11.3	11.3
	(0.305)*	(0.226)*	(0.283)*	(0.276)*	(0.250)*
NOARB	−0.277	−0.691	−1.11	−0.744	−0.782
	(0.201)	(0.206)*	(0.127)*	(0.186)*	(0.176)*
ARBNOFA	−0.107	−0.409	−0.499	−0.318	−0.460
	(0.140)	(0.136)*	(0.108)*	(0.127)*	(0.119)*
R^2	0.855	0.843	0.866	0.877	0.879
$\bar{R}^2$	0.838	0.824	0.850	0.863	0.865
DF	178	178	178	178	177
RSS	31.9	32.6	28.2	27.1	25.9

*Significant at the 0.05 level (2-tail for the constant and 1-tail for the remaining coefficient estimates).
a. Numbers in parentheses are standard errors.
b. See table 8-A for definitions.

Table 8-3. Elasticities over Time, 1965–74

Variable	Range	Scully 1968–69	Current sample									
			1965	1966	1967	1968	1969	1970	1971	1972	1973	1974
BATS[a]	0.02	0.28	0.18	0.15	0.22	0.22	0.23	0.21	0.21	0.22	0.26	0.27
	0.05	...	0.44	0.35	0.52	0.53	0.56	0.52	0.51	0.53	0.64	0.66
	0.08	...	0.69	0.55	0.82	0.82	0.87	0.81	0.79	0.82	0.99	1.03
SLUG[b]	0.30	1.07	0.46	0.40	...	...	...	0.44	0.33	0.51	0.40	0.67
	0.40	...	0.57	0.49	...	...	...	0.54	0.41	0.63	0.49	0.82
	0.50	...	0.66	0.57	...	...	...	0.63	0.48	0.73	0.58	0.96
IP[c]	0.03	0.97	0.27	0.29	0.38	0.32	0.26	0.38	0.42	0.31	0.33	0.36
	0.09	...	0.77	0.83	1.07	0.91	0.75	1.06	1.18	0.88	0.93	1.01
	0.15	...	1.22	1.31	1.70	1.43	1.18	1.68	1.86	1.40	1.46	1.59
SW[d]	0.75	0.81	0.16	...	...	...	...	0.15	0.14	0.33	0.31	0.22
	1.50	...	0.22	...	...	...	...	0.20	0.19	0.47	0.43	0.31
	2.00	...	0.24	...	...	...	...	0.23	0.21	0.52	0.48	0.35

a. Hitter playing time.
b. Lifetime slugging average for hitters.
c. Pitcher playing time.
d. Strikeout-to-walk ratio for pitchers.

Table 8-4. Elasticities over Time, 1986–90

Variable	Range	Scully[a]		Current sample				
		1986	1987	1986	1987	1988	1989	1990
BATS[b]	0.02	0.35	0.29	0.40	0.37	0.44	0.42	0.34
	0.05	0.88	0.73	0.97	0.90	1.07	1.03	0.83
	0.08	1.41	1.17	1.51	1.41	1.66	1.61	1.30
SLUG[c]	0.30	0.57	0.98	...	...	0.62	0.44	0.61
	0.40	0.76	1.30	...	...	0.77	0.55	0.75
	0.50	0.95	1.62	...	...	0.89	0.64	0.88
IP[d]	0.03	0.30	0.22	0.42	0.54	0.52	0.45	0.47
	0.09	0.90	0.66	1.21	1.54	1.47	1.27	1.33
	0.15	1.50	1.10	1.90	2.43	2.32	2.01	2.10
SW[e]	0.75	0.17	0.14	0.33	...	0.44	0.45	0.37
	1.50	0.34	0.28	0.46	...	0.62	0.63	0.52
	2.00	0.46	0.38	0.52	...	0.69	0.70	0.57

a. Scully's estimated coefficients are as follows: 1986, BATS = 17.6, SLUG = 1.90, IP = 10.0, SW = 0.23; 1987, BATS = 14.6, SLUG = 3.25, IP = 7.32, SW = 0.19. Scully (1989).
b. Hitter playing time.
c. Lifetime slugging average for hitters.
d. Pitcher playing time.
e. Strikeout-to-walk ratio for pitchers.

derived in three ways. Let ε = elasticity, S = salary, X = an independent variable, and b represent an estimated parameter. First, Scully's original elasticities (table 8-3) are from regressions of the form $\log S = b \log X$.[18] Raising both sides by the exponential function and taking derivatives directly gives $\varepsilon = b$ (which does not vary with the level of the independent variable). Second, Scully's more recent work on 1986 and 1987 salaries used the form $\log S = bX$.[19] Some simple algebra (raise both sides by the exponential function, take the derivative with respect to X and recognize that $S = e^{bX}$) yields $\varepsilon = bX$ so that elasticities (table 8-4) do vary with the level of the independent variables. In the work here, many of the variables required transformation by adding 1. The elasticity with respect to X is computed as follows. Starting with the form $\log S = b \log (X + 1)$, after applying the exponential function to both sides, one finds that $S = (X + 1)^b$. Taking the partial derivative with respect to X, multiplying both sides by X/S, and recalling that $S = (X + 1)^b$, the result is that $\varepsilon = b\,[X/(X + 1)]$. Thus elasticities vary with levels of the continuous independent variables. For the dummy variables, the coefficients are directly interpreted in percentage change terms and are constant because they represent movements in the intercept of the regression line.

In tables 8-3 and 8-4, the ranges of independent variables chosen for playing time and performance run the gamut from reserves to regulars and reflect the variety of major league ability. Table 8-3 shows that playing-time elasticities reported here are comparable to Scully's findings in the same period for both hitters and pitchers.[20] However, Scully's performance elasticities apply only to superstars. For the free agency period, elasticities are close to Scully's,[21] but are typically larger here.

The elasticity calculations in tables 8-3 and 8-4 reveal no general trends in the determinants of Major League Baseball salaries. Turning first to the 1965–74 period, except for star pitchers' playing time, salary responses all are inelastic with respect to the variables in table 8-3. A barely perceptible increase in elasticities for playing time and on-field performance is apparent in the reserve clause period for hitters but not for pitchers. In the 1986–90 period, salary is generally more elastic with respect to playing time and on-field performance variables, but no trends are apparent. The magnitude of playing-time elasticities rose and fell around 1988 for hitters and 1987 for pitchers. Over the past three years, per-

18. Scully (1974b).
19. Scully (1989).
20. Scully (1974b).
21. Scully (1989).

formance effects dipped in 1989 for hitters but peaked in that year for pitchers.

For the dummy variables, it already has been observed that rookie bonuses have disappeared in the modern period. There appears to be no pattern in the treatment of hopefuls. Except for 1986, when there was no effect, non–free agents are discounted relative to free agents and those ineligible for arbitration at nearly twice the rate of those non–free agents who are arbitration eligible.

Thus, the clearest quantitative result is simply that the magnitude of most Major League Baseball salary determinants has been rising over time. Typically, the lowest levels in the free agency period exceed the highest levels during the reserve clause period. At least two explanations for this come to mind: (1) a redistribution of salary wealth from owners to players, tightening the relationship between salary and MRP, and (2) an increase in the demand for Major League Baseball output over time. Events in Major League Baseball support either of these explanations: free agency and the formation of the Major League Baseball Players Union support the first explanation, and the rise in sale value of major league franchises, evidenced also by the $95 million price tag for 1993 expansion teams, supports the second. Only more work can determine the relative importance of each set of events. However, from this analysis, it is clear that the explanation does not rest with changes in player talent, performance, or experience.

Salary Distribution in Major League Baseball

That owners exploited players, in the sense of holding a monopsony, more completely during the reserve clause period than they have since free agency tells of the distribution of baseball wealth between owners and players. The fact that racial factors have entered into the Major League Baseball salary process reveals another facet of the distribution among players. No general study, however, has appeared about the distribution of salary wealth among players. I aim here to remedy this situation. The analysis of the salary distribution has implications for the process that produces it.

The salary distribution can be thought to depend on the distribution of playing talent and the institutional settings of the Major League Baseball salary process. Scully convincingly demonstrates that the level of offensive and defensive performance in baseball has been affected by changes in playing rules.[22] Offensive performance has improved, and pitching performance has been relatively stable, except for increases in earned run average, over the sample period of interest here. But relevant to the distribution of the returns to talent is the *distribution* of that playing talent. Indeed, the interesting question from this perspective is whether salary distribution, and how it changes over time, is consistent with the distribution of performance and its changes over time.

Equally important are alterations in institutional arrangements, such as the rise of unionism in Major League Baseball. At least two competing theories can be applied when examining the impact of a union on salary distribution. First, unions could work to better the economic welfare of all members and to tighten the relationship between pay and MRP. A competing theory, drawn from the public choice literature, considers a union just another form of representative government. As such, it is subject to special interest effects generated by the rational ignorance and consequent low participation rates of its rank-and-file members. The result is the exploitation both of rational ignorance and of those who do not participate to better the positions of those who do participate, presumably those with the highest salaries. The dispersion of money between the richer and poorer players is intimately tied to both the distribution of talent and the institutions surrounding the Major League Baseball salary determination process. Knowledge of it may point out flaws in the designs of these institutions or the labor negotiation process.

An analysis of the overall salary distribution in Major League Baseball provides insight into the following statement by a well-known baseball agent, Tom Reich: "I believe revenue sharing between players and owners—a salary cap, if you will—is going to be necessary if baseball is to remain financially viable, because the smaller-market teams are going to have major problems in another couple of years down the road."[23] But if salaries are *more* unequal under a cap, then this simply is a self-serving argument for higher commissions for player agents who represent high-priced players.

The first distributional issue to be addressed is the location of the salary distribution over time. Have salaries been rising or falling? Minimum and average salaries over time are shown in table 8-5. Clearly, both have been on the rise, even in real terms. Coupled with the knowledge

22. Scully (1989).
23. The quote is from Nightingale, "Baseball." According to Nightingale, Reich represents Willie McGee, Jack Clark, and Tim Raines.

Table 8-5. *Reported Minimum and Average Salaries in Major League Baseball, Selected Years, 1950–90*
Dollars

Year	Minimum		Average		
	Staudohar[a]	Others[b]	Staudohar	Scully[c]	Others[d]
1950	. . .	. . .	. . .	. . .	11,000
1951	. . .	. . .	. . .	13,300	. . .
1964	. . .	6,000	. . .	. . .	. . .
1965	. . .	6,000	. . .	. . .	. . .
1966	. . .	6,000	. . .	. . .	. . .
1967	. . .	6,000	. . .	19,000	. . .
1968	. . .	7,000	. . .	. . .	. . .
1969	. . .	10,000	. . .	. . .	24,909
1970	12,000	. . .	29,303	. . .	29,303
1971	12,750	. . .	31,543	. . .	31,543
1972	13,500	. . .	34,092	. . .	34,092
1973	15,000	14,000	36,566	. . .	36,566
1974	15,000	. . .	40,839	. . .	40,839
1975	16,000	16,000	44,676	46,000	44,676
1976	19,000	. . .	51,501	51,500	51,501
1977	19,000	. . .	76,066	76,066	76,066
1978	21,000	. . .	99,876	99,876	99,876
1979	21,000	. . .	113,558	113,558[e]	113,558[e]
1980	30,000	. . .	143,756	143,756	150,000[f]
1981	32,500	. . .	185,651	185,651	. . .
1982	33,500	. . .	241,497	241,497	235,000
1983	35,000	. . .	289,194	291,108	. . .
1984	40,000	. . .	329,408	329,408	. . .
1985	40,000	. . .	371,157	371,157	369,000[g]
1986	60,000	. . .	412,520	410,517	410,500
1987	62,500	. . .	412,454	402,094	402,600
1988	. . .	. . .	. . .	449,826	430,700
1989	. . .	68,000	. . .	. . .	489,500
1990	. . .	100,000	. . .	. . .	578,900

a. Staudohar (1989, p. 30).

b. Minimum salaries are in nominal terms. Pre-1969 and 1969 are from Mead (1989, p. 121). Figures for 1973 and 1975 are from Scoville (1976, p. 321). Scully (1989, pp. 34–35) says minimum went from $7,000 to $10,000 under the first Basic Agreement, in 1967, and was raised to $16,000 for the 1975 season. The 1989 minimum was found in Murray Chass, "Call 'Em the High-Dollar Mets: Four on '89 Squad Paid $2 Million," *Sporting News*, November 20, 1989, pp. 42–43. The 1990 figure was quoted in Roy J. Harris, Jr., "Forkball for Dodgers: Cost Up, Gate Off," *Wall Street Journal*, August 31, 1990, p. B1.

c. From Scully (1989, p. 152). Averages are in nominal terms.

d. Figures for 1950 are from Peter Gammons, "1950 vs. 1990: A Tale of Two Eras," *Sports Illustrated*, April 16, 1990, p. 42; 1969–70 are from Scoville (1976); and 1971–79 are from Lehn (1982, p. 348). Scoville (1976) concurs for the early 1970s, but Leigh Montville, "The First to Be Free," *Sports Illustrated*, April 16, 1990, p. 102, says 1976 average was $52,300.

e. Deferred payments were discounted starting in 1979 at 9 percent.

f. From "Now Pro Footballers Want the Big Money," *Business Week*, February 22, 1982, pp. 122–23.

g. Player relations committee (management) for 1985–90, Associated Press report. Dave Nightingale, "Baseball," *Sporting News*, December 31, 1990, p. 29, lists averages for 1989 and 1990 at $497,254 and $597,537, respectively.

of the increase in maximum salaries over time, it is safe to say the entire salary structure of baseball has been rising over time. This is consistent with observations about the rise in salary determinant elasticities observed above.

The tool used here to address the characteristics of the distribution is well known to economists. The Lorenz curve graphically portrays the equality of Major League Baseball salary distribution (see figure 8-1). Only the 1974 and 1990 Lorenz curves are shown because they are representative of their respective periods. On the X-axis is the cumulative percentage of players (the cumulative distribution of salary earners arrayed from poorest to richest), and on the Y-axis is the cumulative percentage of total salaries paid in Major League Baseball (the cumulative distribution of salaries). The latter can be calculated simply as the sum of Major League Baseball salaries for a given year. A Lorenz curve of positive slope equal to 1 would represent a perfectly equal distribution of salaries, whereas complete inequality would be represented by the well-known right-angle Lorenz curve.

The distribution is far from equal; there is a bulge in the Lorenz curves. Table 8-6 reports Gini coefficients, the share of the inequality bulge area relative to the total area below the equality line, for both periods. As the Lorenz curves portray graphically, Gini coefficients reveal that salaries have never been equally distributed in Major League Baseball (the average coefficients for the 1965–74 and 1986–90 periods are 0.354 and 0.505, respectively). A recent undergraduate text reports that U.S. Gini coefficients in 1986 were 0.389 for families and 0.443 for unrelated singles (high for industrial countries, which cluster around 0.300 to 0.350).[24] Thus income inequality in the rest of the U.S. economy pales in contrast to the recent inequality in Major League Baseball salaries.

Equally interesting is how the salary distribution in Major League Baseball has changed over time. Salaries have become less equally distributed and increasingly skewed toward the top end of the salary scale, especially evident when one compares the reserve clause and the free agency periods. The increased inequality from 1974 to 1986 is nearly three times as great as the increased inequality over the ten years during the reserve clause period. Thus, although annual changes have not been great, the cumulative impact of free agency has been dramatic. Coupled with the preceding observation on the magnitude of salary inequality in Major

---

24. Byrns and Stone (1992, pp. 808–11).

Figure 8-1. *Equality of Salary Distribution in Major League Baseball, 1974, 1990*

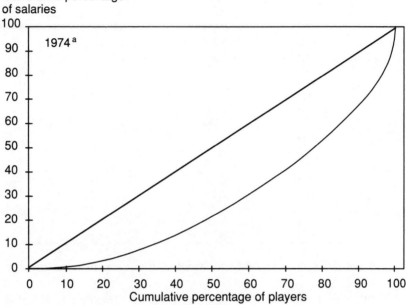

Cumulative percentage
of salaries

1974[a]

Cumulative percentage of players

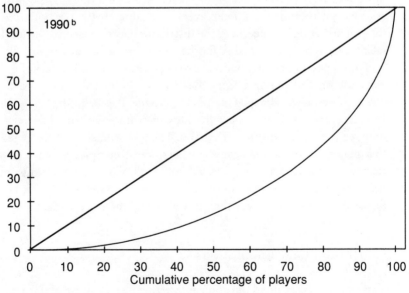

Cumulative percentage
of salaries

1990[b]

Cumulative percentage of players

a. Maximum = $220,000; minimum = $3,700.
b. Maximum = $3,200,000; minimum = $100,000.

Table 8-6. *Gini Coefficients of Major League Baseball Salary Distribution, 1965–74, 1986–90*

Year	Gini	Percentage change
1965	0.363	. . .
1966	0.327	−9.9
1967	0.350	7.0
1968	0.338	−3.4
1969	0.347	2.7
1970	0.328	−5.5
1971	0.350	6.7
1972	0.370	5.7
1973	0.369	−0.3
1974	0.395	7.0
1986	0.488	23.5
1987	0.504	3.3
1988	0.494	−2.0
1989	0.529	7.1
1990	0.508	−4.0

League Baseball, a second conclusion is that inequality has notably increased.

This finding raises two interesting points. The first is revealed by returning to the idea that pay and performance are related. For an increase in salary inequality to occur, player performance should have become more skewed toward higher performance levels, that is, either poor players have gotten worse or good players have gotten better, or both. Given the paucity of data concerning the distribution as opposed to the level of talent over time, this remains another item for further analysis.

The second interesting point has to do with the possible effect of union behavior on the Major League Baseball salary distribution. Although other things have changed in Major League Baseball, the analysis of Lorenz curves tends to reject the idea that union activity has led to a more equitable distribution of salaries. The past studies cited above reveal that players have gained against owners, and some players have gained relative to others based on race. Although all players have been gaining through dramatic increases in both minimum and average salaries, salary disparity is currently larger than it was during the reserve clause period.

Conclusions and Implications

This chapter has pointed out some interesting results of the Major League Baseball salary process over time. First, although some variation in the relative importance of determinants of the salary process has occurred, far and away the most important impact has been the increase in magnitude of all determinants. It is not known what share of the explanation lies with redistribution of income toward players and the overall growth in the demand for Major League Baseball output. Second, although players at every salary level have seen their economic welfare improve over time, an analysis of the Major League Baseball salary distribution reveals that inequality has been increasing over time, despite the advent of free agency and the rise of the players' union.

It is hoped this study will provide impetus for further analysis of the Major League Baseball salary process, for much work remains to be done. First and foremost, an explanation of the rise in demand for the Major League Baseball output will provide fruitful insights into future changes in compensation. Given that structural changes occur regularly, careful checks of data pooling are necessary. The increasing availability of full panel data on Major League Baseball salaries will facilitate exciting new analysis that takes into account changes, such as alterations in the minimum salary, renegotiated basic agreements, and rule modifications.

Major League Baseball also remains a fruitful area for the analysis of larger questions. For instance, one might question the extent to which salary inequality is driven by the underlying variation in playing skill as opposed to the transformation of a player's "gate appeal" into higher salary through the machinations of a union that takes advantage of members' rational ignorance to further its own goals. One might also ask how much worse off players would be in the absence of union activity. Given the insights to be gained both about a functioning labor market that has seen a variety of institutional changes and the policy effects of self-governance through union activity, the field of dreams remains extremely fertile ground for future research.

References

Byrns, Ralph T., and Gerald W. Stone, Jr. 1992. *Economics*, 5th ed. Harper Collins.

Cymrot, Donald J. 1983. "Migration Trends and Earnings of Free Agents in Major League Baseball, 1976–1979." *Economic Inquiry* 21:545–56.

El-Hodiri, Mohammed, and James Quirk. 1971. "An Economic Model of a Professional Sports League." *Journal of Political Economy* 79:1302–19.

Fort, Rodney, and Roger Noll. 1984. "Pay and Performance in Baseball: Modeling Regulars, Reserves, and Expansion." California Institute of Technology, Division of Humanities and Social Science Working Paper 527.

Gwartney, James, and Charles Haworth. 1974. "Employer Costs and Discrimination: The Case of Baseball." *Journal of Political Economy* 82:873–81.

Hill, James R. 1985. "The Threat of Free Agency and Exploitation in Professional Baseball: 1976–1977." *Quarterly Review of Economics and Business* 25:68–82.

Hill, James R., and William Spellman. 1983. "Professional Baseball: The Reserve Clause and Salary Structure." *Industrial Relations* 22:1–19.

———. 1984. "Pay Discrimination in Baseball: Data from the Seventies." *Industrial Relations* 23:103–112.

Lehn, Kenneth. 1982. "Property Rights, Risk Sharing, and Player Disability in Major League Baseball." *Journal of Law and Economics* 25:343–66.

Madura, Jeff. 1980. "Discrimination in Major League Baseball." *Atlantic Economic Journal* 8:70–71.

Mead, William B. 1989. *The Explosive Sixties*. Alexandria, Va.: Redefinition.

Medoff, Marshall H. 1975. "Racial Discrimination in Professional Baseball." *Atlantic Economic Journal* 3:37–44.

———. 1976. "On Monopsonistic Exploitation in Professional Baseball." *Quarterly Review of Economics and Business* 16:113–21.

———. 1986. "Baseball Attendance and Fan Discrimination." *Journal of Behavioral Economics* 15:149–55.

Mogull, Robert G. 1981. "Salary Discrimination in Professional Sports." *Atlantic Economic Journal* 9:106–10.

Neale, Walter C. 1964. "The Peculiar Economics of Professional Sports." *Quarterly Journal of Economics* 78:1–14.

Pascal, Anthony H., and Leonard A. Rapping. 1972. "The Economics of Racial Discrimination in Organized Baseball." In *Racial Discrimination in Economic Life*, edited by Anthony H. Pascal, 119–56. D.C. Heath.

Raimondo, Henry. 1983. "Free Agents' Impact on the Labor Market for Baseball Players." *Journal of Labor Research* 4:183–93.

Rottenberg, Simon. 1956. "The Baseball Players' Labor Market." *Journal of Political Economy* 64:242–58.

Scoville, James G. 1976. "Wage Determination and the Development of Collective Bargaining in Baseball." *Proceedings of the 29th Annual Meeting of the Industrial Relations Association* 317–23.

Scully, Gerald W. 1973. "Economic Discrimination in Professional Sports." *Law and Contemporary Problems* 38:67–84.

———. 1974a. "Discrimination: The Case of Baseball." In *Government and the Sports Business*, edited by Roger G. Noll, 221–73. Brookings.

———. 1974b. "Pay and Performance in Major League Baseball." *American Economic Review* 64:915–30.

_____ . 1989. *The Business of Major League Baseball.* University of Chicago Press.

Sommers, Paul M., and Noel Quinton. 1982. "Pay and Performance in Major League Baseball: The Case of the First Family of Free Agents." *Journal of Human Resources* 17:426–36.

Staudohar, Paul D. 1989. *The Sports Industry and Collective Bargaining*, 2d ed. Ithaca, N.Y.: ILR Press.

Appendix

Table 8-A. *Variable Descriptions*

Variable	Description
Real salary	Log (deflated player salary), deflated by "Value of the Dollar," *Statistical Abstract of the U.S.*, 1989.
Hitters	
AT BATS	Log (1 + lifetime share of team at bats), 0 for pitchers, rookies, and hopefuls (described below).
SLUG	Log (1 + lifetime slugging average), 0 for pitchers, rookies, and hopefuls.
AT BATS+	Log (1 + difference between last year's share of team at bats and lifetime team at bats) if the difference is positive, 0 else, and 0 for pitchers, rookies, hopefuls, and players designated no last year (described below).
AT BATS−	Log (1 + absolute value of the difference between last year's share of team at bats and lifetime team at bats) if the difference is negative, 0 else, and 0 for pitchers, rookies, hopefuls, and players designated no last year.
Pitchers	
IP	Log (1 + lifetime share of total team innings pitched), 0 for hitters, rookies, and hopefuls.
SW	Log (1 + lifetime strikeout-to-walk ratio), 0 for hitters, rookies, and hopefuls.
STARTER	Log (1 + ratio of games started to total appearances), 0 for hitters, rookies, and hopefuls.
IP+	Log (1 + difference between last year's share of total team innings pitched and lifetime share of total team innings pitched) if the difference is positive, 0 else, and 0 for hitters, rookies, hopefuls, and players designated no last year.
IP−	Log (1 + absolute value of the difference between last year's share of total team innings pitched and lifetime share of total team innings pitched) if the difference is negative, 0 else, and 0 for hitters, rookies, hopefuls, and players designated no last year.
All players	
OLD	Log (1 + difference between the player's age and the annual mean age) if the difference is positive, 0 else.
OLD^2	Log (1 + player's age minus the annual mean age), squared.
YOUNG	Log (1 + absolute value of the difference between the player's age and the annual mean age) if the difference is negative, 0 else.
YOUNG^2	Log (1 + absolute value of the difference between the player's age and the annual mean age), squared.
EXPER. RESID+	Log (1 + residual from an annual regression of years in the major leagues on player age) if the residual is positive, 0 else. The residual is calculated as actual minus predicted values from the regression.

Table 8-A *(continued)*

Variable	Description
EXPER. RESID −	Log (1 + absolute value of residual from an annual regression of years in the major leagues on player age) if the residual is negative, 0 else.
Dummies	
HOPEFUL	1 if less than five years in the majors and fewer than 40 (30) at bats (innings pitched) in each season for hitters (pitchers), 0 else. All player statistics are set to 0 for hopefuls.
ROOKIE	1 if one year in the majors and more than 40 (30) at bats (innings pitched) if a hitter (pitcher), 0 else. All player statistics are set to 0 for rookies.
NO LAST YEAR	1 if hopeful = 1, or rookie = 1, or the player had no major league record in the previous season. All variables concerning departures from lifetime averages are set to 0 for players with no last year = 1.
PITCHER	1 if player is a pitcher, 0 else.
NOARB	1 if player's major league years is less than three, 0 else.
ARBNOFA	1 if player's major league years is between three and six, inclusive, 0 else.

Table 8-B. *Experience Regressions, 1965–74, 1986–90*[a]

Year	Constant	Age	R^2	$\overline{R}^2$	DF
1965	−15.3 (1.05)*	0.714 (0.038)*	0.726	0.724	137
1966	−16.8 (1.65)	0.764 (0.057)*	0.603	0.599	117
1967	−16.2 (1.22)*	0.747 (0.043)*	0.671	0.669	149
1968	−17.5 (1.40)*	0.789 (0.048)*	0.688	0.686	123
1969	−17.8 (1.18)*	0.798 (0.041)*	0.668	0.666	189
1970	−18.5 (1.56)*	0.825 (0.054)*	0.570	0.568	175
1971	−18.9 (1.22)*	0.848 (0.043)*	0.668	0.666	192
1972	−18.5 (1.03)*	0.834 (0.036)*	0.711	0.710	215
1973	−18.7 (1.00)*	0.841 (0.035)*	0.733	0.732	213
1974	−21.2 (1.11)*	0.934 (0.038)*	0.781	0.779	171
1986	−21.3 (0.868)*	0.938 (0.030)*	0.836	0.835	198
1987	−21.0 (0.972)*	0.931 (0.034)*	0.794	0.793	198
1988	−22.6 (1.08)*	0.999 (0.037)*	0.783	0.782	198
1989	−21.8 (0.945)*	0.941 (0.032)*	0.812	0.811	198
1990	−22.6 (1.09)*	0.967 (0.037)*	0.777	0.775	198

*Significant at the 0.05 level (2-tail for the constant and 1-tail for the coefficient on age).
a. Numbers in parentheses are standard errors.

Part IV

The Impact of Race on Salaries

CHAPTER NINE

Discrimination in Baseball

Lawrence M. Kahn

E CONOMISTS AND the public at large have become increasingly interested in the issue of discrimination in professional sports. The public perception has to some degree been that sports are an oasis of equal economic opportunity for minorities.[1] Sports teams are sometimes viewed as being engaged in intensive competition in which participants are evaluated solely on their merits. Further, minority representation is higher in major team sports than in the labor force as a whole, reinforcing the idea that sports provide disproportionate opportunities for minorities. For example, among experienced players in Major League Baseball in 1987, 27.8 percent were black; in the National Basketball Association (NBA) in the 1985–86 season, 74.3 percent were black; and in the National Football League in 1988, 56.0 percent were black.[2] These figures are all substantially larger than the percentage of blacks in the civilian labor force, which was 10.9 percent in 1988.[3]

Many of the highest paid athletes in the United States are black. In the National Basketball Association, for example, in the 1988–89 season, 83 percent of the forty-two players earning salaries of at least $1 million were black; in Major League Baseball, of the twelve players making at least $2 million a year in 1988, four were black and one was Hispanic;

This paper reprints portions of the author's article, "Discrimination in Professional Sports: A Survey of the Literature," *Industrial and Labor Relations Review*, vol. 44 (April 1991), pp. 395–418. This material is used with the permission of Cornell University.

1. Eitzen and Sage (1978).
2. These figures were taken from Kahn (1989), baseball; Kahn and Sherer (1988, p. 48), basketball; and Staudohar (1989, p. 86), football.
3. U.S. Bureau of Labor Statistics (1989, pp. 16, 18).

and in the National Football League (NFL), 60 percent of the thirty players making at least $1 million for the 1988 season were black.[4]

Despite this evidence of economic achievement, there is an undercurrent in the public's perception of the treatment of black professional athletes. Until the 1940s, blacks were excluded altogether from professional sports. Since then, the major sports have integrated, although in many instances there was militant resistance to allowing blacks to compete.[5] Although blacks are now well represented among players in major professional sports, they are rarely found in managerial or executive positions.[6] Further, blacks have relatively low representation in such key positions as quarterback in football and pitcher in baseball. Recently, public remarks by a team executive claimed that black athletes did not have the qualities necessary to become managers or executives; and a well-known broadcaster was fired for making racist comments.[7] Anecdotal evidence documents the perception of unequal treatment (relative to whites) among many black athletes.[8]

While the issue of discrimination in sports holds obvious interest for the public, economists have perceived a unique opportunity to study this issue. Economists have usually defined discrimination as unequal treatment (for example, on the basis of race, gender, or age) of equally productive workers.[9] A major difficulty in estimating the extent of discrimination is the problem of measuring productivity. In practice this problem is usually handled by including in wage regressions variables such as education and experience as proxies for productivity.[10] However, such variables are likely to measure productivity with error; further, if this error is correlated with such variables as race or gender, then the procedure will lead to biased estimates of discrimination. A particular advantage of data from professional sports is that there are publicly available extensive measures of performance and compensation of athletes. Although use of such information may still result in biased estimates of productivity (and therefore possibly of discrimination), such mismeasure-

---

4. Salary figures are taken from "Salaries: The Future Is Now," *Sporting News*, January 2, 1989, pp. 56–65.

5. Eitzen and Sage (1978); Okrent and Wulf (1989); Tygiel (1983).

6. In addition, blacks are rarely represented in lucrative sports such as golf and tennis. See Eitzen and Sage (1978); U.S. Tennis Association (1989).

7. Staudohar (1989, p. 58).

8. See, for example, Bradley (1976); Halberstam (1981).

9. Becker (1971).

10. See Cain (1986) for a review of studies on discrimination.

ment is likely to be much smaller than that caused by the exclusive use of education and experience for the labor force in general.

In addition to allowing for relatively precise measures of productivity, a focus on sports permits an estimate of the extent of alternative forms of discrimination beyond that based simply on wages. For example, the high visibility of athletes enables one to examine the phenomenon of customer discrimination, as there are data on revenues in sports and the identity of the workers generating those revenues. Further, there is information on the results of the draft in sports, allowing the issue of hiring standards to be studied in a more precise way than is usually done in the literature on discrimination.

Although the anecdotal evidence on discrimination in sports is suggestive, one needs to know whether the incidents described in it are isolated or, instead, symptomatic of general trends and patterns in professional sports. To answer this question, I survey studies of discrimination in sports that use statistical evidence. In this chapter I examine studies of salaries, hiring standards, positional segregation, and customer discrimination.[11] The focus is primarily on baseball, although some comparisons with basketball will prove useful.

Forms of Discrimination in Professional Sports

Economists have identified a variety of sources and forms of labor market discrimination, which, as suggested earlier, is defined as unequal treatment of equally qualified workers.[12] It is important to identify these sources to analyze the impact of market processes on the persistence of discrimination. Becker argued that labor market discrimination could result from employer prejudice, coworker discrimination, or customer preferences.[13]

In the context of sports, employer (owner) prejudice has been cited as an important reason for the exclusion of black players from Major

11. These studies were concerned with racial or ethnic discrimination.
12. Although among economists this is the dominant definition of discrimination, others have proposed an alternative definition: the setting of unequal standards in allocating job opportunities or pay levels (Conway and Roberts, 1983). This definition is closely related to hiring discrimination, which is discussed below. In addition, there may be discrimination in training opportunities before people enter the labor market. This possibility is also mentioned later.
13. Becker (1971).

League Baseball until 1947.[14] In addition, even after Jackie Robinson broke the color line in 1947, some teams appeared to be more prejudiced against blacks than other teams and were reluctant to field teams with minorities.[15] Moreover, Gwartney and Haworth showed that in the first ten seasons of baseball integration (1947–56), teams that used more black players on average had higher winning percentages than teams that chose not to integrate as quickly. The authors argued that this difference in winning performance illustrated the competitive advantage that Becker noted nondiscriminators would have. Further, one would expect prejudiced teams to trade black players to nonprejudiced teams or, in the era of free agency, blacks to move to nonprejudiced teams. The elimination of pay differentials based on team prejudice, then, depends on the existence of nonprejudiced teams or nonprejudiced potential buyers of teams.[16]

In the case of coworker discrimination, again taking the example of race, whites require a premium for working with minorities. There was much evidence of coworker discrimination as many players resisted Jackie Robinson's entry into the major leagues.[17] For example, several members of his team (the Brooklyn Dodgers) approached the management to protest his place on the roster; the St. Louis Cardinals reportedly threatened to strike rather than play against him. One member of the Dodgers asked to be traded rather than play alongside Robinson, and his request was granted. This trade can be seen as an illustration of the segregation mechanism Becker mentioned as a likely market outcome of coworker discrimination.[18] Free agency can also lead to a similar allocation of players.

Finally, customer prejudice has a long history in sports. In boxing, for example, the wait for the "great white hope" is legendary. Bill Bradley quotes a reporter's view of racism among white fans in the early 1970s: "Take the ordinary ethnic, white, working stiff. . . . There he sees Frazier, this black . . . who is making $300,000 a year for playing. . . . Then there he is, playing poorly. . . . I have watched lots of crowds and those boos for Frazier were vicious."[19] Of course, fans' reaction to the introduction of Jackie Robinson was also in many cases

14. Okrent and Wulf (1989).
15. Gwartney and Haworth (1974); Okrent and Wulf (1989).
16. An exception to this rule has been noted by Goldberg (1982). Specifically, if prejudice takes the form of nepotism for whites (rather than an aversion to blacks), then discriminators and nondiscriminators can coexist.
17. This discussion is based on Okrent and Wulf (1989) and Tygiel (1983).
18. Becker (1971).
19. Bradley (1976, p. 204).

vituperative.[20] Unlike employer or coworker prejudice, market forces will not eliminate discrimination based on customer prejudice.[21] This is the case because teams are rewarded for bidding hardest for the players the fans want to see most.

Just as discrimination can have several sources, so can it take various forms. Perhaps the simplest form is unequal pay for equal work. For example, Pascal and Rapping suggest that white rookies in the 1950s received considerably higher signing bonuses than equally qualified blacks.[22] Discrimination can also take the form of unequal hiring standards. Several authors have alleged that black athletes face higher performance standards than whites for entry into and retention in professional sports (discussed below). An additional form of discrimination that some believe has occurred in sports is positional segregation. Whites have been disproportionately represented at positions such as pitcher and catcher in baseball and quarterback in football. Authors disagree, however, on the extent to which this kind of segregation represents discrimination. Yet to the extent that it does, then comparing salaries for blacks and whites who perform equally may understate discrimination. Further, consideration of endorsement income also suggests that concentrating on salaries may understate discrimination. Specifically, surveys done by sports marketing firms found that in 1987, eight of the ten most popular athletes in the United States were black, yet only one of the ten top sports endorsers (in terms of income) was black.[23]

Salary Discrimination

Studies of salary discrimination in baseball and basketball have used a variety of methodologies to measure the extent of salary discrimination (see table 9-1). The most common method is to regress salary (or its log) on a list of productivity indicators and a dummy variable for race.[24] Such a formulation yields an estimate of the market "discrimination coeffi-

20. Tygiel (1983, pp. 180–208).

21. Kahn (1991).

22. Pascal and Rapping (1972).

23. Joanne Lipman, "Sports Marketers See Evidence of Racism," *Wall Street Journal*, October 18, 1988, p. B1.

24. In some of the studies in table 9-1, race was broken down into three categories: white, black and Hispanic, necessitating the creation of two dummy variables.

Table 9-1. *Studies of Wage Discrimination in Baseball and Basketball*

Study and sport	Sample and date	Results
Baseball		
Pascal and Rapping (1972)	148 players, 1968–69	Nonpitchers: insignificant negative coefficient for whites, 5–6 percent of mean salary; significant negative effect for Latins, 42 percent of mean salary. Pitchers: significant (5–10 percent, 1-tailed) negative coefficient for whites, 13–25 percent of mean salary; insignificant Latin effects, −14 to −11 percent of mean salary.
Scully (1974a)	148 players, 1968–69	Outfielders: insignificant black-white differences in returns to experience and productivity. Infielders: significantly (5 percent, 1-tailed) higher black return to experience. Pitchers: significantly (5 percent, 2-tailed) higher black return to experience.
Mogull (1975)	126 players, 1971	Black returns to productivity and experience generally larger than white returns. No significance tests of differences in black and white coefficients.
Medoff (1975)	62 nonpitchers, 1968	Insignificant, negative black effect on wage change (magnitude is $347).
Mogull (1981)	54 nonpitchers, 1971	Insignificant Chow test for black-white wage equation differences.
Cymrot (1983)	80 free agents, 1976–79	Insignificant race (nonwhite) effect on log salary (effect = 0.02).
Raimondo (1983)	146 players, 1977	Nonwhites get similar returns to performance and experience as whites (no significance tests of differences in coefficients).
Hill and Spellman (1984)	523 players, 1976	Decomposition analysis of separate black-white regressions. Nonpitchers: 7 percentage-point discrimination coefficient against blacks. Pitchers: 5 percentage-point discrimination coefficient against whites.
Cymrot (1985)	885 players, 1978–80	Free agent eligibles: insignificant Chow test for white-nonwhite equation differences. Free agent noneligibles: significant (1–5 percent) Chow tests for white-nonwhite equation differences.
Christiano (1986)	212 nonpitchers, 1977	4.6 percent discrimination coefficient against whites (significant at 10 percent, 2-tailed).

Study	Sample	Findings
Christiano (1988)	356 nonpitchers, 1987	17.0 percent discrimination coefficient against whites (significant at 5 percent, 2-tailed).
Kahn (1989)	575 players, 1987	Nonpitchers: insignificant American black and Hispanic black effects on log salary (coefficients less than 1 percent in magnitude). Pitchers: insignificant American black and Hispanic black effects on log salary (coefficients −13 percent to 30 percent in magnitude).
Basketball		
Rockwood and Asher (1976)	28 players, 1970–71	Insignificant discrimination coefficient against blacks (magnitude is $176).
Mogull (1977)	28 players, 1970–71	White equations generally have higher R^2 than black equations (no Chow tests).
Mogull (1981)	28 players, 1970–71	Insignificant Chow test of black-white equation differences.
Scott, Long, and Somppi (1985)	26 players, 1980–81	Insignificant race coefficient (magnitude is $101,096 in favor of whites; mean of sample = $606,538).
Kahn and Sherer (1988)	226 players, 1985–86	Significant (1 percent, 2-tailed) positive coefficient for white players (magnitude is 21–25 percent).
Koch and Vander Hill (1988)	278 players, 1984–85	Significant (10 percent, 2-tailed) positive coefficient for whites (magnitude is 11.6 percent).
Wallace (1988)	229 players, 1984–85	Significant (10 percent, 2-tailed) positive coefficient for whites (magnitude is 18.3 percent).
Brown, Spiro, and Keenan (1988)	227 players, 1984–85	Significant (5 percent, 2-tailed) negative coefficient for blacks (magnitude is −14.4 percent).

Sources: See References.

cient"—the coefficient on the race dummy variable.[25] It assumes, however, that whites and nonwhites receive the same return to higher performance levels and to other variables that influence salary. As can be seen in table 9-1, some studies examine this assumption by performing a statistical test for the equality of the (nonintercept) coefficients in separate white and black regressions.

As with studies of wage discrimination for the labor force in general, the regression approach to estimating discrimination in sports may lead to biased estimates if the researcher is not able to measure performance accurately. If errors in measuring productivity are (partially) correlated with race, then biased estimates of discrimination will result. As noted, these problems may be less severe in sports because there are much better performance data for it than for other industries. Nonetheless, the studies in table 9-1 use different explanatory variables and to some degree may still suffer from omitted variable bias.

The direction of this bias is unclear. Studies of baseball and basketball generally find that blacks outperform whites when measured productivity characteristics are compared (see table 9-2). If unmeasured productivity moves in the same direction as measured productivity, then the studies in table 9-1 will understate the extent of discrimination. On the other hand, if unmeasured performance is negatively correlated with measured performance, then discrimination against blacks will be overestimated.[26] A final methodological issue in these studies is sample size. In general, earlier studies, particularly those in basketball, had much smaller sample sizes than more recent studies. A larger sample size implies that one can be more confident that a study has captured genuine trends and not merely statistical artifacts of the particular sample analyzed.

Surveying the studies in table 9-1 on baseball, one does not find much evidence of salary discrimination against black players. For example, none of the studies that computed discrimination coefficients found a significant negative effect for blacks. In one case there was a significant Hispanic

---

25. Becker (1971). Ideally, one would like data on all team salary offers, rather than merely on those offers that were accepted; by examining only current players, one obtains a truncated view of the salary offer distribution. Such a truncation can produce biased estimates of discrimination if the propensity to turn down offers differs by race. In the case of professional sports, however, salaries are likely to be much higher for most players than what they could earn elsewhere. Thus, other than the case of injuries or voluntary retirement, the truncation problem is not likely to be important here.

26. For further discussion of the issue of unmeasured productivity and discrimination, see Goldberger (1984).

shortfall for nonpitchers;[27] in several cases there was a significant white shortfall in salary, controlling for measured productivity.[28] In these instances of white salary shortfall, should one conclude that there is discrimination against whites, despite the fact that blacks were barred from Major League Baseball until 1947? A more likely explanation is omitted variables. For example, Pascal and Rapping found white salary shortfalls among pitchers for 1968–69; at this time, there were so few black pitchers (see table 9-2) that those who did pitch probably needed to be especially skilled. Further, though Christiano found significant white salary shortfalls in regressions, Kahn used data similar to Christiano's 1988 study but added more performance measures and found statistically insignificant race differences (with varying magnitudes).[29]

Of the baseball studies in table 9-1 that compared black and white equations, some found significant differences in the coefficients, whereas others did not. Several of the early studies in table 9-1 found that black players in the 1968–71 period had higher returns to experience than white players. Scully argued that such a finding suggested that blacks faced retention barriers: to remain in baseball black veterans had to outperform whites; to produce the higher black experience effect, such barriers would have to grow with experience.[30] Limited evidence for this view can be seen in table 9-2: Scully found that for outfielders, the black performance advantage over whites widens with experience; on the other hand, for infielders, the black performance advantage peaks at six to seven years of experience. However, using more recent data and a larger sample, Christiano did not find consistent evidence of a higher black wage return to experience.[31] Experienced black players in the late 1960s may have faced greater entry barriers (in the 1950s) than experienced players in the 1980s; experienced black players (especially outfielders such as Willie Mays and Hank Aaron) in 1968 may thus have had particularly high unmeasured ability.

It is especially noteworthy that the patterns of results for salary discrimination are similar for the period before free agency (1976) and that after free agency. If some employers discriminated while others did not, then, Cymrot has argued, free agency may reduce such discrimination,

27. Pascal and Rapping (1972).
28. Christiano (1986, 1988); Pascal and Rapping (1972).
29. Christiano (1986, 1988); Kahn (1989).
30. Scully (1974a).
31. Christiano (1988).

as black players would move to nondiscriminating teams.[32] A related hypothesis is that in the era of free agency, if some owners are prejudiced, then there will be more salary discrimination against black players not eligible for free agency than against those eligible.[33]

First, Cymrot estimated separate log salary regressions by race and by free-agency eligibility status. Chow-tests confirmed that, for ineligibles, the coefficients were significantly different between whites and nonwhites; however, such tests accepted the null hypothesis that, for eligibles, there were no significant differences between white and nonwhite coefficients (including intercept terms). He concluded that the competition implied by free agency eliminated the discrimination that presumably would have existed against eligible nonwhites had they not been eligible. Although Cymrot did not compute discrimination coefficients or even the direction of the ceteris paribus white-nonwhite salary differential, his results are consistent with the competition hypothesis. Second, Christiano compared black and white log salary coefficients by eligibility status and could find no strong patterns.[34]

These results suggest that it may be premature to say that there is more discrimination against free-agency ineligibles than against eligibles. Further, one may question the logic behind Cymrot's prediction.[35] Specifically, even in the absence of free agency, one would expect prejudiced owners to trade black players to nonprejudiced teams, leading to an allocation of players similar to what one would find under free agency. To predict that free agency causes a reduction in racial salary differentials, one must argue that free agency allows more player mobility (or potential mobility, through the offer-matching process) than would have occurred through trades alone. There is, however, no evidence on this latter point.[36]

In contrast to the studies of baseball, research on professional basketball players' salaries indicates significant black salary shortfalls in the

32. Cymrot (1985). As I discuss below in the context of basketball, even free agency is not sufficient to eliminate racial pay differentials based on customer discrimination.

33. Cymrot (1985) and Christiano (1988) investigated this possibility.

34. Christiano (1988). He did not perform significance tests for differences in these coefficients.

35. Cymrot (1985).

36. In some conditions, Nash bargaining under the reserve clause can lead to apparently discriminatory pay gaps that would disappear under free agency. Specifically, if blacks have lower "status quo" income than whites (for example, endorsements), then Nash bargaining will leave blacks with lower salaries than equally performing whites, even if owners are not prejudiced (Binmore, Rubinstein, and Wolinsky, 1986). However, if one controls for status quo income, then there should be no race effect. Under free agency, players get their marginal revenue products regardless of their status quo incomes.

1980s. Table 9-1 shows this result for each study that used sample sizes large enough to comprise all or most of the NBA's experienced players. These studies used data from either the 1984–85 or 1985–86 season and found significant discrimination coefficients ranging from 11 to 25 percent against black players.[37] Such results are noteworthy because basketball, like baseball, has had free agency since the 1970s.[38] Although there was a significant ceteris paribus racial pay gap in basketball, the structure of the pay regression other than the intercept term was not significantly different for blacks and whites in basketball.[39]

Hiring Discrimination

Because black athletes were virtually barred from participation in major professional sports until after World War II, it is not surprising that many researchers have examined the issue of hiring discrimination (see table 9-2). One intuitive definition of hiring discrimination is unequal job offer probabilities facing different applicants with the same ability.[40]

To obtain information about hiring discrimination, one needs information on workers in the hiring pool for professional sports. That is, one would like to know if black players at the margin of acceptance or rejection by the sport face tougher admission standards than whites. Several studies examine this issue in the context of basketball.

First, Kahn and Sherer used 1985–86 data and found no significant racial differentials in the order in which NBA players were drafted, con-

37. Earlier studies surveyed in table 9-1 on basketball were inconclusive but used samples of only twenty-six to twenty-eight players.

38. Staudohar (1989, p. 120). Although these studies all used a long list of explanatory variables, they may still suffer from omitted variable problems. One technique for dealing with such problems, suggested by Conway and Roberts (1983) is to regress qualifications on (log) salary and race—the "reverse regression" technique. However, Goldberger (1984) has argued that such a technique is no less likely to give a biased estimate of discrimination than the usual ("direct") salary regression. Nonetheless, when the reverse regression technique was used by Kahn and Sherer (1988) as an additional check on their results, the implied discrimination coefficients were still significant and actually larger in magnitude than those obtained by the direct regression.

39. Kahn and Sherer (1988).

40. This definition misses the phenomenon by which, say, black workers may be discouraged from applying for employment by anticipated discrimination. Courts in discrimination cases have taken account of this phenomenon by requiring firms to hire minorities (and women) in proportion to their availabilities in the relevant labor market (Flanagan and others, 1989). Studies of professional sports do not even have data on rejected applicants, much less the appropriate hiring pool (which would include presumably discouraged applicants).

Table 9-2. *Studies of Hiring Discrimination in Baseball and Basketball*

Study and sport	Sample and date	Results
Baseball		
Pascal and Rapping (1972)	429 nonpitchers, 1968	At each position, blacks have higher batting average than whites, significant at 5 percent (one-tailed) in 6 of 12 cases.
Scully (1974a)	148 players, 1968–69	Outfielders: black performance advantage over whites widens with experience. Infielders: blacks outperform whites at all experience levels; differential peaks at 6–7 years. All positions: black performance advantage negatively correlated with black representation.
Gwartney and Haworth (1974)	Team data 1950–55; individual player data 1950, 1955	Teams with more black players on average have higher winning percentages; at each position, blacks have higher slugging averages than whites.
Medoff (1975)	174 nonpitchers, 1967	National League nonwhites significantly outperform whites and American League nonwhites; accept null hypothesis that American League whites and nonwhites have equal productivity.
Hill and Spellman (1984)	516 players, 1976	Blacks outperform whites in 4 of 6 positions; differences generally not significant.
Jiobu (1988)	1,113 nonpitchers, 1971–85	Controlling for performance, blacks have a significantly higher (hazard) rate of exit from baseball than whites; Hispanics' hazard rate, controlling for performance, is insignificantly different from whites'.
Basketball		
Johnson and Marple (1973)	337 pro and 2,254 college players, 1970–71	Black players outscore white players; marginal white pro players have longer careers than marginal black players.
Scully (1973)	ABA and NBA players, 1971–72	Blacks have significantly higher points scored per minute of play than whites; blacks also outrebound whites, but the difference is sometimes not significant.
Kahn and Sherer (1988)	226 NBA players, 1985–86	At the same salary, blacks significantly outperform whites; however, controlling for college performance, there are no significant race differences in the order in which players are drafted by NBA teams.
Brown, Spiro, and Keenan (1988)	227 NBA players, 1984–85	Black benchwarmers generally have insignificantly better performance than white benchwarmers; for all players, blacks generally significantly outperform whites.

Sources: See References.

trolling for college performance.[41] In fact, all else equal, black players were drafted slightly (and, as noted, insignificantly) earlier than whites. Although this study did not look at those players rejected by the NBA, it provides no evidence of hiring barriers. Second, Brown, Spiro, and Keenan compared the performance in the 1984–85 season of black and white "benchwarmers" in the NBA.[42] They found generally insignificant performance differences for these groups, although for the league as a whole, blacks outperformed whites.[43] These results again suggest the absence of hiring barriers at the margin of entry into the league, although joint tests of differences in individual performance indicators would have perhaps provided a fairer test. On the other hand, Johnson and Marple found for the 1960–71 period that marginal white pro players had longer careers than marginal black players, suggesting that the latter faced retention barriers.[44]

Unlike these studies, which examine the selection process, most research on hiring discrimination in professional sports merely compares black and white performance levels (see table 9-2). If blacks outperform whites, then this finding is taken to be evidence of hiring barriers. Yet because many players are likely to have more ability than those at the margin of entry into the major league level, such studies do not provide direct evidence on hiring barriers. If, say, the best black outfielder is better than the best white outfielder, can one say that the former faced entry barriers?[45] There usually are many more marginal players than stars, suggesting that teams do have substitution possibilities at the margin. An implication of the presence of barriers is that teams are hiring lower-quality whites even though there are more highly qualified blacks who are attempting to gain entry. Despite the methodological difficulty with using overall performance comparisons, such studies have yielded some interesting insights.

As noted, in all the major U.S. professional sports, there were racial barriers to entry until after World War II. The purpose of many of the studies in table 9-2 is to determine the degree to which these barriers

41. Kahn and Sherer (1988).
42. Brown, Spiro, and Keenan (1988).
43. As can be seen from table 9-2, other studies of the NBA also found that, overall, blacks outperformed whites.
44. Johnson and Marple (1973). Although mobility may be voluntary (in the case of some retirements), the high incomes earned by professional athletes suggest that much turnover is involuntary.
45. Of course, other information could indicate hiring discrimination against such a player; however, the concern here is with the interpretation of performance differentials.

have eroded. The early studies of baseball, based on data from the 1950s and 1960s, indicated important performance differentials in favor of blacks. For this period, however, Medoff found that, although black National Leaguers significantly outperformed whites, in the American League there were no significant racial performance differences. Because the National League integrated before the American League, in the 1940s and 1950s, and took advantage of the accumulated black playing talent previously barred from the major leagues, Medoff argued that the American League was the appropriate setting in which to examine barriers in the 1960s.[46] The lack of a performance differential in the American League indicated to him a lack of hiring barriers. One must use caution in interpreting his findings, however, because only twenty-six nonwhites were included in his American League sample. This small sample size could be the result of racial exclusion. By 1976 racial performance differentials were less noticeable in baseball: Hill and Spellman found that blacks outperformed whites in four of six positions but that these differences were generally not significant.[47] A joint significance test of such differences would have been informative, however.

The studies reviewed above are concerned with entry barriers in baseball. Jiobu, however, studied racial retention barriers.[48] Among a sample of 1,113 players from 1971 to 1985, he found that given the same performance level, position, and age at entry, blacks on average had a significantly higher exit rate from baseball than whites. This finding was similar to that of Johnson and Marple for benchwarmers in basketball (see above). Hispanic-white differences were small and insignificant. Because high salaries suggest that baseball players are not likely to quit unless injured, Jiobu reasoned that the racial difference in exit was akin to a higher discharge rate for blacks, all else equal. Further, because whites are likely to have better nonbaseball opportunities than blacks, one might expect in the absence of salary discrimination to find earlier retirement rates among white players. Although his finding assumes no differences in injuries, it does suggest that teams are more likely to keep an aging white player than an aging black player. If a player's skills deteriorate near the end of his career,[49] then the racial difference in exit rates could

46. Medoff (1975). That is, the black performance differential in the 1960s reflected the talents of the black players brought in during the early period of integration, not current hiring standards.

47. Hill and Spellman (1984).

48. Jiobu (1988).

49. Kahn (1989).

by itself yield an average performance advantage in favor of black players. Again, one must use caution in interpreting performance differentials.

Positional Segregation

Related to the issue of barriers to entry is that of segregation by position. Table 9-3 contains results from studies of this issue. In baseball, there is evidence that blacks are underrepresented at pitcher, catcher, and infield positions (other than first base).[50] In basketball, the evidence is less strong, although in the 1980s blacks appear to be slightly overrepresented at guard.

Although the existence of positional segregation in baseball is not a controversial issue among researchers, its explanation has been the subject of some debate. On the one hand, some have argued that blacks are kept out of positions involving leadership and critical thinking.[51] According to this argument, this exclusion is based on negative stereotypes about black players' intelligence or leadership abilities. It is also consistent with the idea introduced earlier of coworker discrimination: white players may resist taking orders from black players. Baseball managers and coaches, when they were players, more often played infield than other positions; if black players are excluded from these areas as players, then they will receive less "training" for managerial jobs than white players. Thus, even if positional segregation did not lead to any salary differentials, it could still adversely affect the careers of blacks after retirement as players. On the other hand, it has been suggested that black underrepresentation in central positions is the result of discrimination in training opportunities available to young athletes (that is, "pre–labor market" discrimination).[52] According to such an argument, positions such as pitcher, catcher, and infielder in baseball require more training and equipment than other positions. Inequality in training resources provided by schools can lead blacks to disproportionately choose noncentral positions.

At present, there is insufficient evidence to allow rejection of one of these explanations in favor of the other. On the one hand, in basketball in the 1970s there was no evidence of segregation,[53] and in the 1980s blacks were disproportionately represented at guard, the leadership po-

50. One exception to this generalization is Hill and Spellman (1984), who find slight black overrepresentation at second base and shortstop for 1976 (see table 9-3).
51. See, for example, Curtis and Loy (1978); Scully (1974a); and Yetman (1987).
52. Medoff (1986).
53. Curtis and Loy (1978).

Table 9-3. *Studies of Positional Segregation in Baseball and Basketball*

Study and sport	Sample and date	Results
Baseball		
Pascal and Rapping (1972)	784 players, 1968	Blacks underrepresented at pitcher and catcher; blacks overrepresented at outfield and first base.
Scully (1974a)	Players, 1960–71	Blacks overrepresented at outfield, underrepresented at infield.
Hill and Spellman (1984)	516 players, 1976	Blacks underrepresented at pitcher, catcher; overrepresented at outfield, first base, second base, and shortstop.
Medoff (1986)	Players, 1970 and 1984	Black representation lowest for positions with highest training and equipment costs; as blacks' access to training rises, so does their representation in these positions.
Christiano (1988)	356 nonpitchers, 1987	Blacks overrepresented at outfield, underrepresented at infield and catcher.
Basketball		
Curtis and Loy (1978)	Review of studies on college and pro players, 1970–72, 1974–75	No stacking pattern on pro teams; blacks underrepresented at center and guard in college, 1970–71; no college stacking pattern, 1974–75.
Kahn and Sherer (1988)	226 NBA players, 1985–86	Blacks underrepresented at center and forward.

Sources: See References.

sition.[54] Such evidence is not consistent with the "negative stereotypes" argument. In the 1980s black representation at pitcher in baseball appeared to be increasing, although blacks were still underrepresented at this position.[55]

Customer Discrimination

Testing for the existence of customer discrimination is important because, unlike employer or coworker prejudice, competition will not eliminate this form of discrimination within an industry. To the extent that one finds customer prejudice, one cannot rely on market forces to eliminate unequal treatment of black and white athletes. Table 9-4 shows the results of studies of customer prejudice in baseball and basketball. These studies typically control for team or player performance.

In baseball in the 1950s, black players raised home attendance, all else equal. Gwartney and Haworth attributed this to the presence of black superstars in the incoming cohort of black players and to new black customers attracted by the integration of baseball.[56] By the 1960s, there was evidence that the presence of black players significantly lowered team revenue, all else equal.[57] Presumably these latter findings reflected preferences of white fans. By 1976–77, however, there was no evidence that the racial composition of baseball teams had any impact on revenues.[58] These differences in findings across decades could reflect changes in fans' attitudes or differences in empirical methods used in the studies. On the latter point, there are no obvious methodological biases in these studies that would be expected to produce the results obtained. However, if white players become increasingly scarce, one might expect future findings of pay gaps related to fan prejudice.

In the 1980s, there is some evidence of fans' racial preferences, although there is no evidence of the impact of such preferences on revenues. Nardinelli and Simon's finding that, in 1989, white players' baseball cards sold for higher prices than those for equally qualified blacks is suggestive of racial attitudes among fans.[59] Further, Johnson found that in 1987, black players' salaries were significantly and negatively affected by the

54. Kahn and Sherer (1988).
55. Medoff (1986).
56. Gwartney and Haworth (1974).
57. Scully (1974a, 1974b).
58. Sommers and Quinton (1982).
59. Nardinelli and Simon (1990).

Table 9-4. *Studies of Customer Discrimination in Baseball and Basketball*

Study and sport	Sample and date	Results
Baseball		
Scully (1974a)	1967 fan attendance for 57 starting pitchers	Other things equal, black pitchers draw significantly (10 percent, 2-tailed) fewer fans than white pitchers (magnitude is 8.0 percent of first-place team's average attendance).
Scully (1974b)	Team data, 1968–69, 43 teams	Black players significantly (1 percent, 2-tailed) lower team revenue (a 1 percentage-point rise in percent of players who were black lowered revenue $59,000).
Gwartney and Haworth (1974)	Teams, 1950–59	Black players raise annual team attendance (significant, 5 percent, 2-tailed for 1950–59; insignificant for 1950–55); magnitude is 16,000–29,000 fans per additional black player.
Noll (1974)	Teams, 1970–71	Higher black population in team's SMSA significantly lowers annual attendance (10 percent, 2-tailed); replacing 1 million white residents with 1 million black residents lowers attendance by 168,000.
Sommers and Quinton (1982)	Teams, 1976–77	Black players have insignificant effect on team revenue (magnitude is −$2,500 per percentage-point increase in black players).
Nardinelli and Simon (1990)	1989 baseball card prices for 577 cards issued in 1970	Nonpitchers: controlling for performance, black or Hispanic players have significantly (10 percent, 1-tailed, to 5 percent, 2-tailed) lower baseball card prices; magnitude is −14.2 percent to −9.8 percent. Pitchers: controlling for performance, black or Hispanic players have significantly (10 percent, 1-tailed, to 1 percent, 2-tailed) lower card prices; magnitude is −31.3 percent to −15.8 percent.
Johnson (chap. 10)	306 players, 1987	Number of blacks on team significantly (1 percent, 2-tailed) lowers black salaries; magnitude is −5 percent black salary effect for each additional black player. Number of blacks on team has significantly positive effect (1 percent, 2-tailed) on white salary; white salary magnitude is 5.4 percent for each additional black player.

Basketball

Study	Sample	Findings
Noll (1974)	1969–71 teams (NBA and ABA)	Higher black population significantly (1 percent, 2-tailed) lowers attendance; replacing 1 million white residents with 1 million black residents lowers attendance by 6,535.
Vining and Kerrigan (1978)	NBA teams, 1964, 1968, 1970–77	Black players not randomly distributed across teams; significance level 5 percent in 5 of 10 years.
Scott, Long, and Somppi (1985)	NBA teams, 1978–81	Black players significantly raise revenue (1 percent, 2-tailed); magnitude is $4,300 for each percentage-point increase in black representation.
Schollaert and Smith (1987)	NBA teams, 1969–82	Black players have insignificant effects on attendance; beta coefficients range from −0.086 to 0.077.
Kahn and Sherer (1988)	NBA teams, 1980–86	White players raise attendance (insignificant to significant at 2 percent, 2-tailed tests); replacing a black with a white player raises attendance by 5,700 to 13,000 fans per year.
Koch and Vander Hill (1988)	NBA teams, 1984–85	Simple correlation between percent of team that is white and percent of population in team's area that is black is −0.19, significant at 1 percent.
Brown, Spiro, and Keenan (1988)	NBA teams, 1983–84	Percent of playing time played by blacks has insignificant, negative effect on attendance; magnitude is 8,400 fans lost by replacing one full-time white with one full-time black player.
Brown, Spiro, and Keenan (1988)	NBA teams, 1988	Percent black players on three most "white" teams is significantly different (1–3 percent level) from that of three most "black" teams.
Burdekin and Idson (1991)	NBA teams, 1980–86	Percent of white SMSA population has significant (1 percent, 2-tailed) positive effect on black representation on team. Closeness of racial match between team and SMSA significantly (5 percent, 2-tailed) and positively affects attendance.

Sources: See References.

number of black players on the team; white players' salaries were significantly and positively affected by this variable. These findings are consistent with the existence of fans' racial preferences and suggest that such preferences do not necessarily result in aggregate racial salary differentials.[60] Thus, although there is some suggestion of customer racial preferences in the 1980s, as yet there is no evidence on the impact in the 1980s of black baseball players on team revenues or attendance.[61]

In contrast to baseball, there appears to be evidence of customer discrimination in basketball in the 1980s. Although studies based on data from 1978 to 1981 and from 1969 to 1982 did not produce evidence that black players lowered revenues or attendance, data from 1980 to 1986 did find that attendance was negatively affected by the black players, all else equal (see table 9-4). Further, there is evidence from the 1980s (as well as 1964–77) that the racial composition of NBA teams is significantly affected by the racial composition of the areas in which they are located. These latter results suggest the presence of customer prejudice and indicate a response on the part of NBA teams to such prejudice. In addition, the closeness of the racial match between the team and the area positively affects attendance.[62] The share of NBA players who are black has risen from roughly 58 percent in 1970–71 to about 74 percent in 1985–86.[63] As white players have become more scarce, white fans may have become more responsive to the presence of additional white players. That is, prejudiced fans' utility depends on both winning and the presence of white players; further, the existence of diminishing marginal returns in such utility functions would explain the increased evidence of customer discrimination in the 1980s relative to the 1970s. A test of this idea could

60. Johnson's findings (see chap. 10 in this volume) are also consistent with the coworker discrimination model, which predicts that, say, white players require a premium to work alongside members of minority groups. The customer prejudice model is consistent with Johnson's results to the extent that fan utility with respect to team racial composition is subject to diminishing marginal returns.

61. As noted in table 9-4, Noll (1974) found that in both baseball and basketball, a higher percentage of the area's population that was black lowered attendance, all else equal. However, he concluded that this variable was primarily a proxy for the quality of the neighborhood in which the team's stadium was located rather than solely evidence of an aversion on the part of white fans to the presence of black fans. Although some white potential fans might be deterred by the presence of black fans, Noll concluded from his parameter estimates that such a factor could not be the whole explanation for the black population effect.

62. Burdekin and Idson (1991).

63. For 1970–71 data, see Johnson and Marple (1973, p. 11); for 1985–86, Kahn and Sherer (1988, p. 48).

involve the impact of a quadratic term for local racial composition in an attendance model. It is also possible that the close proximity of the crowd to the players and the greater degree of exposure of the players to the crowd in basketball heightens racial consciousness among the fans more than in other sports.

Conclusions

Currently there is little evidence of salary or hiring discrimination in Major League Baseball. Consistent with these findings for baseball salaries, there is no evidence that customer discrimination has affected team revenues since free agency, although customer discrimination does affect baseball card prices. Further, customer preferences may affect baseball players' salaries without causing a racial salary differential. Finally, there are unexplained racial differences in career length and persistent, though slowly falling, segregation by position. Both career length and positional segregation help explain the low incidence of black managers, although it is unclear whether positional segregation reflects team discrimination, pre–labor market discrimination, or occupational choice.

In contrast to baseball, in basketball there is evidence of salary discrimination as well as customer prejudice; it is likely that the revenue produced by fans' preferences for white players enables the discriminatory salary differential for white players to exist. The fact that blacks make up a higher proportion of NBA players than of players for other sports may explain the great impact additional white players have on fans.[64]

This review of the literature has uncovered varying patterns of evidence on discrimination in professional sports. Most economic analyses predict an end to discriminatory pay differentials based on employer or coworker prejudice, as long as some nonprejudiced employers are in the market or are free to enter the market. Such differentials can persist, however, if all employers are prejudiced, if some have a positive preference for whites,[65] or if there is customer discrimination. The evidence for customer discrimination appears stronger for basketball than for baseball, as does the evidence of salary discrimination. In light of the predictions of economic

64. There is indirect evidence of customer prejudice in professional football and hockey. See, for example, Jones and Walsh (1988) for a study of hockey, and Kahn (1992) for a study of football.
65. Goldberg (1982).

theory, this combination suggests the particular importance of customer discrimination in sports.

The findings cited here on salary discrimination in team sports have for the most part been obtained using far more detailed performance or productivity data than are typically available for the labor force in general. They are thus likely to be much freer of omitted variable bias than estimates of discrimination using standard databases such as the Current Population Survey. For that reason alone, the studies surveyed here would be of interest to labor economists. In addition, the evidence reviewed here yields some substantive lessons for those interested in issues of race differentials in labor market outcomes.

First, the consistent evidence of customer preferences for white players has been obtained in the most recent studies of the issue. These racial attitudes among white customers in the 1980s, as reflected in these studies, may well carry over into other areas of the labor force in which there is contact between producers and customers. Such fields include law and medicine, as well as a variety of services. The growth of the service sector suggests ample opportunity for such attitudes to adversely affect black workers in the future.[66] Second, the continued, albeit slowly declining, positional segregation in baseball suggests the persistence of negative stereotypes of blacks or unequal access to training facilities. If the latter phenomenon is the explanation, it is a reminder that pre–labor market discrimination can still be a powerful force creating racial income differentials, even if there is no evidence of employer discrimination. Third, the presence of retention barriers facing black athletes in baseball and basketball is reminiscent of the major cause of high unemployment rates for nonwhite males in the United States: a high probability of leaving employment (voluntarily or involuntarily) to become unemployed.[67] Thus, several of the findings in this review are consistent with existing research on the labor force as a whole.

Findings in this chapter suggest further avenues for research on discrimination in sports. First, customer discrimination can be tested in more detail using methods that survey the race of particular fans. With such information, one could examine whether white fans or nonwhite fans respond to the race of the players providing entertainment. Second, co-

66. For evidence that customer discrimination has noticeable effects on the economy, see Borjas and Bronars (1989).

67. Ehrenberg (1980). There is evidence that for young workers, black quit rates are no different from whites'; however, black permanent layoff rates are substantially higher than whites'. See Blau and Kahn (1981a, 1981b).

worker discrimination is a relatively unexplored area in sports and deserves further study. Third, the low representation of blacks among managers and coaches in baseball has not yet been subjected to close scrutiny.

Finally, the issue of collective bargaining and discrimination in sports is an unexplored area. Collective bargaining is undoubtedly responsible for the advent of free agency, yet the impact, if any, of collective bargaining institutions such as salary arbitration or salary caps on racial salary differentials has not yet been researched.

References

Becker, Gary. 1971. *The Economics of Discrimination*, 2d ed. University of Chicago Press.

Binmore, Ken, Ariel Rubinstein, and Asher Wolinsky. 1986. "The Nash Bargaining Solution in Economic Modelling." *Rand Journal of Economics* 17:176–88.

Blau, Francine D., and Lawrence M. Kahn. 1981a. "Causes and Consequences of Layoffs." *Economic Inquiry* 19:270–96.

———. 1981b. "Race and Sex Differences in Quits by Young Workers." *Industrial and Labor Relations Review* 34:563–77.

Borjas, George J., and Stephen G. Bronars. 1989. "Consumer Discrimination and Self-Employment." *Journal of Political Economy* 97:581–605.

Bradley, Bill. 1976. *Life on the Run*. Quadrangle/New York Times.

Brown, Eleanor, Richard Spiro, and Diane Keenan. 1988. "Wage and Nonwage Discrimination in Professional Basketball." Pomona College, Department of Economics.

Burdekin, Richard C. K., and Todd L. Idson. 1991. "Customer Preferences, Attendance and the Racial Structure of Professional Basketball Teams." *Applied Economics* 23:179–86.

Cain, Glen. 1986. "The Economic Analysis of Labor Market Discrimination: A Survey." In *Handbook of Labor Economics*, edited by Orley Ashenfelter and Richard Layard, 693–785. Amsterdam: North-Holland.

Christiano, Kevin J. 1986. "Salary Discrimination in Major League Baseball: The Effect of Race." *Sociology of Sport Journal* 3:144–53.

———. 1988. "Salaries and Race in Professional Baseball: Discrimination 10 Years Later." *Sociology of Sport Journal* 5:136–49.

Conway, Delores, and Harry V. Roberts. 1983. "Reverse Regression, Fairness, and Employment Discrimination." *Journal of Business and Economic Statistics* 1:75–85.

Curtis, James E., and John W. Loy. 1978. "Race/Ethnicity and Relative Centrality of Playing Positions in Team Sports." In *Exercise and Sport Sciences*

Reviews, edited by Robert S. Hutton, vol. 6, 285–313. Philadelphia: Franklin Institute Press.

Cymrot, Donald J. 1983. "Migration Trends and Earnings of Free Agents in Major League Baseball, 1976–1979." *Economic Inquiry* 21:545–56.

———. 1985. "Does Competition Lessen Discrimination? Some Evidence." *Journal of Human Resources* 20:605–12.

Ehrenberg, Ronald G. 1980. "The Demographic Structure of Unemployment Rates and Labor Market Transition Probabilities." In *Research in Labor Economics: An Annual Compilation of Research*, edited by Ronald G. Ehrenberg, vol. 3, 241–93. Greenwich, Conn.: JAI Press.

Eitzen, D. Stanley, and George H. Sage. 1978. *Sociology of American Sport.* Dubuque, Iowa: Wm. C. Brown.

Flanagan, Robert J., Lawrence M. Kahn, Robert S. Smith, and Ronald G. Ehrenberg. 1989. *Economics of the Employment Relationship.* Scott, Foresman.

Goldberg, Matthew S. 1982. "Discrimination, Nepotism, and Long-Run Wage Differentials." *Quarterly Journal of Economics* 97:307–20.

Goldberger, Arthur S. 1984. "Reverse Regression and Salary Discrimination." *Journal of Human Resources* 19:293–318.

Gwartney, James, and Charles Haworth. 1974. "Employer Costs and Discrimination: The Case of Baseball." *Journal of Political Economy* 82:873–81.

Halberstam, David. 1981. *The Breaks of the Game.* Alfred A. Knopf.

Hill, James R., and William Spellman. 1984. "Pay Discrimination in Baseball: Data from the Seventies." *Industrial Relations* 23:103–12.

Jiobu, Robert M. 1988. "Racial Inequality in a Public Arena: The Case of Professional Baseball." *Social Forces* 67:524–34.

Johnson, Norris R., and David P. Marple. 1973. "Racial Discrimination in Professional Basketball: An Empirical Test." *Sociological Focus* 6:6–18.

Jones, J. C. H., and William D. Walsh. 1988. "Salary Determination in the National Hockey League: The Effects of Skills, Franchise Characteristics, and Discrimination." *Industrial and Labor Relations Review* 41:592–604.

Kahn, Lawrence M. 1989. "Managerial Quality, Team Success and Individual Player Performance in Major League Baseball." University of Illinois, Institute of Labor and Industrial Relations.

———. 1991. "Customer Discrimination and Affirmative Action." *Economic Inquiry* 29:555–71.

———. 1992. "The Effects of Race on Professional Football Players' Compensation." *Industrial and Labor Relations Review* 45:295–310.

Kahn, Lawrence M., and Peter D. Sherer. 1988. "Racial Differences in Professional Basketball Players' Compensation." *Journal of Labor Economics* 6:40–61.

Koch, James V., and C. Warren Vander Hill. 1988. "Is There Discrimination in the 'Black Man's Game'?" *Social Science Quarterly* 69:83–94.

Medoff, Marshall H. 1975. "A Reappraisal of Racial Discrimination against Blacks in Professional Baseball." *Review of Black Political Economy* 5:259–68.

_____. 1986. "Positional Segregation and the Economic Hypothesis." *Sociology of Sport Journal* 3:297–304.

Mogull, Robert G. 1975. "Salary Discrimination in Major League Baseball." *Review of Black Political Economy* 5:269–79.

_____. 1977. "A Note on Racial Discrimination in Professional Basketball: A Reevaluation of the Evidence." *American Economist* 21: 71–75.

_____. 1981. "Salary Discrimination in Professional Sports." *Atlantic Economic Journal* 9:106–10.

Nardinelli, Clark, and Curtis Simon. 1990. "Customer Racial Discrimination in the Market for Memorabilia: The Case of Baseball." *Quarterly Journal of Economics* 105:575–95.

Noll, Roger G. 1974. "Attendance and Price Setting." In *Government and the Sports Business*, edited by Roger G. Noll, 115–57. Brookings.

Okrent, Daniel, and Steve Wulf. 1989. *Baseball Anecdotes.* Oxford University Press.

Pascal, Anthony H., and Leonard A. Rapping. 1972. "The Economics of Racial Discrimination in Organized Baseball." In *Racial Discrimination in Economic Life*, edited by Anthony H. Pascal, 119–56. D.C. Heath.

Raimondo, Henry J. 1983. "Free Agents' Impact on the Labor Market for Baseball Players." *Journal of Labor Research* 4:183–93.

Rockwood, Charles E., and Ephraim Asher. 1976. "Racial Discrimination in Professional Basketball Revisited." *American Economist* 20:59–64.

Schollaert, Paul T., and Donald Hugh Smith. 1987. "Team Racial Composition and Sports Attendance." *Sociological Quarterly* 28:71–87.

Scott, Frank A., Jr., James E. Long, and Ken Somppi. 1985. "Salary vs. Marginal Revenue Product under Monopsony and Competition: The Case of Professional Basketball." *Atlantic Economic Journal* 13:50–59.

Scully, Gerald W. 1973. "Economic Discrimination in Professional Sports." *Law and Contemporary Problems* 38:67–84.

_____. 1974a. "Discrimination: The Case of Baseball." In *Government and the Sports Business*, edited by Roger G. Noll, 221–73. Brookings.

_____. 1974b. "Pay and Performance in Major League Baseball." *American Economic Review* 64:915–30.

Sommers, Paul M., and Noel Quinton. 1982. "Pay and Performance in Major League Baseball: The Case of the First Family of Free Agents." *Journal of Human Resources* 17:426–36.

Staudohar, Paul D. 1989. *The Sports Industry and Collective Bargaining*, 2d ed. Ithaca, N.Y.: ILR Press.

Tygiel, Jules. 1983. *Baseball's Great Experiment.* Oxford University Press.

U.S. Bureau of Labor Statistics. 1989. *Employment and Earnings* 36:16–18.

U.S. Tennis Association. 1989. *1989 Official USTA Tennis Yearbook.* Lynn, Mass.: H.O. Zimman.

Vining, Daniel R., Jr., and James F. Kerrigan. 1978. "An Application of the Lexis Ratio to the Detection of Racial Quotas in Professional Sports: A Note." *American Economist* 22:71–75.

Wallace, Michael. 1988. "Labor Market Structure and Salary Determination among Professional Basketball Players." *Work and Occupations* 15:294–312.

Yetman, Norman R. 1987. " 'Positional Segregation and the Economic Hypothesis': A Critique." *Sociology of Sport Journal* 4:274–77.

CHAPTER TEN

Team Racial Composition and Players' Salaries

Bruce K. Johnson

SINCE IT became fully integrated in the 1950s and 1960s, Major League Baseball has seemed to many a shining triumph of equal opportunity, its athletes played and paid according only to performance.[1] Econometric studies of major league salaries show no evidence of pay discrimination against black players after the 1960s.[2] Casual observation corroborates the finding of the formal analyses. Some of the highest paid players in the major leagues are black, and the average salary of veteran black players exceeds that of veteran whites.[3] Previous studies of the impact of race on baseball salaries have focused on the race of the individual player.[4] Given two otherwise identical players, one white and one black, they ask if the white player is paid more than the black. But that may not be the correct question. As shown below, whether discrimination occurs as a result of preferences by fans, players, or owners, a player's salary depends not only on the player's own race but also on the racial composition of his entire team. After determining the theoretical implications of team racial composition on player salaries, this chapter tests whether two identical players of the same race earn different salaries if they have different numbers of black teammates. The models and the results suggest that the

The author thanks Robert Brownlee, Philip Holleran, William Huneke, Harry Landreth, W. Robert Reed, Roger Sherman, Jonathan Skinner, and William C. Wood for their helpful suggestions and James K. Johnson for research assistance but retains all responsibility for any errors.

1. See Scully (1974, pp. 221–22) for a description of this belief.
2. For an extensive economic bibliography on discrimination in baseball and other professional sports, see Kahn (1991).
3. See table 10-1.
4. Kahn and Sherer (1988) have shown that attendance in the National Basketball Association varies directly with the percentage of white players on a roster, but they have not investigated the effect of team racial composition on salary.

standard method for detecting racial discrimination misses the true effect of discrimination on salaries.

The Models

Discrimination can come from three sources—the fans, the players, and the owners. This section develops three models to evaluate the effects of team racial composition on players' salaries.

Fan Discrimination

Anecdotal and econometric evidence can be found showing that professional sports fans discriminate. Some sports writers and player agents and others closely involved with professional sports believe fan discrimination affects salaries. Bob Woolf, an agent for professional basketball players, has said: "Remember, this is an entertainment industry. You have to draw fans. [Owners] might pay a little extra to put a white player on the bench."[5] Baseball cards of black players sell for lower prices than cards of comparable white players, probably because of fan discrimination.[6] For the 1967 season, fewer fans attended games pitched by black starters than those by white starters.[7]

Suppose the utility fans derive from watching baseball depends on two factors—the team's racial composition and the players' ability. Prejudiced fans prefer to watch players of their own race, ceteris paribus, so the marginal utility of another black player is negative for white fans and positive for black fans. The substitution of a black player for a white player reduces a white fan's utility unless the black player's ability compensates for the change in race by being sufficiently higher than the white's. In other words, fans are willing to substitute greater ability for undesirable race. A black fan's utility is similarly affected by the addition of white players. Of course, if fans are not biased, race has no effect on utility.

The effect of team racial composition on players' salaries can be examined with this simple model. Assume each player's salary depends

5. Shaun Powell, "Williams Roasts Heat with Charge of Racism," *Sporting News*, August 29, 1988, p. 44.

6. Nardinelli and Simon (1990).

7. Scully (1974, pp. 221–33).

positively on his marginal revenue product (MRP).[8] For simplicity, assume also that all team revenue comes from ticket sales.[9] Let

$$(1) \qquad\qquad R = TP,$$

where T is the number of tickets sold and P is average revenue, including the price of the ticket plus concessions. Furthermore, $T = T_w + T_b$, where T_w is ticket sales to white fans and T_b is ticket sales to black fans. For a given ticket price, $T_w = T_w(A, B)$ and $T_b = T_b(A, B)$, where A is ability and B is the number of blacks on the roster. So,

$$(2) \qquad\qquad R = P[T_w(A, B) + T_b(A, B)]$$

$$(3) \qquad \partial R/\partial B = P[\partial T_w/\partial B + (\partial T_w/\partial A)(\partial A/\partial B)$$
$$+ \partial T_b/\partial B + (\partial T_b/\partial A)(\partial A/\partial B)].$$

What does this model suggest? If a team replaces a white player with a black player of identical ability, total ticket sales change by $\partial T_w/\partial B + \partial T_b/\partial B$. If the number of tickets sold to whites drops by more than the number of tickets sold to blacks rises, revenue falls; the MRP of the black player is less than that of the white player replaced. In other words, the MRP of the racial characteristic "black" is negative.

But if the rise in ticket sales to blacks more than offsets the drop in sales to whites, the MRP of the black player exceeds that of the white player he replaces. Although 93 percent of ticket-buying fans are white,[10] blacks may respond more to changes in the number of black players and have a greater marginal effect on team revenues than the more numerous white fans. In the 1950s, the five teams with the highest percentage of black players drew significantly more fans than the other teams, possibly

8. Free agency and salary arbitration make competitive salaries more likely now than in the late 1960s and early 1970s, when many of the other econometric studies were conducted.

9. Teams also receive substantial revenue from concessions, local broadcast royalties, and national network broadcast royalties. Concessions are closely related to ticket sales. Local broadcast revenues presumably are affected by the same factors as ticket sales. Fans who do not like a team's players will not buy as many tickets, watch them as often on television, or listen to them as often on radio. Because all teams share national broadcast revenue equally, it does not vary with team characteristics.

10. Brent Staples, "Where Are the Black Fans?" *New York Times Magazine*, May 17, 1987, p. 28.

because more blacks were attracted than whites were driven away.[11] In the early years of integration, many blacks attended major league games to see Jackie Robinson and other black players.[12] Thus, if salaries equal MRPs, black players may earn more than comparable white players. If black and white fans are prejudiced, the salary premium earned by blacks would diminish with each additional black player until, at some critical number of blacks, the MRP of blacks would fall below that of whites. That blacks could earn more than otherwise identical whites runs counter to the most common notions of discrimination.

Although blacks' salaries may in some cases exceed whites' salaries, black players' salaries will, ceteris paribus, vary inversely with the number of blacks on the roster. A black on a team with two blacks, for instance, would earn more than he would on a team with three or more blacks because each additional black player is worth less to black fans and each additional white player replaced is worth more to white fans. Thus white salaries will rise with the number of black teammates while black salaries will fall, if fans are prejudiced.

Player Discrimination

Players themselves may discriminate on the basis of race. If white players prefer playing with other whites and blacks prefer playing with other blacks, they may adjust their labor supply curves according to team racial composition. A white player on an otherwise entirely black team would require a higher salary than he would on an entirely white team. A player's reservation wage would depend on his ability, with better players demanding higher pay, and on team racial composition.

Let W_w be the reservation wage of a white player and W_b be the reservation wage of a black player. Then

(4) $$W_k = f(A, B) \qquad k = w, b$$

where, as before, A is ability and B is the number of blacks on the roster. For prejudiced players,

(5) $$\partial W_w / \partial B > 0 \qquad \text{and} \qquad \partial W_b / \partial B < 0.$$

11. Gwartney and Haworth (1974).
12. Miller (1990, p. 17).

The player discrimination model implies the same relationship between player salaries and team racial composition as the model of fan discrimination. White players' salaries will rise and black players' salaries will fall as the number of blacks on a team increases.

Over time, in a league with no barriers to player mobility, player discrimination could lead to racially segregated teams, because segregation would minimize wage bills. But barriers to player mobility do exist. Most players enter professional baseball through the amateur draft and must sign a contract with the team that selects them. Once in the professional ranks, players are bound to the organizations that own their contracts until they achieve free agent status, after six or more years of major league service. In 1987 only about 44 percent of those on opening-day rosters or disabled lists had been in the majors for at least six years. Even free agents are limited in the number of clubs they can bargain with.[13]

Furthermore, the distribution of blacks across positions is skewed. Most blacks play in the outfield, while few pitch or catch. Most blacks would have to play with white teammates even if all players had perfect mobility.

Owner Discrimination

Suppose major league club owners, none of whom are black, discriminate on the basis of race. If they simply favor whites over blacks, a dummy variable may capture the effect, and this is the model of discrimination at least implicitly underlying most of the previous studies of racial discrimination in baseball and other professional sports.[14] Certainly, before the Brooklyn Dodgers fielded Jackie Robinson in 1947, the major leagues practiced the most extreme form of discrimination against blacks: total exclusion. But even well into the 1950s, despite the ready availability of cheap, skilled players from the Negro leagues, some major league clubs remained unintegrated, costing them wins on the field and fans in the stands.[15]

Times have changed. Today club owners who blatantly discriminate or express racist views risk public condemnation. To quell the public's anger in 1987, the Dodgers fired general manager Al Campanis within

13. Scully (1989, p. 38).
14. Cairns and others (1986, pp. 49–50).
15. Gwartney and Haworth (1974).

days of his saying on national television that he thought blacks lack the ability to handle managerial jobs in baseball.[16]

An all-white team might also attract unwanted accusations of racism. To protect themselves against such charges, owners may value racially mixed teams. Owners may also want integrated teams because of sincere beliefs about the desirability of integration.

If such an owner has too few blacks on his team, he will place a high marginal value on additional blacks. But an owner with "too many" blacks will place a low marginal value on additional blacks, preferring to hire whites at a higher salary. Wages offered to white and black players will depend on their ability, their race, and the team's racial composition. As with the fan and player discrimination examined above, the salaries of blacks would decline as the number of black players on the team rose, while the salaries of white players would increase.

Measuring Discrimination

According to each of the three models described above, a player's salary depends on his ability, his race, and the racial composition of his team, regardless of whether the source of the discrimination is fans, players, or owners. Discrimination need not come solely from one source. All three types of discrimination may occur together. But looking for discrimination with an intercept dummy variable or any other technique positing a constant difference between white and black salaries may obscure the true effect of race on salaries.

To sort out the effects of ability, race, and racial composition, the following equation was estimated separately for black and for white non-pitchers.[17]

$$(6) \quad LOGSAL_i = B_0 + B_1 BLACKS_i + B_2 YRS_i + B_3 YRS2_i$$

$$+ B_4 ABBAR_i + B_5 OA_i + B_6 FREE_i$$

$$+ B_7 GOLD_i + B_8 BBOF_i + B_9 BBIF_i + B_{10} DEFIF_i$$

$$+ B_{11} NONARB_i + e_i,$$

16. Lynn Rosellini and others, "Strike One and You're Out," *U.S. News and World Report*, July 27, 1987, pp. 52–57.

17. Because only 17 of the 215 pitchers on opening-day rosters in 1987 were black, and pitcher performance is measured with entirely different statistics, pitchers are not included in the regression. Separate regressions were run for pitchers, however, and are discussed briefly in the section on results.

where

$LOGSAL_i$	=	natural logarithm of 1987 salary, in thousands of dollars, for player i;
$BLACKS_i$	=	number of black players, including pitchers, on player i's team;
YRS_i	=	years of major league experience for player i;
$YRS2_i$	=	years of major league experience squared for player i;
$ABBAR_i$	=	average number of at bats per year for player i;
OA_i	=	lifetime offensive average, a measure of offensive ability. It is calculated as $1{,}000 \times$ (total bases + bases on balls + stolen bases)/(at bats + bases on balls);
$FREE_i$	=	1 if player i has ever been granted free agent status;
$GOLD_i$	=	1 if player i has ever earned a gold glove;
$BBOF_i$	=	1 if player i played at least 75 percent of his 1986 games in the outfield (stands for big bat outfield position);
$BBIF_i$	=	1 if player i played at least 75 percent of his 1986 games at first or third base (stands for big bat infield position);
$DEFIF_i$	=	1 if player i played at least 75 percent of his 1986 games at catcher, second base, or shortstop (stands for defensive infield position);
$NONARB_i$	=	1 if player i has fewer than three years of major league experience, making him ineligible for final-offer arbitration;
e_i	=	a normally distributed random error.

To allow for superstar effects, the natural logarithm of salary is used as the dependent variable.[18]

The variable $BLACKS$ is included in equation 6 to measure the effects of team racial composition on salaries. In the fan discrimination model, the coefficient on $BLACKS$ should capture the change in MRP as a result of altering the number of blacks on a team. In the player discrimination model, it shows the effect of racial composition on the reservation wage, and in the owner model, it shows racial composition's effect on the marginal value of additional blacks.

How should ability be measured? Baseball players have two broad types of skill: offensive and defensive. Teams record a plethora of offensive statistics for each player, including batting average, slugging average, and home runs, among others. No measure, however, captures all of the

---

18. Scully (1974).

important ways a player may contribute to the team's offense. The value of two .300 hitters is not identical if one hits thirty doubles and thirty homers and the other hits ten doubles and five homers. Although use of slugging averages instead of batting averages would better distinguish between two such players, it would not allow a distinction between players who walk or steal a lot and those who do not. The offensive average used here reflects all these contributions to offense. The average number of at bats per year reflects the importance of a player to his team and may be an index of ability. Better players bat more and contribute more to a team during a season.

To reflect defensive skills, the regressions include four dummy variables.[19] Exceptional defensive prowess is measured by *GOLD* for players who have ever been selected as the league's best fielder at a position in a season. The other defensive dummies, *BBIF*, *BBOF*, and *DEFIF*, attempt to differentiate between defensive skills by position. Teams value talented glovemen in the key positions of catcher, second base, and shortstop so highly that they often tolerate weak hitters there.[20] Heavy hitters are more likely to man the other, less crucial, positions. Nonetheless, the defensive skills required for first and third bases differ from those required for the outfield—hence the distinction between *BBIF* and *BBOF*. Utility players and designated hitters have zeroes entered for all of the positional dummies.

Years of experience, or *YRS*, may capture other facets of player ability not reflected in the offensive and defensive variables. Players with longer tenures in the major leagues have had more time to establish a following among fans. They may provide valuable stability and leadership. But aging stars may have great career statistics from their glory years, even though their current productivity is falling and their salaries may also be falling, or growing more slowly. So *YRS2* is included to account for a possible nonlinear relation between experience and salary.

Does free agency affect salaries? If bidding for players is competitive and salaries equal MRPs, the coefficient on *FREE* should be 0. But players

19. Fielding average is not used because few in baseball believe it is a good index of defensive skill.

20. Many would include center field as well. The data on games played by position, however, make no distinction between center, right, and left fields. This may reflect the common belief that left fielders and center fielders are more interchangeable than first basemen and shortstops. The correlation coefficient between the defensive infield dummy and offensive average for all players in the sample is -0.530.

have accused owners of monopsony collusion in the free agent market,[21] which could result in a negative coefficient. Some economic evidence suggests the players' claims are correct.[22]

The variable *NONARB* should have a negative coefficient. Players with only two years of major league experience are contractually bound to their teams and have no right to final-offer arbitration. They find themselves dealing with a pure monopsonist.

Description of the Sample

Data on player salaries and race came from the 1987 baseball salary survey issues of the *Sporting News* and *Sports Illustrated*, which reported the 1987 salaries of every player on an opening-day roster or disabled list in the major leagues.[23] *Sports Illustrated* included a color photograph of every player, from which the race of individual players was determined. Data on all other baseball variables were collected or computed from the 1987 *Baseball Encyclopedia* and *Official Baseball Register: 1987 Edition*.[24] Players with less than two years of experience were excluded because their salaries showed little variation (most made the major league minimum salary of $62,500), and many of them had no career statistics for the major leagues.

Table 10-1 presents summary statistics for all players in the sample.

Results

The results of the *OLS* estimation of equation 6 appear in table 10-2. For both white and black players, team racial composition affects salary as predicted by the three models of discrimination. White players' salaries rise with the number of blacks on the roster, whereas blacks' salaries fall. Blacks pay a large penalty for each additional black teammate. Consider

21. Hal Lancaster, "Baseball Players Contend Owners Continue to Thwart Free Agency," *Wall Street Journal*, January 15, 1988, p. 21.

22. Scully (1989, pp. 166–67).

23. Murray Chass, "57 Millionaires, 66 Who Make Minimum $62,500 on Opening-Day Rosters," *Sporting News*, April 27, 1987, pp. 18–19; Ivan Maisel, "Baseball Salaries '87," *Sports Illustrated*, April 20, 1987, pp. 54–81.

24. Siegel (1987).

Table 10-1. *Black and White Players' Salaries: Summary Statistics*

Variable	White[a]		Black[b]	
	Mean	Standard error	Mean	Standard error
SALARY[c]	489.3	440.4	539.7	483.6
BLACKS	4.8	1.9	5.8	1.8
ABBAR	282.5	138.9	320.6	156.5
OA	460.3	60.1	476.9	67.5
YRS	7.7	4.5	7.0	4.3
FREE	0.195	0.397	0.138	0.346
BBOF	0.200	0.401	0.509	0.502
BBIF	0.226	0.420	0.103	0.306
DEFIF	0.374	0.485	0.267	0.444
GOLD	0.142	0.350	0.155	0.364
NONARB	0.100	0.301	0.112	0.317

Sources: Salaries from Murray Chass, "57 Millionaires, 66 Who Make Minimum $62,500 on Opening-Day Rosters," *Sporting News*, April 27, 1987, pp. 18–19; *GOLD* from Sloan (1989, pp. 275–77); all other data from 1987 *Baseball Encyclopedia*.
a. $N = 190$.
b. $N = 116$.
c. In thousands of dollars.

the case of an average black outfielder, with offensive statistics equal to the averages for all black players.[25] If he is one of two blacks on the team and has played seven years in the majors, he will earn about $697,000. The addition of a third black to the team would reduce his salary by almost $35,000. If this player were one of nine blacks, his salary would be more than $209,000 lower than with just two blacks.

White players gain from an increase in the number of black teammates. If the player described above were white rather than black, he would earn about $475,000 on a team with two blacks. The addition of a third black would raise his salary by about $26,000. With nine black teammates, his salary would rise by almost $213,000.[26]

Do blacks earn less than whites? Not necessarily, as seen in the above examples. When five or fewer blacks are on a team, the average black outfielder or defensive infielder, for example, earns more than his similar white teammate. Only with the addition of a sixth black does the white player's salary rise above the black player's. Figure 10-1 shows how the

25. Note in table 10-1 that the average white player's *OA* and *ABBAR* are lower than the average black player's. Scully (1989, pp. 174–75) and others have observed the difference and concluded that barriers to entry confront black ballplayers.

26. Separate and pooled regressions for white and black pitchers reveal similar results. The coefficients on *BLACKS* in the pitcher regressions take the expected signs but are not significant at the 90 percent confidence level.

Table 10-2. *Results of Salary Regressions for White and Black Players*[a]

Explanatory variables	Whites	Blacks
Constant	2.035	1.915
	(0.3334)	(0.3758)
BLACKS	0.0525	−0.0511
	(0.0156)	(0.0193)
YRS	0.2995	0.3833
	(0.0350)	(0.0418)
YRS2	−0.0131	−0.0167
	(0.0017)	(0.0022)
NONARB	−0.1349	−0.2319
	(0.1323)	(0.1386)
ABBAR	0.0037	0.0030
	(0.0003)	(0.0003)
OA	0.0024	0.0040
	(0.0007)	(0.0007)
FREE	−0.1421	−0.3928
	(0.0990)	(0.1287)
GOLD	0.0465	−0.0029
	(0.0992)	(0.1042)
BBOF	0.1566	−0.1460
	(0.0998)	(0.1237)
BBIF	0.1551	−0.2282
	(0.0954)	(0.1565)
DEFIF	0.2313	0.0233
	(0.0869)	(0.1426)
$\bar{R}^2$	0.8087	0.8612
Sample size	190	116
Standard error of estimate	0.4038	0.3650

a. Ordinary least-squares estimation of the natural log of salary. The numbers in parentheses are standard errors.

black player's salary compares with the white player's when the number of blacks on the team varies.

That blacks could earn more than whites runs counter to most popular notions of racial discrimination. If any or all of the types of discrimination described in this chapter occur in the Major League Baseball players' labor market, testing for discrimination with an intercept dummy may not detect any effect of race on salary. The models of discrimination developed in this chapter, however, explicitly allow for such a possibility.

The other results also indicate differences in the ways the two races are paid. The coefficients on the defensive dummies show that a defensive specialty earns whites, but not blacks, a premium over utility players and

Figure 10-1. *Black and White Outfielders' Average Salaries, by Number of Blacks on Team*

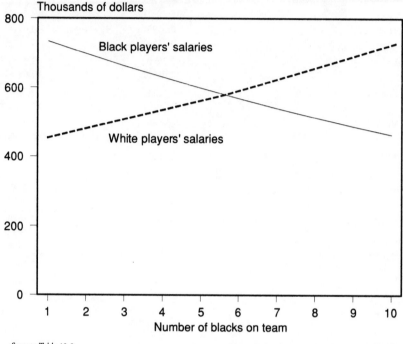

Source: Table 10-2.

designated hitters. The null hypothesis that all four of the defensive dummies are 0 for the black regression cannot be rejected. The results may show the effects of positional segregation in the major leagues noted by many other observers.[27] Most blacks play in the outfield, most whites in the infield (see table 10-1).

Both white and black players are paid for offensive contributions to the team. As expected, the signs on offensive average and average at bats are positive. Experience exerts a strong positive, nonlinear influence on the log of salaries. Blacks seem to gain more from extra years and a higher offensive average, whereas whites benefit more from extra at bats.

Both white and black free agents pay a penalty for exercising their freedom, perhaps indicating monopsony collusion. Blacks, however, apparently suffer a greater penalty than whites.

27. See, for instance, Scully (1989, pp. 176–77).

Conclusion

The results support the hypothesis that team racial composition affects Major League Baseball players' salaries. They show that whites on teams with few blacks may earn less than blacks of comparable ability. Previous econometric studies of the effect of race on baseball salaries have neglected to consider the importance of team racial composition. They asked only whether blacks are paid less than whites, implicitly assuming that neither black fans nor black players discriminate and that owners do not value racial diversity.

The results do not allow a conclusion as to the source of the discrimination; fans, players, and owners may all discriminate. But whatever the source of the discrimination, the importance of the results cannot be dismissed. Testing for discrimination with an intercept dummy variable for race may obscure discrimination's true effect on earnings.

The significance of these findings transcends baseball and provides insight into the racial attitudes of society as a whole. After decades of change in race relations, people are still not color-blind. Even baseball, regarded by many as a meritocracy, reflects lingering prejudices. This will hardly be news to many, but baseball provides a rare opportunity to measure such effects. Other industries, where consumer or employer utility depends in part on the racial composition of the employees, may exhibit similar patterns of salary differences.

References

The Baseball Encyclopedia. 1987. 7th ed. Macmillan.

Cairns, J., N. Jennett, and P. J. Sloane. 1986. "The Economics of Professional Team Sports: A Survey of Theory and Evidence." *Journal of Economic Studies* 13:3–80.

Gwartney, James, and Charles Haworth. 1974. "Employer Costs and Discrimination: The Case of Baseball." *Journal of Political Economy* 82:873–81.

Kahn, Lawrence M. 1991. "Discrimination in Professional Sports: A Survey of the Literature." *Industrial and Labor Relations Review* 44:395–418.

Kahn, Lawrence M., and Peter D. Sherer. 1988. "Racial Differences in Professional Basketball Players' Compensation." *Journal of Labor Economics* 6:40–61.

Miller, James Edward. 1990. *The Baseball Business: Pursuing Pennants and Profits in Baltimore.* University of North Carolina Press.

Nardinelli, Clark, and Curtis Simon. 1990. "Customer Racial Discrimination in the Market for Memorabilia: The Case of Baseball." *Quarterly Journal of Economics* 105:575–95.

Scully, Gerald W. 1974. "Discrimination: The Case of Baseball." In *Government and the Sports Business*, edited by Roger G. Noll, 221–73, Brookings.

———. 1989. *The Business of Major League Baseball*. University of Chicago Press.

Siegel, Barry, ed. 1987. *The Sporting News Official Baseball Register: 1987 Edition*. St. Louis: Sporting News Publishing Co.

Sloan, David, ed. 1989. *The Sporting News Official Baseball Guide, 1989*. St. Louis: Sporting News Publishing Co.

Contributors

Paul L. Burgess
Arizona State University

George G. Daly
University of Iowa

Rodney Fort
Washington State University

David M. Frederick
University of Colorado

Bruce K. Johnson
Centre College

William H. Kaempfer
University of Colorado

Lawrence M. Kahn
University of Illinois

Daniel R. Marburger
Arkansas State University

Philip K. Porter
University of South Florida

David J. Salant
GTE Laboratories, Inc.

Paul M. Sommers
Middlebury College

John A. Vernon
National Archives and Records Administration

Richard L. Wobbekind
University of Colorado

Andrew Zimbalist
Smith College

Index

Aaron, Hank, 171
Alchian, Armen A., 21
Andreano, Ralph, 110
Antitrust laws, 2
Arbitration, 2, 29–30, 123n; arbitrators' behavior in, 32–34; conventional binding arbitration, 31; and discrimination, 185; evidence in arbitration hearings, 51; final-offer arbitration, theory of, 31–34, 52–53; players' behavior in, 34–38; process of, 51; teams' behavior in, 38–39. *See also* Bargaining-power effect of arbitration eligibility; Repeat arbitration
Archival records on baseball, 92–93, 105–06
Attendance: and ticket prices, 79–80, 88; and winning, 69–75

Bargaining-power effect of arbitration eligibility, 5–6, 50; and collusion by owners, 58; eligibility requirements, 51; for hitters, 54–55, 56; measurement of, 54; for pitchers, 56–58
Bargaining power of players, 50; and reserve clause, 51. *See also* Bargaining-power effect of arbitration eligibility; Free agency
Baseball card industry: collateral businesses, 103–04; commercialization of card collecting, 104; growth in *1980*s, 103
Baseball card prices, and fan prejudice, 179, 183, 190
Baseball card restraint of trade case, 6, 91–92; archival records on, 92–93,

105; charges brought by Fleer, 98; complaint filed by FTC, 98–99; contracts with players, 95, 97–98, 99, 100; court rulings, 103; Fleer's attempts to enter market, 97–98; reversal of ruling against Topps, 102; ruling against Topps, 100–01; Topps's defense of its position, 99–100; Topps's domination of market, 94–97
Basic Agreement of *1973*, 2, 51
Basic Agreement of *1976*, 3
Basic Agreement of *1990*, 109, 110
Basketball. *See* National Basketball Association
Baylor, Don, 111
Becker, Gary, 165, 166
Bird, Larry, 83
Boddicker, Mike, 113
Boggs, Wade, 121
Boston Celtics, 83, 84, 88
Boston Red Sox, 81, 84, 121, 136
Bouton, Jim, 103
Boxing, discrimination in, 166
Bradley, Bill, 166
Brooklyn Dodgers, 166, 193
Brown, Eleanor, 175
Buffalo Bills, 82
Busch, August, 70

Campanis, Al, 193–94
Canseco, Jose, 109
Chelius, James R., 53
Chicago Cubs, 84
Christiano, Kevin J., 171, 172
Clemens, Roger, 109, 113, 134